Few themes run with consistency all the way through the history of the British Isles, save the land itself. It is the product of the interaction over time between the internal, mental world of men and women, their hopes, ideas and ambitions, and their external, physical environment.

The five books in this new series examine the varied and complex relationship between man and his environment, and show how the landscape of Britain has acquired its rich historical density. They illustrate the way in which men and women have shaped and occupied the country, and how society has been moulded by the opportunities and constraints imposed by the landscape. Man is the agent of change within the landscape, so that behind a simple hedgerow, a country cottage, a mean street in some grimy industrial town, lie the modes of thought, the unconscious attitudes and the habits and expectations of past generations.

The Author

Born in Shrewsbury, Trevor Rowley attended the local grammar school, and then read geography at University College, London, and modern history at Linacre College, Oxford. He is currently Staff Tutor in Archaeology at the University of Oxford Department for External Studies, and was formerly Honorary Secretary of the Council for British Archaeology. His previous publications include *The Shropshire Landscape* (1972), *Landscape Archaeology* (co-author with Michael Aston, 1974), *Villages in the Landscape* (1978), and many articles and papers on archaeology, local history and the management of the historic environment.

D0452956

The Making of Britain
1066–1939

General Editor: Andrew Wheatcroft

The Norman Heritage Trevor Rowley
The High Middle Ages Trevor Rowley
The Age of Exuberance Michael Reed
The Georgian Triumph Michael Reed
The Transformation of Britain Gordon Mingay

TREVOR ROWLEY

The Norman Heritage
1066–1200

Granada Publishing

Paladin Books
Granada Publishing Ltd
8 Grafton Street, London W1X 3LA

Published by Paladin Books 1984

First published in Great Britain by
Routledge & Kegan Paul plc 1983
as a title in THE MAKING OF BRITAIN series

Copyright © Trevor Rowley 1983

ISBN 0-586-08401-0

Reproduced, printed and bound in Great Britain by
Hazell Watson & Viney Limited,
Aylesbury, Bucks

Set in Palatino

Contents

	Illustrations	4
	Acknowledgments	7
	General Editor's preface	8
	Preface	10
1	The coming of the Normans	13
2	The Norman dynasty in England	43
3	Castles of the Conquest	57
4	The English landscape at the time of the Conquest	85
5	The towns of the Conquest	115
6	The impact of the Conquest on the church	155
7	Forest, park and woodland	197
8	The Norman impact on Wales and the Welsh borderlands	217
9	The Norman heritage	243
	Appendix 1	263
	Appendix 2	267
	Appendix 3	269
	Further reading	273
	Index	277

Illustrations

Plates

1	An extract from the Domesday Book	12
2	Harold swearing allegiance to William from the Bayeux Tapestry	14
3	Death of Harold from the Bayeux Tapestry	15
4	The Jew's House, Lincoln	19
5	Boothby Pagnell manor house, Lincolnshire	20
6	William I silver penny	21
7	Preparations for the battle of Hastings from the Bayeux Tapestry	27
8	Horses from the Bayeux Tapestry	28
9	Norman knights	30
10	The exchequer, Caen castle, Normandy	33
11	Cainhoe castle, Bedfordshire	53
12	Burwell castle, Cambridgeshire	54
13	The White Tower, Tower of London	60
14	Ewyas Harold, motte, Herefordshire	61
15	Church Brough and Market Brough, Westmorland	62
16	Pleshey, Essex	64
17	Yelden earthworks, Bedfordshire	66
18	Building Hastings castle from the Bayeux Tapestry	72
19	The hall of Chepstow castle	76
20	Rochester castle, Kent	77
21	Dover castle	78
22	Norwich castle	79
23	Castle Rising, Norfolk	80
24	Richmond castle, Yorkshire	81
25	Porchester castle, Hampshire	82
26	Bury St Edmunds, Suffolk	108
27	Aerial view of Shrewsbury	116
28	Wallingford Saxon *burgh*	119
29	Old Sarum, Wiltshire	127
30	Devizes, Wiltshire	129
31	Eye, Suffolk	132
32	Clare, Suffolk	133

33 New Buckenham, Norfolk   134
34 Kilpeck, Herefordshire   135
35 Ludlow, Shropshire   140
36 Norman chapel in Ludlow Castle   143
37 Chipping Campden, Gloucestershire   152
38 St Mary's church, Iffley, Oxford   162
39 Tympanum at Aston Eyre, Shropshire   164
40 Leominster Priory church, Herefordshire   166
41 Sawley Abbey, Yorkshire   171
42 Fountains Abbey, Yorkshire   174
43 Durham   183
44 Worcester cathedral   187
45 Stretton Sugwas tympanum, Herefordshire   189
46 Hook Norton font, Oxfordshire   191
47 Barford St Michael, Oxfordshire   192
48 Kilpeck, Herefordshire   193
49 Parish church, Melbourne, Derbyshire   194
50 Illustration of a hunting scene   200
51 Rhuddlan castle   222
52 Pembroke   228
53 Caus castle and failed borough, Shropshire   234
54 More castle, Shropshire   237
55 Tin-mining earthworks, Dartmoor   258
56 Medieval bell-pit coal mines, Clee Hills, Shropshire   259

Figures

 1 Normandy and north-west France in the eleventh century   23
 2a Distribution of pre-Conquest dioceses in England   34
 2b Distribution of post-Conquest dioceses in England and
    Wales   35
 3 The Norman Empire   40
 4 Norman kings family tree   44
 5 Drawings from the Bayeux Tapestry showing a house
    being burnt by Norman soldiers   45
 6 Waste vills recorded in the Domesday Book (1086)   47
 7 Castles of the Conquest   58
 8 Plan of a motte and bailey   67
 9 Plan of excavations at Hen Domen   70
10 William's early campaigns in England and Wales   71
11 Plan of the Tower of London   75
12 Plan of Great Shelford, Cambridgeshire   96
13 A planned village of the early Middle Ages   98
14 Late eleventh-century vineyards   103
15 Plan of Bury St Edmunds   109
16 Plans of Viroconium and Shrewsbury   117

17 Plan of Winchester   118
18 Plan of Wallingford, Oxfordshire   120
19a Site at Devizes, Wiltshire   128
19b Plan of Devizes castle town   130
20 Plan of Nottingham   136
21 Ludlow Shropshire, the 'classic' medieval planned town   141
22 Clun, Shropshire, medieval castle borough   144
23a Siting of Old Sarum, Salisbury and Wilton   146
23b Salisbury, a planned town   148
24 Plans of Stratford-upon-Avon, Warwickshire and
    Thame, Oxfordshire   150
25 Monastic houses in 1066   157
26 Plans of the churches of St Martin, Tours and Battle,
    Sussex   167
27 Monastic establishments and houses of regular canons
    in England, c. 1200   168
28 Canals and artificial waterways of Rievaulx Abbey,
    Yorkshire   172
29 Plan of Fountains Abbey, Yorkshire   175
30 Nunneries in England, c. 1200   178
31 Plan of Westminster Abbey and Edward the Confessor's
    church in the eleventh century   182
32 The distribution of Royal Forests, 1066–1200   198
33 The Northamptonshire Royal Forest   203
34 Ongar, an early medieval park   207
35 Distribution of deer parks in eastern England   209
36 Devizes castle town and deer park   214
37 The early stages of the conquest of Wales   220
38 Wales in the early thirteenth century   224
39 Plan of Brecon   230
40 Richard's Castle, Herefordshire   235
41 Medieval colonization of the waste in south Lincolnshire   255

Acknowledgments

I would like to thank all those who have made the writing of this book possible, in particular Lucienne Walker for undertaking much of the background research and preparing plans and Melanie Steiner also for preparing plans. I have received advice from many colleagues on aspects of the Norman legacy and I would like to thank Professor L. Cantor in particular for permission to reproduce Table 1. I would also like to thank Shirley Hermon and Linda Rowley for the preparation of the typescript.

The author and publishers would like to thank the following for permission to reproduce illustrations: Phaidon Press, nos 2, 3, 7, 8 and 18; Bodleian Library, no. 50; the Trustees of the British Museum, no. 6; the Burrell Collection – Glasgow Museums and Art Galleries, no. 9; Cambridge Committee for Aerial Photography, nos 11, 12, 15, 16, 17, 26, 27, 28, 29, 30, 31, 32, 33, 34, 35, 37, 40, 41, 51, 52, 53, 54, 55, 56; National Monuments record, nos 4, 5, 13, 20, 22, 23, 24, 25, 43, 44, 46, 49; Oxfordshire Museums Service, no. 38; Public Records Office, no. 1. The remaining, uncredited, photographs are from the author's collection. Thanks are also due to the following for permission to reproduce the figures: P. Barker for figure 9; I. Burrow for figure 16; and M. Aston for figure 39.

General Editor's preface

To the archaeologist, the notion of material culture, of a society exemplified by its artefacts, is commonplace. To historians it has traditionally had less appeal, although Professor Fernand Braudel's *Civilisation matérielle et capitalisme* marks a foray into unknown terrain. The intention of this series, which follows chronologically from another of more directly archaeological approach*, is to see the history of Britain from the Norman Conquest to the Second World War, partly in human terms – of changing cultural, social, political and economic patterns – but more specifically in terms of what that society produced, and what remains of it today.

Few themes run with consistency through the history of the British Isles, save the land itself. This series seeks to show the way in which man has shaped and occupied the country, and how society has been moulded by the opportunities and constraints imposed by the landscape. The broad theme, is of man's interaction with his environment, which is carried through the series.

As editor, I have tried to allow each author to write his approach to the subject without undue interference. Ideally, such a study would have appeared as a large single volume but we have sought to make the divisions less arbitrary by allowing authors to cover a broad body of material in more than one book. Thus the volumes dealing with the medieval period come from the same hand, as do those spanning the sixteenth to the nineteenth centuries.

Britain before the Conquest, 5 vols, Routledge & Kegan Paul, 1979–81.

8

The effects of the Norman Conquest in England were pervasive, as Trevor Rowley makes clear early in his book, altering the whole framework of active life. The Conquest spawned a deep division in the way Englishmen regarded their past, some seeing in it a civilizing process, while others, like Tom Paine, writing in 1776 in *Common Sense*, looked upon it as the foundation of all our ills: 'A French bastard landing with an armed banditti and establishing himself King of England, against the consent of the natives, is, in plain terms, a very paltry, rascally original.' The basis for a rational judgment of the effects of the Conquest is more difficult to formulate, since so much of the documentary evidence is fragmentary or ambiguous. Thus the importance of the type of analysis made by Trevor Rowley of the landscape and material features often provides the only certain basis which we possess for understanding many aspects of our Norman heritage.

The achievement of the Normans becomes all the more remarkable given the relative brevity of the *Norman* period. In two generations the throne had passed to the first of the Plantagenets, Henry of Anjou, with little of the Norman in him either by blood or upbringing. Moreover, the first years after the Conquest were dominated by consolidation, and defence against Saxon revolt. The surge of building, of administrative and social reconstruction, and the extension of Norman power on the periphery, into Wales and Scotland, was concentrated into a short timespan under the Conqueror himself and his only English-born son, Henry I. The ferocious energy displayed by the Normans, not only in the British Isles but in all their domains, was the key to their success.

Andrew Wheatcroft

Preface

1066 is the best-known date in English history, and marks the end of the Anglo-Saxon period and the beginning of the Middle Ages. The battle of Hastings brought the Normans into Britain and literally changed the course of European history. However, despite their very obvious achievements, the castles, the churches, the new towns, the monasteries, much about the Normans remains enigmatic. Historians of various persuasions have argued continuously about the nature of their contribution to English society, its law, its economy, its wealth, and its political structure. This is perhaps because the Norman Conquest meant different things to different people, both at the time and subsequently, and no single statement can encompass the whole truth.

In writing this book I have followed in the steps of the giants of English medieval scholarship such as F. W. Maitland and F. M. Stenton. It has not been my intention to attempt to supersede their work or that of their successors; I have been more concerned to place their findings within a broader framework and to take an overview of the Norman heritage. Much of this heritage is to be found in the unwritten record of the landscape, in the shape of town and village, road and river alignments, in place-names, and in boundary patterns.

The quality and quantity of this landscape evidence has perhaps been underestimated in the past. We should perhaps examine the impact of the Norman Conquest very critically using the solid body of documentary, archaeological, architectural and linguistic evidence available as a means of understanding earlier non-documented invasions. For the purposes of this book I have retained the pre-1974 county boundaries. This is because Normans were largely responsible for the maintenance and the strengthening of the traditional county structure and because local English historical scholarship has been organized on a county basis for well over a century before local government re-organization.

Trevor Rowley

To Richard and Susannah

De tra ñ de Lanpe ten de epo Rotbt. x. hid. Saulod
iii. hid. Wills. iii. hid. Aluyed. focul cã. vi. hid
Ibi funt in dñio. x. car. 7 xvi. uilli cu xxi. bord viii. ferui
hñt. x. car. Totum ualet. xx. lib.

In Middeltone ten de epo Aluric. vi. hid. Willm. iii. hid
iii. v. Ibi in dñio fuñ. ii. car. 7 x. uilli cu. vi. bord
iiii. ferui hñt. iiii. car. Ibi molin de. vii. fol. Tot ual. vi. lib.

De tra ñ Banesberie ten de epo Rotbt. iii. hid. Goiffen
v. hid. Robtus ate. ii. hid. dñi. Wills. v. hid. Turmod dñi
hid. Tra e. xii. car. dim. Ibi fuñ in dñio. vii. car. xx. uilli
cu. v. bord. xii. ferui hñt. iiii. car. Ibi molin uni car
de. v. fol. iiii. denr iiii. ac tra.   xxiii. lib.
Tot T.R.E. ualb. xi. lib. 7 x. fol. Cu recep. xx. lib. 7 x. fol. Modo

De tra ñ Cropelie ten de epo Ansfred. x. hid.
Gislebtus. v. hid. Teodric. ii. hid. Ricard. iii. hid. Eduard
vi. hid. Roger. iii. hid. una grex Rotbt. ate Rotbt
iii. hid. una v. mñ. Tra e. xxv. car. In dñio fuñ. xiii.
car. 7 xx. viii. uilli cu. xviii. bord 7 un. francig. 7 x. ferui
hñt. xxvi. car. Ibi. iii. molin de. xxv. fol. iiii. denr
7 xx. ac tra. 7 v. ac graue.   xx. fol.
Tot T.R.E. ualb. xx. vi. lib. Cu recep. xx. xv. lib. Modo xxx. lib.

Roger ten de epo Harduintone. h est de peda Egelsham
Ibi fuñ. x. hide 7 dim. Tra e. ix. car. Ne in dñio. ii. car.
7 x. uilli cu. xii. bord hñt. vii. car. iiii. ac tra. xx. mñ.
7 qd xx ac pasture. Sibi qda maino habuit. hb.
7 quo uolt ire poterat. Tot T.R.E. ualb. x. lib.
Modo cu piscaria 7 cu paf. ual. xvii. lib.

Robt ten de epo inland epi. i. hid. in Widele. Tra e. ii. car.
Ne in dñio. ii. car. 7 iiii. ferui. 7 vi. uilli cu. ii. bord dñi
Ibi molin de. xxx. folid. Valuit. lx. fol. Modo. c. folid.

Saulod ten de epo Strodi. h. e. de feudo mātris Lincole.
Ibi. v. hide. Tra e. v. car. Ne in dñio de hac tra. iii. hide
7 ibi. ii. car. 7 molin. xx. fold. vi. den. 7 vi. ferui. 7 xx. vi.
ac tra. Valuit. xx. fold modo. l. fold. Almoi lebe tenuit.

In Baldendone ten de epo Ilernard. v. hid. Bristeua
ii. hid. 7 dimid. Tra e. vii. car. ibi. x. uilli cu. iii. ferui
hñt. vi. car. ibi. ii. ac pri. T.R.E. ualb. iiii. lib. Modo. vii. lib.

TERRA EPI BAIOCENSIS.

Epo Baiocensis ten de rege Cube. Ibi e. i. hida
Tra e. ii. car. Ne in dñio. ii. car. 7 ii. ferui. 7 vi. uilli
cu. v. bord hñt. vi. car. Ibi molin de. vi. fol. 7 xx. ac
tra. Silua. i. leu dim. tg. amd lat. Valuit. vi. lib. m. x. lib.
Aluuin. Algar lebe tenuit.

Iete epo ten Badintone. Ibi fuñ. xxxvi. hide. Tra e. xxx. car.
In dñio fueñ. ii. hide 7 dim. 7 aliã inland. Modo fñ in dñio
xxiiii. hide 7 dimid. 7 ibi fñ. x. car. 7 v. ferui. 7 xlviii.
uilli cu. x. bord hñt. xxx. car. ibi. iiii. molin de xlii. fol.
7 c. anguill.

7 ibi. c xl. ac tra. 7 xxx. ac pasture. Valuit. x. fol.
T.R.E. 7 post. ualb. xl. lib. Modo. lx. lib. Rumquini.

Item eps ten Scattone. Ibi. xxvi. h 7 q geldt T.R.E.
Tra e. xxiii. car. Ne in dñio de hac tra. i. hida 7 una v.
pter inland. 7 ibi. ii. car. 7 xx. ferui. 7 vi. uilli hñt
xxvi. bord hñt xxvi. car. Ibi. iiii. molin de. xl. fol.
7 ii. piscarie de. xxx. folid. 7 c. ac tra. 7 c. ac pasture.
Silua. i. leu tg. 7 dim leu lat. cu onerat ual. xx. fol.
T.R.E. 7 post. ualuit. xxx. lib. Modo. l. lib. Alnod lebe
tenuit.

Item eps ten Fewar. Ibi fñ. xxvi. hide. Tra e. xxvi. car.
Ne in dñio. vi. car. 7 xiiii. ferui. 7 xxx. uilli cu. viii. bord
hñt. xvi. car. Ibi. ccc. ac tra. xii. mñ. 7 ci. ac pasture.
T.R.E. 7 post. ualuit. xx. lib. Modo. xl. lib. Alveuechol honc

Libered de Laci ten de epo Baieoli. ii. hið. 7 dim in Bagin
torp. Tra e. iii. car. Ne in dñio. i. car. 7 un. uilli hñt alia.
Ibi. ii. ac tra. Valuit. lx. fol. Modo. xl. fol.

Widard ten. i. hið. 7 xii. ac. ex q ead ii. geld aii medi uilla
Tra e. ii. car. Ne in dñio. i. car. ii. ferui. 7 ii. uilli hñt
alia. Ibi. x. ac tra. Valuit. lx. fol. Modo. xl. folid.

Herueus ten Haselie. Ibi e. x. hide. Tra e. vi. car.
Ne in dñio. iii. car. 7 ii. ferui. 7 vi. uilli cu. iiii. bord
hñt. vi. car. Ibi. xxx. ac tra. Valuit. vi. lib. m. vii. lib.

Ide herueus ten. ii. hið in Bartewelle. Tra e. vi. car.
Ne in dñio. ii. car. 7 vi. uilli cu. v. bord hñt. iiii. car.
Ibi molin de. xx. denar. 7 vi. ac tra. 7 xx. ac filue.
Valuit. l. fold. Modo. lx. folid.

Roger ten. i. hið. 7 ciã parte. i. v. in Covele.
Tra e. ii. car. h e ibi in dñio. cu. iiii. bord. ii. ferui.
Ibi. iiii. ac tra. 7 ii. ac pasture. Valuit. xx. fol. m. xl. fol.

Rainald ten de epo Sunermone. Ibi fñ. xv. hide.
Tra e. xv. car. Ne in dñio. ii. car. iii. ferui. 7 xxvi. uilli
cu. xv. bord hñt. vi. car. Ibi molin de. xx. fol. 7 cccc.
anguill. 7 xl. ac tra. 7 cl. ac. ac pasture.
Valuit. x. lib. Modo. xij. lib.

Ide ten. vi. hið in Pearewelle. Tra e. iii. car. Ne in
dñio. ii. car. iii. ferui. 7 uii. uilli cu. ii. bord hñt. i. car.
7 dim. Ibi. ii. xii. ac tra. Valuit. 7 ual. iii. lib.

Adã ten de epo. ii. hið in Spineltone. Tra e. ii. car. haf
hnt. vi. uilli. Valuit. xl. fold. modo. lx. folid.

Aluyed ten de epo. i. hið in Spineltone. Tra e. i. car.
7 dimid. Ne in dñio br. i. car. 7 un. uilli cu. iii. bord
hñt. i. car. Valuit. ual. xxx. folid.

Widard ten de epo Fersnetford. Ibi fñ. vii. hið. Tra
e. viii. car. Ne in dñio. iii. car. 7 xxx. ferui. 7 xxvi. uilli
cu. viii. bord hñt. ix. car. Ibi. ii. molin. x. fol. Valuit. 7 ual
In ead uilla ten. ii. hið. 7 dim. Tra e. iii. car. Long. lib.
7 ipsa. ac tra. cu. vi. hid. Valuit. xx. fol. modo. xl. lib.
Robt ten de epo. ii. hið in Sulerge. Tra e. ii. car.
Ibi hñt hoof. ii. ii. car. Valuit. xxx. fol. modo. xl. fol.
Roger ten de epo Fostel. Ibi fñ. ii. hide. Tra e. iii. car.

1 The coming of the Normans

Introduction

There are seldom absolute full stops in history or entirely new chapters. One event, however, which has been almost universally accepted in such terms, from the greatest scholars to the humblest schoolchild, is the Norman Conquest of England in 1066. Not only was this the last time that England was successfully invaded, but it was followed by a complete change in the ruling dynasty, the introduction of military feudalism, the reform of the church and the rapid expansion of monasticism. Such social and political changes were accompanied by dramatic architectural and topographical developments: the introduction of the castle, the spread of new towns and the erection of hundreds of new ecclesiastical establishments, all executed in a new style of architecture. Whatever moral reservations must be expressed about the activities of the Normans in England there is no doubt that through their energy and administrative ability they transformed the face of town and country alike.

Two unique sources of historical evidence have contributed greatly to this impression of profound change: the Domesday Book, which was compiled some twenty years after the Norman Conquest, and the Bayeux Tapestry, which was probably completed within a decade of the Conquest. The Domesday Book (1086) provides us with the most comprehensive survey of the English landscape and

1 An extract from the Domesday Book covering lands held by the Bishops of Lincoln and Bayeux in Oxfordshire in 1086. See Appendix 1 for translation of this section of the survey

VBI hAROLD:SACRAMENTVM:FECIT: hIC hAROLD:DVX
VVILLELMO DVCI:-

2 This scene showing Harold swearing an oath of allegiance to William while touching a reliquary (left) and the altar (right) is a critical one in the Bayeux Tapestry's account of William's accession to the English throne

society ever executed. Although doubts may be expressed about the proper interpretation of its contents, the survey represents the first historical reference to the vast majority of English settlements and therefore intrinsically it represents an historical beginning.

The Bayeux Tapestry is a confident account of the Conquest which incorporated a justification of William's claim to the English throne. A claim which scholars have argued about over the centuries. It seems probable that the tapestry was embroidered in England, perhaps at St Augustine's, Canterbury, for William's half brother, Bishop Odo of Bayeux, and was intended to be hung in Bayeux Cathedral. There has been considerable controversy over the dating of the tapestry, but it seems most likely that it was completed in time for the consecration of Odo's new cathedral in Bayeux in 1077. The tapestry narrates in ostensibly simple terms the events leading up to the Conquest and the story of

14

3 Death of Harold at the battle of Hastings as shown in the Bayeux Tapestry. Traditionally Harold has been regarded as the figure falling with an arrow apparently piercing his eye. There has been considerable scholarly controversy over this interpretation, but it remains the most probable explanation

the battle of Hastings itself. The story is quite clearly told from the Norman viewpoint and appears to be based largely on the accounts of two of William the Conqueror's contemporary hagiographers, William of Jumièges and William of Poitiers, as well as a version of the Anglo-Saxon Chronicle.

In brief the tapestry tells of Harold leaving Edward the Confessor's court and undertaking the journey to Normandy, where, after being seized by Count Guy of Ponthieu, he is taken to William's palace at Rouen. Harold then joins William in a successful campaign against the Breton border towns of Dol and Dinan. At Bayeux Harold takes an oath of obedience to William – an event which was pointedly of considerable significance in the light of subsequent events. On returning to England Edward dies and Harold accepts the crown. At this point the vision of Halley's comet which appeared that year is seen as a terrible omen. On hearing of the news of Harold's accession William prepares a fleet and then sails for England, where, after building a castle at Hastings, he goes into battle against Harold. Some of the most vivid scenes then follow, portraying aspects of the battle in considerable detail, including a brilliantly depicted cavalry attack, and Harold's death. The final section which presumably showed William being crowned at Westminster is missing. Thus the actual event which led to Norman domination in England is graphically illustrated. No other event in English medieval history received such singular treatment, but it is ironic that this, the finest surviving example of English medieval embroidery, was also to be the last. Subsequently both embroidery and the allied art of manuscript illumination were to be starker and cruder as a result of the Conquest.

Attitudes to the Norman Conquest
Almost without exception the chroniclers of the eleventh and twelfth centuries regarded the Norman Conquest of England in a favourable light. They did not question William's right to the throne, nor his method of obtaining and maintaining it. Not surprisingly the views of these contemporary historians have had an important part to play in the way in which subsequent historians have looked at the Conquest and its impact. As is the way with such accounts too much weight has been placed upon their accuracy and historians have tended to quarry in them for information which would strengthen their own view of events. Many political and legal historians have 'taken sides', viewing the Conquest either as an unmitigated disaster on the one hand; or as the re-establishment of civilized order on the other.

Although Victorian historians viewed the Roman Conquest of Britain as an unparalleled success bringing civilization and eventually Christianity, albeit temporarily, to a backward pagan country, their attitude to the Normans was more ambivalent. A. E. Freeman in his monumental *History of the Norman Conquest of England: Its Causes and Its Results*

(1867–79), believed in the basic continuity of English society and saw the Norman Conquest as a temporary set-back: 'The fiery trial which England went through was a fire which did not destroy, but only purified. She came forth once more the England of old.' J. H. Round, as a genealogist disagreed; in *Feudal England* (1895) he argued his belief that the Normans were essentially superior and that 'There must be surely, an instinctive feeling that in England our consecutive political history does in a sense, begin with the Norman Conquest.'

In 1908 Sir Frank Stenton wrote *William the Conqueror*, in which he followed Round and claimed that England prior to the Conquest had 'no administration worthy of the name' and to compare it with contemporary Normandy seemed like a move 'from decadence to growth'. Two world wars later Stenton was to alter his views radically and in *Anglo-Saxon England* (1943), he wrote: 'in comparison with England, Normandy in the mid 11th century was still a state in the making', and that the Normans were 'a harsh and violent race, they were the closest of all western people to the Barbarian strain in the continental order. They had produced little in art or learning and nothing in literature that could be set beside the work of Englishmen.' Subsequently the pendulum swung even further against the Normans and in 1963 H. G. Richardson and G. O. Sayles in the *Governance of Mediaeval England from the Conquest to the Magna Carta* wrote: 'For half a century or so, from 1066 the English way of life was not sensibly altered, the Normans had very little to teach even in the art of war, and they had very much to learn. They were Barbarians who were becoming conscious of their insufficiency.' While in the *Medieval Foundations of England* (1974) Sayles systematically attempted to destroy any claims the Normans might have had for any social, political, economic or military innovation and development. In essence, he believed that the Normans were rather an unpleasant irrelevance!

As far as historians are concerned the Battle of Hastings still rages. In 1976 in *The Normans and their Myth* R. H. C.

Davis bypassed the old argument, by admitting the achievements of Anglo-Norman England, but in a disquieting way questioning the very existence of the 'Normans' as an identifiable separate people. The pendulum is now somewhere in the middle, and in a thoughtful essay written in 1966 to mark the 900th anniversary of the Conquest, F. Barlow suggested there was a basic continuity from Anglo-Saxon England to Anglo-Norman England, but that we should look mainly to Normandy for the influences that in the later eleventh century modified the indigenous pattern (*The Norman Conquest its setting and Impact*, T. Chevallier *et al.* 1966). Scholars increasingly are attempting the difficult task of distinguishing between the purely Norman contribution to Anglo-Norman England and those developments whose entry was simply facilitated by the Conquest.

There remain, however, fundamental unanswered and perhaps unanswerable questions. While, for instance, the virtually total replacement of the English aristocracy by Normans is quite clear, the scale of the Norman impact upon other Anglo-Saxon institutions is far less obvious. How many of the changes which we are able to detect would have occurred anyway? How far did the Normans simply provide a vehicle for the introduction of new ideas from the continent and how many of the apparent changes we think we can see after 1066 are in fact illusory? Nevertheless English society in the mid-eleventh century *did* experience a decisive change, the remains of which are visible all around us.

The sources

In order to reconstruct a picture of Norman England we have to rely on a wide variety of very different source materials. The documentary evidence for the century and a half succeeding the Conquest is regrettably erratic, both in content and quality. Despite the Domesday Book, we are largely without that wealth of documentary evidence that characterizes the thirteenth and first half of the fourteenth century. Central government records only begin with the

4 The Jew's House, Lincoln. A rare example of surviving non-military, Norman vernacular architecture

Pipe Rolls in 1130, and even then it is not until 1156 that there is a continuous surviving record. We are therefore largely dependent upon local charters and the fragmentary surviving estate accounts.

The writings of the chroniclers and annalists are of immense interest, but have to be treated with extreme caution. They tend to be partial, repetitive and sometimes bizarrely inaccurate. Most of the contemporary writers were Norman or pro-Norman, such as Florence of Worcester, Henry of Huntingdon, William of Jumièges and William of Poitiers, although the Anglo-Saxon Chronicle was continued in English at Peterborough Abbey until 1154; a Saxon Eadmer, wrote *The Life of St. Anselm* and Ordericus Vitalis of mixed parentage produced his *Historia Ecclesiastica*. William of Malmesbury, who died about 1143, was a monk who did

5 Boothby Pagnell, Lincolnshire. A fine example of a Norman manor house

something to redress the balance by reporting the Conquest and its aftermath, in retrospect, more from the English viewpoint.

The surviving architectural evidence provides us with the soundest information about the physical appearance of military and ecclesiastical structures of the period, but the evidence is less helpful when it comes to domestic architecture and lesser buildings. The architectural remains tend to reflect that section of society, i.e. the aristocracy, where we know that there was maximum change. Nevertheless the wealth of Norman architectural remains represents the most tangible legacy of the Conquest and provides us with the best opportunity of understanding their cultural and artistic development.

When it comes to the archaeological record we are faced with something of a dilemma. There is no branch of medieval archaeology labelled 'Norman'. This is because the century of Norman rule in England has left no distinctive artefactual record, which would demonstrate that a significant change had taken place in the lives of the majority of people. It is true that examples of churches, castles and monasteries of Norman build which were subsequently destroyed, have been excavated, but the results of this work tend to complement what is already known from standing structures. Neither were the Normans responsible for introducing any significant technological innovations. Agricultural and industrial processes were unaffected by the Conquest as far as we can see.

The changes wrought by the Conquest were too subtle to be detected in the below-ground evidence – ceramics, metal and glass objects were not really affected by the Conquest, either in fabric or design, even Norman coins continued in the Saxon style. To the question, 'would the archaeologist recognize the Norman Conquest in the absence of documentary evidence?', the strict answer must be 'no'. However, taken in a broader landscape context, the proliferation of castles and churches, the acceleration of urbanization, changes in place-names and extensions of trading practices seen in the archaeological record of the twelfth and thirteenth centuries would indicate that there had in reality been profound economic, social and political changes, many of which would not have occurred, at least in the form they took if there had been no Conquest.

6 A silver penny of William I minted at Dover. Apart from the change of head Norman coins did not significantly change in design from their Saxon predecessors

Who were the Normans?

Perhaps one of the reasons for the lack of agreement over the Norman impact is due to the difficulty of defining precisely who the Normans were. They were an enigmatic people, whose monarchy had ceased to rule in England within a century of the battle of Hastings, and whose scattered empire, which at its largest included land from Wales to Syria, had all but evaporated by 1200. Normandy itself ceased to exist as an independent entity in 1204 when it was absorbed into France after the fall of Chateau Gaillard and Rouen. We should therefore perhaps begin by examining the early development of the Normans in order to understand who they really were, how they saw themselves, and how others saw them. Normandy does not constitute a natural geographical region; the north-east (Haute Normandie) is made up of undulating chalk and limestone while the west (Basse Normandie) forms part of the *armorican massif* consisting of hard sandstone, slate and granite.

The territory of historical Normandy sits astride the lower Seine river, which provides a natural and historically well-used access to the very heart of France. By the late Iron Age the region was well peopled with a series of regional tribal centres. When the Romans conquered Gaul they built upon the existing settlement pattern creating a province known as the second Lyonnaise. They built a military road roughly parallel to the Seine from Paris to Lillebonne (*Juliobona*) and on to the harbour at Harfleur. Rouen (*Rotomagus*) sitting on the road was made capital. Another Roman road, from the Loire valley, passed through Sées and Bayeux (*Augustodonum*). Before the Romans withdrew from Gaul in the fifth century AD, the northern province had settled very much into the political entity that was to become Normandy.

Rouen had become an important bishopric before the end of the fourth century and in the fifth century further bishoprics were founded at Bayeux, Avranches, Évreux, Lisieux, Coutances and Sées. This ecclesiastical pattern, based firmly upon that of Roman civil government, was to withstand subsequent Germanic and Scandinavian incursions. Already in the third century, Germanic tribes of Visigoths, Vandals and Huns were making forays into Gaul. In the fifth century another German group, the Franks, had taken

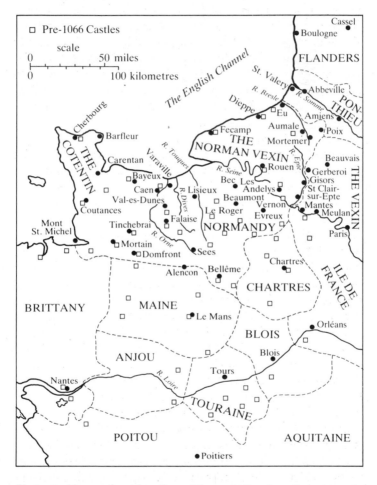

Figure 1 Normandy and north-west France in the eleventh century, also showing castles recorded before 1066. The heavy concentration of castles in the Norman domain in France was repeated in England after the Conquest

23

control and, under Clovis, with the help of the Gallo-Roman bishops, unified the whole kingdom by the end of the century. His son Clothaire became king of the Western Country or Neustria, which included two-thirds of the territory we know as Normandy. Late medieval writers romanticizing over Norman glories created the myth that Normandy and the grand sounding Neustria were co-extensive; in reality, however, the new duchy coincided with the metropolitan see of Rouen, which itself was formed from the Roman province.

It was the Seine which attracted Norse pirates in the ninth century; two campaigns in particular in 856–61 and 885–91 saw extensive Scandinavian activity in north-western France. With considerable ferocity they laid siege to Paris and overran Neustria, burning and looting churches and monasteries. The traditional story of the creation of Normandy was that in 911 Charles the Simple, the King of the Franks, ceded a large territory on the lower Seine at the same time as giving his daughter in marriage to a Norseman called Rolf or Rollo by the Treaty of St Clair-sur-Epte. The cession is generally regarded as the foundation of Normandy as a marcher duchy. Although there is some dispute about the precise status of the duchy, significantly one of the clauses in the treaty gave Rollo the right of fighting Brittany, which at the time was an independent kingdom. Initially the territory consisted of Upper Normandy, centring on the estates of Rouen, and bounded by the rivers Bresle, Epte, Avre and Dives. Lower Normandy, including the Le Bessin and Maine, was added by two consecutive grants of 924 and 933. Thus by the middle years of the tenth century the *Terra Northmannorum* or the *Northmannia* had been established. It was a 'state' with well-defined borders and internal administrative divisions and this secular and ecclesiastical administrative heritage was to be of considerable benefit to the dukes in their creation of the Norman Empire. Normandy was born out of a mixture of Roman, Carolingian, Frankish and Scandinavian elements: a strange pedigree, but one which was to prove extraordinarily potent in the hands of its single-minded leaders.

Surviving documentary evidence for the emerging Normandy in the tenth century, is tantalizingly thin and we have only a blurred picture of the nature of Scandinavian settlement. In the light of later development in England one particularly pertinent question to be asked is how much was the creation of Normandy accompanied by large-scale folk movements from the north and how much was the Norse settlement simply the imposition of an alien aristocracy on to the indigenous population. We do have some indication through the evidence of language and place-names that French remained the dominant language, which is an indication of limited early settlement. In the early eleventh century contemporary writers recorded that 'Roman' rather than Danish was the language of Rouen, although reputedly Scandinavian was being spoken in Bayeux.

The analysis of place-name evidence is revealing. Many names which were once regarded as purely Scandinavian have been found to have parallels in non-Scandinavian parts of France. For instance, Dieppe can mean 'deep' in English or Frisian as well as in Scandinavian, and place-names such as 'Fecamp' could equally be of Germanic or Scandinavian origin. The same difficulty of interpretation is to be found in distinguishing between Scandinavian and Germanic personal names. The Franks had ruled the country for more than four centuries before the Norse settlement and many of the recorded personal names could be either Germanic or Scandinavian.

More important, however, is the fact that the vast majority of Scandinavian place-names in Normandy are hybrids. Whereas in northern England Scandinavian settlement resulted in a pattern of distinctive Scandinavian place-names, there is no equivalent distribution in Normandy. Names which incorporate a Scandinavian personal name such as *Grimon*ville and *Tour*ville suggest that a still romanized peasantry referred to the villa or farm of a Scandinavian lord simply by adding the French suffix to his name. The picture that emerges from the place-name evidence of tenth and early eleventh century Norman society is of a Scandinavian hierarchy ruling over a population whose language was neither Frankish nor Scandinavian, but French. Recent analysis of the scanty documentary evidence also points to a considerable degree of continuity between the estates of the Carolingians and the Normans.

Archaeologically, too, the evidence for a large-scale folk movement is sparse, but perhaps this point should not be overstressed, in view of the fact that Scandinavian archaeological remains in England had not been located in any quantity until relatively recently. None the less it is worth noting that so far very few incontestable Scandinavian buildings or burials have been found in Normandy. Scandinavian coins from the tenth century are quite common in Normandy as they are throughout maritime northwestern Europe. But the quality and distribution of coinage in the period c. 1000–20 suggests an increasing detachment from Scandinavia and a strengthening of ties with the Romantic world.

Early Norman chroniclers enjoyed telling of the devastation brought about by the Scandinavian settlement; all the evidence, however, indicates a considerable degree of continuity between Frank and Norman and tends to suggest that there was no great exodus of population from Scandinavia into Normandy in the ninth and tenth centuries. The Norsemen married freely with non-Scandinavians, indeed none of the dukes' wives came from Scandinavia or England. By the first half of the eleventh century their family connections were typically French, and Professor R. H. C. Davis has pointed out that it was only in the eleventh century, when the Normans were no longer Scandinavian, that they began to acquire some of their most 'Norman' characteristics. As the great families emerged, so did the great abbeys, with their distinctive style of art and architecture. F. W. Maitland in his usual perceptive fashion remarked: 'It is now generally admitted that for at least half a century before the battle of Hastings, the Normans were Frenchmen, French in their language, French in their law

7 This part of the Bayeux Tapestry shows the careful military preparations made by the Normans before the sailing of the fleet for England. Such preparations were an important element in the military success of the Normans

... and the peculiar characteristics which mark off the custom of Normandy from other French customs seem due much rather to the legislation of Henry of Anjou than to any Scandinavian tradition.' So the Norsemen had to a great extent been absorbed by the indigenous inhabitants of Normandy, but as we shall see the Normans still retained some distinctive features which appear to have reflected Scandinavian influence. Not least of which, was a degree of ruthlessness and flexibility which enabled them to take over existing institutions and use them very effectively for their own ends.

What were the other chief characteristics of the Normans in the eleventh century? By the early eleventh century they had a well-organized state and a powerful army which enabled the Norman dukes to play an influential role in the politics of northwestern Europe, and to intervene militarily in the affairs of other duchies. Although the organization of civil and ecclesiastical institutions was important, it was

8 Depiction of horses during the battle of Hastings on the Bayeux Tapestry. Horses appear throughout the length of the tapestry and often they are treated more sympathetically than the human characters

perhaps the army which was their strongest asset. The Normans clearly recognized the value of efficient military organization – the Bayeux Tapestry dwells on the organization of supplies, helmets, hauberks, swords, lances, axes, barrels and skins of wine, and the building of the invasion fleet, which was apparently completed in eight months.

The Norman love of horses was legendary and the tapestry dwells lovingly on equestrian detail. The military used a horse known as a 'destrier'; these were reputed to be nimble even when carrying a heavily armed rider, and some scholars have attributed Norman military success to this capacity. However, the argument that a victorious army succeeded because it had better horses is a familiar one and can rarely be verified.

The Normans recruited skilled soldiers from outside the province. Earlier in the eleventh century families such as the Bellêmes who were Frankish and the Tessons from Anjou were recruited into the military service of the Norman dukes, and William the Conqueror was only following the policy of his predecessors when he recruited knights from Brittany, Flanders, Artois and Picardy for the invasion of England. Many of the 'foreign' knights were rapidly assimilated into the Norman aristocracy. Few of the great baronial families that were subsequently to feature so prominently in English history had acquired their Norman lands before the 1030s. It was the emergence of the new noble families, such as the Beaumonts, Bohuns and the Warennes, which marked the real break between the sub-Carolingian and the authentic Norman period, and by the mid-eleventh century this ruling group had begun to develop the symptoms of territorial feudalism found in the rest of France.

The church was to be the other major institution which contributed towards Norman supremacy. Just as the ruling and military classes were re-organized and strengthened with the introduction of outsiders in the early eleventh century, so, too, was the church. Although the Norsemen rapidly embraced Christianity and re-established the monastic foundations, which only a few years earlier they had been plundering, the tenth-century Norman church was not inspiring. Apart from the community at Mont-St-Michel on the border between Normandy and Brittany, which showed exceptional zeal for collecting and copying manuscripts, there was little evidence of artistic or architectural merit in the duchy. Indeed there were clear symptoms of decadence by the end of the millennium. The decisive change came in 1001 when Duke Richard II, probably inspired by developments in Burgundy, decided to replace the secular clerks of Fécamp with a monastic community. The duke looked abroad for help and succeeded in attracting a noted ecclesiastical reformer, an Italian called William of Volpiano, or William of Dijon as he became known. William had been trained at Cluny where he had effected widespread monastic change and, once established at Fécamp, he used it as a base to systematically develop the church throughout the duchy. He played an important role in the re-organization of the dioceses of Bayeux and

Coutances by acquiring estates, by establishing a church for the communities there and assisting in the foundation of new monasteries. His work had a fundamental impact both on the quality of the religious life of the Norman church and on the influence of the church in the community. The number of monasteries increased rapidly from five in 1000

9 Three Norman knights – a twelfth-century bronze fragment, probably part of a casket, known as the Temple Pyx

to thirty or more by 1066, and it has been estimated that William of Dijon was directly involved in the foundation of twenty-one of these.

Just as re-organization of the Norman aristocracy in the early eleventh century was to provide a model for what was to later happen in England, so, too, the reformed Norman church was to play a vital part in the subsequent creation of Norman England. The churchmen of Normandy gained a wide reputation as reformers, and their scholars were amongst the finest in Europe. The most important of the foreign recruits was an Italian called Lanfranc who transformed the abbey at Bec from a place of obscurity into one of the most famous abbeys of Europe. Pupils from many countries were attracted to it, the most notable being two Italians, Anselm of Lucca, the future Pope Alexander II, and Anselm of Aosta. The latter was to prove himself to be one of the greatest intellects of the Middle Ages and succeeded Lanfranc as Archbishop of Canterbury.

When Lanfranc first settled in Normandy c. 1039, the monasteries under their great foreign abbots – fellow Italians, like John of Fruttuaria at Fécamp, Suppo of Fruttuaria at Mont-St-Michel, and Isembard Teutonicus at Holy Trinity, Rouen – had become centres of prestige, wealth, learning and spiritual excellence. These provided a direct link with the great monasteries of Burgundy, northern Italy and with Rome. Lanfranc was to act as William's agent in developing and strengthening the episcopacy and fashioning it as a tool of government. By appointing William's nominees to vacant sees, such as Odo of Bayeux (1049) and Geoffrey of Coutances (1048), Lanfranc was able to ensure control of the allegiance of the bishops and effective geographical control of their estates. As prior of St Étienne (1063–70) he was to play an important role in developing Caen as William's alternative urban power base to Rouen.

The revival of the importance of the episcopacy was followed by the construction of new cathedrals on a scale commensurate with that of the monasteries. By the 1050s and 1060s new abbey churches were being built at Mont-St-

Michel, Remy, Jumièges and Caen and, although borrowing heavily from Burgundian sources, they displayed the beginnings of the distinctive Norman style of architecture which was to reach its height in Norman England.

Thus in the eleventh century building on an underlying demographic and administrative continuity Normandy developed a new and vital aristocracy, church, monasticism and culture. In the words of Professor Davis: 'As a result the Normans had produced a new state and new society which no longer belonged to the Scandinavian world but was in the forefront of the military and cultural development of the French.'

William and the Conquest of England.

Duke William II, or William the Conqueror as he was known after the battle of Hastings, was born at Falaise in 1027/8, the bastard son of Duke Robert I, or Robert the Magnificent as he was popularly known. Robert's death in 1035 while returning from a pilgrimage to Jerusalem, resulted in a politically troubled situation. William succeeded to the dukedom as a minor and there followed a period of near anarchy during which two of his guardians were assassinated. William survived this tumultuous period and formally came of age in 1044. Almost immediately he was involved in an internal revolt which was finally crushed at the decisive battle of Val-ès-Dunes in 1047.

William's long apprenticeship at the seat of power was to serve him well. In the following twenty years he consolidated his control and developed skills which he was later to apply with great success in England. Although regrettably the details are only scantily recorded in the early part of this period a strengthening of feudal ties was accompanied by a general tightening up of ducal administration, most notably in the area of military service, providing the Norman duke with the strongest army in Europe. At the same time William insisted on exercising his right to garrison the castles of his strongest barons, and it was probably at this time that the castle became a particularly important element

10 The exchequer in Caen castle, Normandy. This is one of the few surviving Norman buildings in the much altered fortification

in William's military strategy.

William embarked on a series of successful and by all accounts brutal campaigns which eventually brought the whole of Maine under Norman control, and subdued Brittany over which he claimed lordship. Thus by 1066 William had established himself as master of north-west Gaul, a powerful European sovereign in all but name.

Town life flourished and in particular William deliberately fostered the development of Caen between Bayeux and Rouen on an island at the confluence of the rivers Orne and Odon. William saw Caen as a new military stronghold with the geographical advantages of Rouen, mainly access to the sea, but without Rouen's vulnerability to attack. Caen also lies in the very heart of the narrow belt of Jurassic limestone, which provided the main source of Caen stone for the construction of castles, churches and monasteries both in Normandy and England.

By 1060 William had built a stone castle there, traces of which have recently been located to the east of Henry I's *aula*, as well as the abbey of Holy Trinity (the Abbaye-aux-

Dames) to the east of the castle and by 1063 St Étienne (the
Abbaye-aux-hommes) to the west. These two fine abbeys
which dominated the city were constructed as part penance
for the uncanonical nature of William's marriage to
Matilda, daughter of Baldwin V, Count of Flanders, in the
early 1050s. This marriage, which for rather obscure reasons
was opposed by Pope Leo IX, brought to the Norman court a
descendant of both Charlemagne and King Alfred. The
ostensible reason for the papal ban was that the couple were

Figure 2a   Plan of pre-Conquest (*c.* 950) dioceses in England

too closely related, but this was palpably untrue. Papal opposition to the marriage was only lifted in 1059 after Lanfranc's intercession on behalf of William.

William's claim to the throne of England lay principally through his grandfather's sister, Emma, who was married to two consecutive kings of England, Ethelred and Cnut. Emma who was sister to Duke Richard II (966–1026), and the mother of Edward the Confessor, was largely responsible for bringing Normans and Norman customs into the

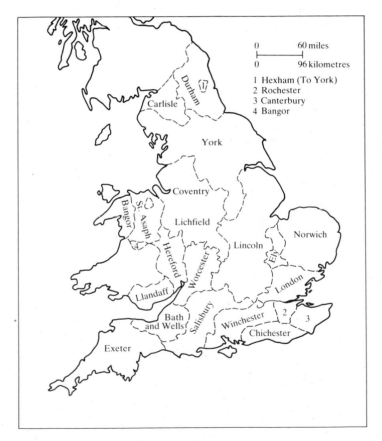

Figure 2b Plan of twelfth-century dioceses in England and Wales

English court. Edward spent half his life in exile in the duchy and in the first years after succeeding to the throne relied on the political and military advice of his Norman comrades and generally throughout his reign maintained close personal contact with Normandy. It seems reasonably clear that Edward the Confessor had recognized William as his successor in the early 1050s, and probable that Harold's journey to Normandy in 1064 was to confirm this recognition. On hearing of Edward's death on 5 January 1066 and Harold's accession, William had no doubt about his course of action and set in motion the diplomatic and military preparations necessary for the invasion of England.

The political details of the immediate events leading up to the Conquest of England need not detain us here, nor shall we rehearse the story of the famous battle itself. Suffice it to say that William's preparation and organization, the characteristics of which were to be the hallmark of his rule as King of England, played a decisive role in his victory. Seldom can the events of one day – Saturday, 14 October 1066 – have had such a profound effect on the political geography of Europe. William of Poitiers wrote that, with his success at the battle of Hastings, Duke William had conquered all of England in a single day 'between the third hour and evening'. In reality, however, although this battle saw the end of united and national resistance to William, local resistance and piecemeal risings continued and it was not until after the notorious 'harrying of the North' (1068–70) that the *pax Normanica* prevailed.

The immediate impact of the Conquest
The Norman occupation of England was virtually a re-run of the Scandinavian settlement in Normandy. England received a new royal dynasty, a new aristocracy, a virtually new church, a new art and architecture and, in official circles, a new language. By 1086 only half a dozen of the 180 greater landlords or tenants-in-chief were English. The Crown itself held one-fifth of the land and a considerable percentage of the remainder was held by a few of William's

favourites, who had come with him from France. It has been estimated that about half the country was in the hands of ten men, most of whom were William's relatives. The power and wealth of the country was held by a small Norman elite, and as if to demonstrate the change of management castles were built throughout the kingdom. Within twenty years of the Conquest they dominated all the shire towns and within half a century sat in virtually every settlement of importance in the country. By 1090 only one of the sixteen English bishoprics was held by an Englishman and six of those sees had been moved from their historic centres to large towns where they subsequently remained. By the end of the twelfth century virtually every Anglo-Saxon cathedral had been removed and rebuilt in Anglo-Norman style, as well as hundreds of new abbeys, and parish churches.

It should, however, be remembered that Norman domination was largely confined to the upper echelons of society. Although groups of French settlers did move into England and were found in many towns particularly in the Welsh borderlands, the level of folk penetration was far less even than that perpetrated by the tenth-century Norsemen in Normandy. Indeed recent analysis of place-names in Normandy suggests that there might even have been a modest movement of English settlers into Normandy after the Conquest.

The Norman Conquest of England was in no way a folk movement to be compared with the Anglo-Saxon or Scandinavian settlements. Similarly, the place-name evidence demonstrates precisely the same pattern of hybridization that had already occurred in Normandy. Norman family names were attached to already existing Anglo-Saxon place-names and there was a considerable restyling of place-names to Norman design. Despite the use of French in polite society it never reached much beyond that, and although a considerable number of French words found their way into the English language, they did not change it profoundly. One reason for this was that the Normans transacted most of the written communication in Latin and not French, but in the process did displace Anglo-Saxon as the official language.

Norman control of England

Once William had successfully quelled all opposition he was able to create a state in England which was far stronger and more unified than anything that had gone before. The secret of this was his complete domination of the country through feudal institutions. Before 1066 feudalism was more developed in Normandy than in England, military obligations in return for land, known as Knights' service was already a recognized institution and many feudal quotas had already been established. In the process of the Conquest, not only was the Norman model introduced into England, but it was made far more effective and systematic than it had ever been in Normandy. This was largely because, as conqueror, William quite literally claimed the whole of England as his own. He dispossessed all but a handful of English lords and gave lands to his own men, insisting that he, as king, was the only person allowed to regard land as his absolute property; everyone else was merely a tenant who paid rent, normally in the form of knights' service. This was even the case with the English bishoprics and abbeys who also became Crown tenants and had to provide service. He was therefore both king and feudal lord of absolutely all the land in his kingdom, and consequently he controlled the sole source of wealth as well as the font of justice. England became the supreme example of a feudal military monarchy. The Crown and the Norman aristocracy found themselves extremely wealthy, wealth which was rapidly translated into buildings – cathedrals, abbeys, parish churches, castles and new towns.

It is a paradox that although it was in England that the Normans achieved their greatest success in all fields, in the long run the Conquest of England turned them into Englishmen. Although the new Norman aristocracy largely despised the English and their customs, they were operating essentially within an English matrix. Because their penetration of English society was at such an elevated level it was always probable that English traditions and institutions would survive in some form, and eventually absorb the Norman masters. By the end of the twelfth century the Normans in England were ceasing to call themselves Normans and from 1154 even the kings were no longer Norman. Henry II was an Angevin of the Plantagenet family – only one of his eight grandparents had been Norman.

King John's loss of Normandy in 1204 merely placed the final seal on a process of territorial evaporation which was already well advanced. The French Conquest of Normandy this time moving westwards down the Seine valley, proved to be almost as easy as the Norman Conquest of England. Those lords who had lands on either side of the Channel had to choose, not between England and Normandy, but between England and France. Although the French continued to refer to Normandy and recognized it as a distinct province observing its Norman customs or laws, all the evidence suggests that, in the words of Professor Davis:

> the kings of England and France had forced the barons of Normandy to choose between their two countries, no one stood up to protest that he was neither English or French, but Norman. On the contrary the English became more English and the French more French and the Normans as history had known them disappeared.

The Norman Empire
It is indisputable that the Normans played a major, and in some cases, decisive role in European politics during the eleventh and twelfth centuries. The term 'Norman Empire' has been applied in various ways: to describe their domination of north-western France in the eleventh century, to cover the Anglo-French territories of the later twelfth century, and to cover the scattered lands held by Norman lords throughout the world in the twelfth century. It is true that from time to time Norman-dominated territories acted in military unison, but in reality there was never any question that those territories which were simultaneously ruled by

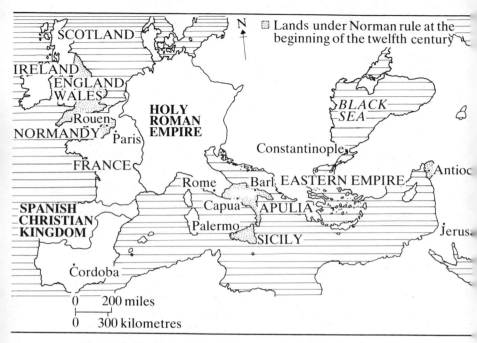

Figure 3 The Norman Empire. Normans also ruled in Malta and along stretches of the North African coast in the twelfth-century

Normans formed part of a homogeneous Norman empire. Although there was intermittent continuing contact between clerics, scholars and even soldiers, the Normans themselves never saw these links as constituting a cohesive cultural and political structure. Even during those short stretches of time where England and Normandy had the same head of state they were ruled completely independently. It was the chronicler Ordericus Vitalis who was mainly responsible for welding the various episodes of Norman opportunism together in order to create a coherent narrative, and in so doing created a Norman world which many later historians accepted at its face value. Nevertheless it is informative to look at the Normans abroad in order to understand something of their attitudes to the lands which they ruled albeit temporarily.

40

The Normans were a warrior people, and in the eleventh century when war was endemic in Europe they were constantly in conflict with their neighbours, both in France and in Britain and further afield. In the first part of the eleventh century a number of Normans had ambitions further south. In about 1020 a strong contingent of Normans took part in what was virtually a crusade to the Iberian peninsula. This was not the first time that the men of the north had ventured southwards: Norse raids in the ninth and tenth centuries had extended around the whole of the Iberian peninsula into the Mediterranean, attacking Christian and Arab alike. There was certainly something of this same opportunist piratical spirit operating under a Christian banner that attracted, amongst others, Norman barons to the vulnerable kaleidoscope of states that made up the central and eastern Mediterranean.

As early as 1016 a party of Norman pilgrims returning from the Holy Lands landed at Apulia in Italy and found a political situation ready for exploitation. They travelled back to Normandy, gathering reinforcements and intervened, ultimately decisively, in a struggle between Byzantine, Moslem, Lombard and Papal interests. For nearly two generations before the Conquest of England active Norman military leadership was transforming the political shape of southern Italy. In 1059 Robert Guiscard, the 'wizard', was recognized by the pope as Duke of Apulia and Calabria. From this secure base the Normans conducted the conquest and settlement of Sicily between 1071 and 1092. Sicily had previously been ruled by Moslems for two centuries and had a large Berba population with a lively Arab culture. The island was acquired under the auspices of a Christian Crusade, and in the late eleventh century the Normans became the self-appointed champions of a new concept of Holy War: a variation on the theme of 'private war' of which they were by then the undoubted European masters. During the twelfth century Sicily, under a Norman king, enjoyed an important political role in the central Mediterranean, and, by an alliance with the Papacy, at one stage had designs upon the eastern Roman Empire. Ultimately, however, in 1194 the Normans lost control of the island to the Holy Roman Empire.

Following the appeal of Pope Urban II at Clermont in 1095 the Normans were in the vanguard of the first crusade, with one powerful contingent from Normandy led by Duke Robert 'Curthose', William's eldest son, and another even more powerful one from Norman Italy and Sicily under Bohemond of Hauteville, a son of Robert Guisgard, and Bohemin's nephew, Tancred. Jerusalem was taken from the Moslems in 1098. In the meantime a Norman lordship was established by Beaumont at Antioch, and the Norman dynasty here, which formed part of the Latin kingdom of Outremer, outlasted those in England, Sicily and southern Italy. From 1123 to 1160 an alliance between Norman Antioch and Norman Sicily even enabled them to occupy a considerable length of the North African coast.

The Mediterranean Norman rulers, however, were Norman only in name: the ancestors of the kings of Sicily and the empires of Antioch had already left Normandy in the first half of the eleventh century, before Norman culture had fully developed its distinctive characteristics. They maintained only tenuous links with their 'homeland' in northwestern Europe. Both their political and cultural achievements, should, in fact, be seen much more in the literally 'Byzantine' context of the Mediterranean lands which they occupied. Perhaps a brief glance at the extraordinary twelfth-century architecture of the Norman territories will suffice to underline the ingurgitatory nature of the Norman character. The Norman buildings of Sicily are built in a western European style, but are a bizarre mixture of Moslem, Greek and Byzantine influence both in design and execution.

2 The Norman dynasty in England

The royal Norman dynasty in England survived for less than ninety years after the battle of Hastings. The Norman Conquest of England was simply their largest and most surprising territorial expansion, but in retrospect it can be seen as the watershed that marked the emergence of a new European power. Although the battle of Hastings turned out to be decisive, William's arrival did not immediately put a stop to the constant political and military manoeuvring which had been and remained a feature of European political life throughout the Middle Ages. William felt confident enough to return to Normandy in 1067, but although a rising at Dover was successfully subdued he found it necessary to build further castles on his return later that year. A castle was constructed at Exeter after a rising led by Harold's mother, Gytha, was put down following a siege of Exeter castle which involved the first recorded use of mining as a siege tactic. In order to subdue the much more serious opposition of the Northern earls, Morcar and Edwin, castles were built at Warwick, Nottingham, York, Huntingdon and Cambridge in the spring of 1068. A Danish invasion fleet landed in Yorkshire in 1069 and York castle was burnt, but soon rebuilt. Taking advantage of the unsettled situation, the Welsh under Edric the Wild attacked the Marches, Shrewsbury was besieged and Norman castles were erected at Chester, Stafford and Worcester.

The threat of a foreign invading force allying itself with northern dissidents prompted William to employ the 'scorched earth policy' that he had developed in the process of defeating Maine and was to use on subsequent occasions

43

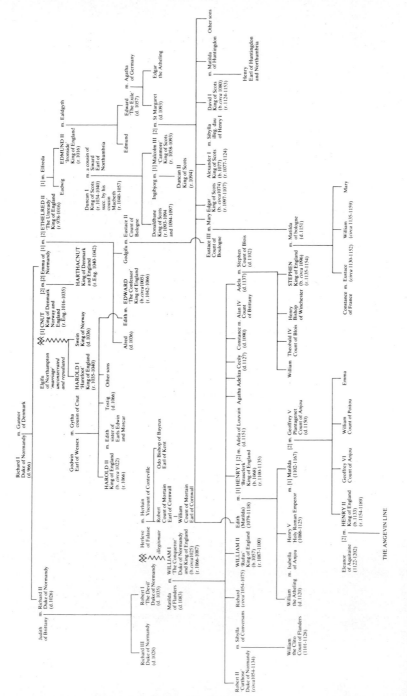

Figure 4 The descent of the Norman kings of England and Scotland

to great effect. Even by the fairly barbaric standards of the age, the 'harrying of the North' (1068–70) must be judged as savage. Ordericus Vitalis, normally a sympathizer of the Conqueror, was provoked to report the views of a Norman monk:

> On many occasions I have been free to extol William according to his merits, but I dare not commend him for an act which levelled both the bad and the good in one common ruin by a consuming famine . . . I am more disposed to pity the sorrows and sufferings of the wretched people than to undertake the hopeless tasks of screening one who was guilty of such wholesale massacre by lying flatteries. I assert moreover that such barbarous homicide should not pass unpunished.

Simeon of Durham supplied more precise details of the horrible incidents of the destruction and recalled the rotting and putrefying corpses which littered the highways of the afflicted province. Inevitably the massacres resulted in pestilence and an annalist of Evesham tells how refugees in the last state of destitution poured into the town.

Figure 5 A scene from the Bayeux Tapestry showing soldiers burning a house. Such explicit references to the Norman 'scorched earth' strategy are rare

It is not possible to dismiss these accounts as rhetorical exaggeration, for twenty years later the Domesday Book shows the evidence of the persisting effects of the devastation by the Normans as rulers. The Conquest and subsequent rebellion affected a minimum of twenty-five counties. In the Welsh border and the north many of the villages which were recorded as being wholly or partially waste in 1086 were the result of the crushing of the rebellion by William's army during the years 1068–70. The account for Cheshire gives details of waste not only for 1066 and 1086, but also for the date when the Norman owner received the estate. Out of a total of 264 estates, 52 were wholly or partially waste in 1066, and by 1070 the figure had increased to 162. By 1086, however, some of the estates had been restored and there were only 58 estates that were recorded as wholly or partly waste. It is clear that in places where these extra figures do not exist we may be missing much of the evidence of the damage which had already been repaired by 1086.

It was in northern England that the most severe effects of William's punishing activities can be identified from the records. The Anglo-Saxon Chronicle in 1069 simply states of Yorkshire that the king had 'laid waste all the shire'. And seventeen years later entry after entry for the northern estates said '*wasteas est*'. As well as estates specifically described as waste, there were others which had no recorded population, and these, too, we must suppose were the result of William's campaigns. One enigma is that many of the waste settlements recorded in Domesday lie in remote upland areas, while much of the adjacent lowland appears relatively unscathed. One plausible, but undocumented, explanation for this discrepancy is that the lowland areas were depopulated during the raids, but the Normans organized forced migration from the untouched poorer upland settlements to the vacated farms below. Thus the concentration of Domesday waste in the uplands could paradoxically still represent lowland devastation. Such was the effectiveness of William's strategy that castles were largely superfluous. The northern problem, which had long been a thorn in the side of successive Anglo-Scandinavian monarchs, had been eliminated at a stroke in the most brutal way imaginable.

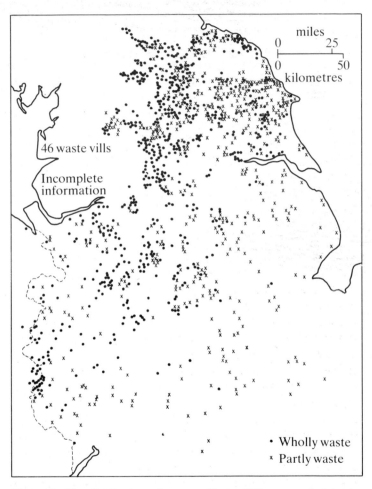

Figure 6 The distribution of waste vills in 1086 as recorded in the Domesday Book. The existence of so much waste twenty years after the conquest is regarded as a testament to the severity of 'the harrying of the North' (after Darby)

The last of the serious risings following in the wake of the Conquest was in the fenland of East Anglia and associated with the English folk hero, Hereward, who was joined by Earl Morcar. This, too, was decisively crushed and the Normans were subsequently in possession of a politically passive England, from which they could turn their attention to Scotland, and in particular to Wales (see Chapter 8). William's personal interest, however, was not directly with the border, his main concern being with England south of York and his native Normandy, where he spent more than half of the last sixteen years of his life.

During the remainder of William's reign there were only two further serious internal threats to Norman peace. The first in East Anglia, which necessitated the heightening of the motte at Norwich. After the suppression of the rebellion Lanfranc, who was acting as 'the protector of England', wrote to William:

> Norwich castle has fallen and its defenders have sworn to leave England within forty days. The mercenaries who served the traitor Ralph have begged a similar indulgence. The castle itself is occupied by Geoffrey of Coutances, William of Warenne, and Robert Malet, with 300 heavily armed men, slingers and many siege-engineers. By God's mercy the clamour of war has entirely ceased on English soil.

This rising was the occasion of the execution of Waltheof, the only English nobleman to suffer that fate. Throughout his reign William was anxious not to create martyrs, and consistently employed diplomatic leniency in his treatment of rebel leaders at least. The second rebellion was again in the north, in Northumbria, where William had employed the same tactics of delegating military responsibility which had been so successful in the Welsh Marches. Following the assassination of the marcher-bishop of Durham, Walcher, in 1080 William strengthened the defences at Durham and concentrated his hold on the town of Newcastle where he constructed a new castle.

Although internal uprisings were not a major feature of the last years of William's reign, there was a persistent threat of invasion by Cnut of Denmark between 1081 and 1087. In response to this threat Colchester Castle and a number of east coast castles were constructed, and yet again the danger of English support was reduced by the application of the 'scorched earth' policy along the east coast. William crossed from Normandy with, according to one contemporary, 'a larger force of mounted men and foot soldiers than had ever come into this country'. In the event they were unnecessary; Cnut was murdered at Odensee in Denmark, and the army he had assembled for the invasion dispersed. But, as usual, another threat had presented itself, this time back in Normandy and William returned to Normandy to regain the Vexin, which had been taken by the French king, Philip. Using his, by now familiar, savage tactics William regained and sacked the towns of Mantes, Chaumont and Pontoise. It has been speculated that at this stage William even had his eyes on Paris, only thirty miles away, and with it the French throne. This sack of Mantes, however, was to be the last of the Conqueror's military actions. He was taken ill in the town and taken to the priory of St Gervais, which lay on a hill in the suburbs of Rouen. The dying William was attended by two clerics known for their medical skills, Gilbert Maminot, Bishop of Lisieux, and Gontard, Abbot of Jumièges.

On Thursday, 9 September 1087, in a year notorious for fires, pestilence and famine, King William I of England, Duke of Normandy, died. Several obituaries of William survive, including one by an anonymous monk of Caen which appears to have been based on personal observations:

> In speech he was fluent and persuasive, being skilled at all time in making clear his will. If his voice was harsh, what he said was always suited to the occasion. He followed the Christian discipline in which he had been brought up from childhood, and whenever his health permitted he regularly, and with great piety, attended Christian worship each morning and evening and at the celebration of mass.

Other opinions on the nature of William's character vary

considerably, but all agree that he was a pious and able man. Piety, administrative ability, resourcefulness and ruthlessness were qualities which might not have made William an attractive man, but were just what were required to enable him to dominate first Normandy and then England.

William II
William was buried at the church which had been built partly as a sepulchre, St Étienne, Caen, to which he had given the Crown, Lance and Sceptre of England after the Conquest. On his death Normandy passed to his eldest son Robert, and England to his second surviving son, William Rufus, but Normandy was eventually restored to the fold of the Anglo-Norman monarchy after the battle of Tinchebrai (1106). William II's accession was a signal for renewed dissent in England based largely around Norman nobles and clerics supporting Robert, and in 1088 Durham Castle was besieged and several royal castles were captured, including one of the strongest, Bristol, which fell to Bishop Geoffrey of Coutances and his nephew Robert de Mowbray, Earl of Northumberland. Amongst other rebels was William the Conqueror's half-brother, Odo of Bayeux, who eventually negotiated a surrender outside Rochester Castle.

William Rufus was involved in campaigns in Normandy in 1090–1, but in 1092 he turned his attention to western Cumberland and Westmorland which were still under Scottish control. A castle and colony were planted at Carlisle (1092) and he began to colonize the area with English settlers. The remainder of William II's reign was characterized by intrigue, dispute and threat of external attack. As a response to this it also saw the consolidation of the Norman control of England, and military expeditions into Scotland and Wales. Both developments were accompanied by the construction of castles. William Rufus, like his father, was an expansionist and at the time of his death in August 1100 he was already expressing interest further afield, in Aquitaine. According to one story, on the day before he was killed while hunting in the New Forest, William was asked where he would spend Christmas that year, and he replied, 'Poitiers' – an ambition not realized by an English king until later in the twelfth century after the Norman dynasty had been replaced by the Angevin line.

Henry I

The youngest of William the Conqueror's sons, Henry I, succeeded his brother William Rufus, to the throne. Although Henry was more anglicized than his two Norman predecessors – he also married an Anglo-Saxon princess, Matilda – his reign was characterized by the strengthening and formalization of many Norman institutions, for example, the Forest Laws. They were probably at their most severe during his reign and he has also become associated with the creation of legal procedures and the courts with which to execute them.

There was no serious internal unrest but political troubles did continue throughout his reign, both in England and in France, and there followed a further period of military consolidation. Construction and refortification was concentrated on coastal defences and along the border with Scotland and Wales; important strategic castles were rebuilt in stone, and some town wall circuits, like that at Carlisle, were constructed. A change in the route of cross-channel traffic which came about soon after the accession of Henry I (between Purbeck and the Cotentin peninsula) resulted in the building of major castles at Corfe, Wareham, Porchester and Carisbrooke to guard the new important coastal area.

Most of this military consolidation was carried out by the king, but the White Ship disaster of 1120, in which Henry lost his only son, created a disputed succession. It is significant that despite the reputation Henry I gained for suppressing the power of the barony it is only after this date that we hear of major castle-works carried out by private individuals.

Stephen and the Anarchy

Henry I died in 1135 and was succeeded by his nephew,

Stephen of Blois, Count of Mortain and Boulogne, and feudal lord of half a million English acres from Lincolnshire to Kent. There followed the long period known as 'the Anarchy' – nineteen years of civil war between the supporters of Stephen and the supporters of the other principal contender for the throne, Henry I's daughter, the Empress Matilda. One chronicler complained that the land was filled with castles – few of them were erected with the king's permission, and fewer still at his command. During the Anarchy, as well as the extensive construction of siege works, churches and monastic sites were fortified. The monks were ejected from the Bridlington and Coventry priories, and Romsey Abbey, while ringworks were thrown up around churches at places such as Merrington, Durham, and St Martin, Thetford.

Many castles which had been built by Stephen's predecessors passed from his control either into Matilda's hands, or into those of men like Rannulf, Earl of Chester, for whom the civil war presented an opportunity to consolidate their own authority in that part of the country where they already possessed estates. Such men included Baldwin de Redvers at Exeter, Earl Miles at Gloucester and Hereford, Earl Simon at Northampton, Hugh Bigod at Norwich, and at Lincoln, Earl Rannulf himself. Even the Tower of London was, until 1143, under the control of Geoffrey de Mandeville, whose allegiance varied from year to year. The lords, it was claimed, 'burdened the country with forced labour on their estates'. The royal control over private fortification had broken down, and everywhere hastily constructed or 'adulterine' castles were being thrown up.

Though no longer the master of his kingdom, Stephen was by no means an incompetent general, and if many royal castles were lost, others were gained to take their place. In 1136 he captured Exeter Castle from the rebellious Baldwin de Redvers, and compelled him to surrender Carisbrooke. In 1138 he took Bedford Castle from Miles de Beauchamp, and Shrewsbury from William fitz Alan. In 1139 he forced Roger, Bishop of Salisbury, and Alexander, Bishop of

11 Cainhoe castle, Bedfordshire. The extensive earthworks of an early medieval motte and bailey castle, with traces of settlement and agricultural activities showing in the same field

Lincoln, to surrender the castles which they had strengthened: Malmesbury, Sherborne, Devizes, and Salisbury, belonging to the former, and Newark and Sleaford belonging to the latter. Only Nigel, Bishop of Ely, resisted, but Stephen, having made his way across the marshes, had

12 Burwell castle, Cambridgeshire. An unfinished castle of the period known as 'the Anarchy', which overlies earthworks indicative of an earlier settlement

little difficulty in capturing this newly fortified castle and garrisoning it with his own knights.

Not all these castles remained permanently in royal possession, but even in those which did, there are few structural features that can be attributed to Stephen. In 1142, he is recorded to have fortified Wilton (Wiltshire) and in 1150 he raised a castle within the precincts of Reading Abbey, but in neither case is there any suggestion of permanent construction in stone. In 1149 he went to Beverley with the intention of building a castle to control the hostile citizens, but was deterred by what John of Hexham believed to be the personal intervention of the local saint.

Stephen was better known as a besieger than as a castle builder and during his campaigns he tore down the defences of many 'adulterine' strongholds, some of which were apparently abandoned at the mere news of his approach. A properly fortified stone castle, however, was a more serious proposition, and in such cases Stephen tended to establish a temporary earthen castle to contain the garrison and to serve as a base for operations. He adopted such tactics at Castle Cary and Harptree in 1138, at Ludlow in 1139, at Wallingford in 1139 and 1146, and at Worcester in 1151. In 1144 nearly eighty of his workmen were killed while constructing a fortification of this type against Lincoln Castle. The earthworks which he threw up in front of Corfe Castle in 1139 are known as 'Stephen's Rings', and as H. M. Colvin remarks these: 'may not inappropriately serve as a memorial to a king who must have been something of an expert in the siting and construction of such ephemeral earthworks.'

Henry II and Richard I
On 6 November 1153 the civil war was ended by the Treaty of Winchester, when Henry I's grandson, Henry Plantagenet, was acknowledged as the heir to the throne. Within a year Stephen was dead and the Norman dynasty had ended in what appeared to be ruin. However, Henry II, the first of the Angevin kings, rapidly restored order. The laws and institutions were revived and expanded into the foundations of a legal system that was to rival that of Rome and through the acquisition of territories by marriage, diplomacy, and force of arms, the Angevin heir to the Norman throne became master of western Europe from the Cheviots to the Pyrénées.

Historians have placed considerable emphasis upon the premature end of the Norman rule in the mid-twelfth century, but the Norman style of government survived. We only have to look briefly at the career of the second of the Angevin kings to recognize the complete shift of emphasis in European affairs that had been brought about by the Norman Conquest. Richard I, 'Richard Coeur de Lion' (1189–99) was and has remained a national hero, but he visited England only twice as king, once for three months and later for two. Richard's great grandfather was Henry I, and Richard acted in the manner of a Norman monarch – as a crusader and as a territorial entrepreneur for whom national boundaries had little significance. It seems appropriate to finish this brief political survey by observing that in 1200 the affairs of England and France were interlinked in a fashion that would have been unthinkable if the Conquest had not taken place. Ironically, in view of their origins, one of the major lasting contributions attributable to the Norman Conquest, was that it completely severed the political links between England and Scandinavia, that had been so much a feature of the later Anglo-Saxon period. To underline this point no more need be said than that Richard I left behind him in government as regents, William Longchamp, Bishop of Ely, and Walter of Coutances, Archbishop of Rouen.

3 Castles of the Conquest

The story of the Norman castle in England in the eleventh and twelfth centuries mirrors faithfully the turbulent political events of the period. The earliest castles were those associated with the conquest of southern England in the months following the battle of Hastings, built at the same time as the Anglo-Saxon nobles were making their reluctant peace with William. In the next few years castles were built at major centres all over the country, both to consolidate the peace and in response to local risings. To many Englishmen the physical impact of the Conquest was manifested in the great feats of construction – the churches and the cathedrals, and, most of all, the castles. It was the latter which provided tangible and irrefutable evidence of Norman political and military domination, and many must have seen their triumphal spread as confirmation of William of Malmesbury's bitter comment about the Normans: 'they are a race enured to war and can hardly live without it.'

Unquestionably the major impulse for the creation of fortifications, on royal and baronial estates alike, came with the arrival of the Normans in England. The historian Ordericus Vitalis believed that it was the castle which enabled the Normans to establish themselves in England: 'the fortifications called castles by the Normans were scarcely known in the English provinces, and so the English – in spite of their courage and love of fighting – could put up only weak resistance to their enemies.' Contemporary chroniclers sometimes implied that the castle was a secret weapon which gave the Normans an unfair advantage, and in 1137, during the Anarchy, the Anglo-Saxon chronicler was suf-

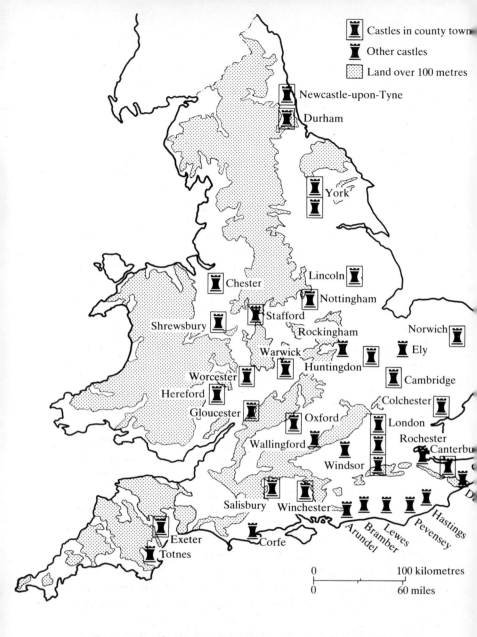

Figure 7 The distribution of early Norman castles in England showing a concentration in county towns, and along the south coast and the Welsh Marches

ficiently moved to complain: 'They sorely burdened the unhappy people of the country with forced labour on the castles. And when the castles were made they filled them with devils and wicked men.'

From the time William the Conqueror inherited Normandy in 1035, castles had played a major role in the warfare on the southern borders of his duchy. The first castles were built in the frontier districts, for instance, in Maine at the time Geoffrey Martel, Count of Anjou began to push northwards. The castles were manned by *vicomtes* loyal to the duke, but William was well aware of the danger implicit in the uncontrolled spread of private fortifications. Accordingly the Custom of the Duchy of Normandy (first formally recorded in 1091) forbade the erection of castles without licence. It specified that ditches were not to be dug so deep that the spoil could not be thrown out without staging and that the building of high palisades and bastion galleries was forbidden. These laws prohibited defence construction on rocks or islands, and stated that, whenever necessary, the duke could take possession of any castle. As so often happened, events in eleventh-century Normandy foreshadowed what was to happen in England during the following century when similar restrictions were imposed in England by the Norman kings in various attempts to maintain strong centralized authority. Indeed uncontrollable castle building was to be the hallmark of the Anarchy in the mid-twelfth century.

Although the majority of castles built in the eleventh and twelfth centuries enjoyed only a very brief life, they still form one of the largest categories of surviving archaeological monuments in England and Wales. To quote from Hadrian Alcroft's classic book, *Earthwork of England* (1908): 'Next to the Briton the Norman has left the most enduring, the most numerous and the most impressive marks upon our soil.'

The most imposing of all the monuments of the Conquest were London and Colchester castles, whose cultural predecessors were the Carolingian castle-palaces. It has been

13 The White Tower, Tower of London – the most formidable military
building in Norman England, begun in 1078

14 The motte at Ewyas Harold, Herefordshire. There was probably a pre-Conquest fortification here, but the mound almost certainly dates from the period 1066–71 when it was refortified by William fitz Osbern

suggested that the idea of a stone keep might originally have been imported into Europe from the Middle East; but the earliest reference to a stone castle in France, that at Doué-la-Fontaine built about 950, pre-dates the most quoted Syrian example, that at Saône, near Antioch which was constructed *c*. 976. Fulk Nerra, Count of Anjou, built a two-storey hall tower at Langeais in Tourraine, *c*. 992 and William the Conqueror was born in a castle at Falaise (1027/8). Duke Richard's fortress at Rouen, which has long since disappeared, but is depicted on the Bayeux Tapestry, appears to have provided the immediate inspiration for the great tower keeps. Other castles in France, which incorporated stone portions, including great towers or donjons were known at Brionne and Ivry. The donjon at Ivry is attributed to the wife of the late tenth-century Comte d'Ivry. She is said to have subsequently beheaded the architect lest he should build another like it for anyone else.

Fortification in late Anglo-Saxon England has been predominantly of a communal nature. Alfred and the late Saxon kings developed a system of interconnected urban defensive centres known as *burhs*, fortified against Scan-

15 Church Brough and Market Brough, Westmorland. The castle, which was probably built by William II as part of his northern campaigns, sits within the rectangular earthworks of a Roman fort – both fortifications were built to control the northern route. The village of Church Brough grew up outside the castle gates, while Market Brough developed on lower ground to the north, in order to accommodate a developing trading community

dinavian attack. Urban fortifications were also developed in the area of the Danelaw. References to pre-Conquest private defended enclosures or castles are rare, and where castles were recorded in the mid-eleventh century, they were associated with Edward the Confessor's Norman favourites who established a Norman colony in the Welsh Marches. In September 1051 the Anglo-Saxon Chronicle records: 'The foreigners had built a castle in Herefordshire in Earl Swein's territory and inflicted all injuries and insults they possibly could upon the king's men in that region.' This is generally believed to be a reference to a fortification at Hereford. Other castles in the region appear to have been constructed at Ewyas Harold and Richard's Castle, c. 1050, but were probably suppressed well before the Conquest.

Recent excavations in the Welsh Marches and elsewhere have failed to identify private defensive structures on any real magnitude prior to the Conquest, although evidence of enclosures in the form of a simple ditch and bank have been located at Goltho (Lincolnshire), Sulgrave (Northampton-shire) and Middleton Stoney (Oxfordshire). Certain thegns had the right to possess a gatehouse which implied that they constructed enclosures, and it is fair to assume that modest 'manorial' compounds were far more common in the tenth and eleventh centuries than has hitherto been suspected. It is possible that in parts of the country there may be a link between such pre-Conquest enclosures and the siting of Norman churches. However, relatively few of these structures have been systematically investigated and there remain intriguing questions in this area which can only be resolved by further topographical analysis and excavation.

The impact of the Norman castle
On a number of sites the Norman castle was indeed super-imposed on an already existing enclosure. In some in-stances this was a much earlier prehistoric or Roman forti-fication, as at Church Brough (Westmorland), and in other cases a Saxon village enclosure, as at Pleshey (Essex), or a pre-Conquest seigneurial enclosure, as at Middleton Stoney.

The impact of the construction of castles in towns is graphically recorded in the Domesday Book. Many early castles erected inside existing towns destroyed large areas: at York one of its seven wards had been wasted, at Lincoln 160 houses were destroyed, at Norwich 98 houses, at

16 Pleshey, Essex. A twelfth-century settlement whose topography is completely dominated by the castle

Shrewsbury 51 houses all to accommodate the castles. There had been smaller scale destruction by the building of castles at Cambridge, Canterbury, Gloucester, Huntingdon, Stamford, Wallingford and Warwick. Indeed devastation due to one cause or another was entered for almost a third of the boroughs mentioned. Oxford, for example, suffered badly, and out of about 100 properties recorded in 1086, half were wasted or destroyed to such an extent that they rendered nothing.

Castles were often physically imposed on villages in much the same way that they were imposed on towns. During the Anarchy Eudo Dapifer, the king's steward, built himself a castle at Eaton Socon (Bedfordshire) which strati-graphically sealed a late Saxon church and cemetery, together with other village buildings. Excavated evidence of this character is rare, but in some places the fieldworker can see a similar story told through the medium of earthworks. In 1143 Geoffrey de Mandeville marched an army into the fenlands and captured the Isle of Ely, and in an attempt to contain him, King Stephen ordered the construction of a number of castles along the fen edge. The best known of these is Burwell (Cambridgeshire), and the castle earth-works here, massive as they are, tell the story that the edifice was never actually finished. Neither the moat nor the castle mound were completed (See Plate 12), and furthermore it is quite clear from examining its relationship with adjacent earthworks that the castle was built over an already existing settlement. There is a similar tale of an unfinished castle overlying village remains at Rampton, another Cambridgeshire fen-edge settlement. Similarly at Yeldon (Bedfordshire) the massive remains of a mid-twelfth century castle can be seen from aerial photographs to cover a substantial area of former settlement. Earthworks recog-nizable as those of village property boundaries clearly run underneath the castle, the builders of which took in more than half of five crofts, supplanting the houses to which they belonged.

The castle was not merely a defensive stronghold but was also a firm base for active operations. Prominent in any garrison was the cavalry who could respond swiftly and decisively to an uprising by dominating the surrounding countryside, in addition to making sorties against besieging forces. The scale and the speed of castle building in the immediate post-Conquest period is revealed by the almost casual reference to some fifty castles in the Domesday Book. The distribution of these castles to some extent reflects the various uprisings against Norman control, for instance in the southwest and the Welsh Marches. But underlying this distribution there is clearly a pattern of political centraliz-ation not merely in response to specific uprisings, but also

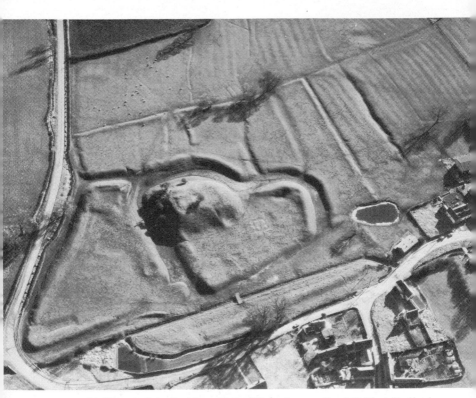

17 The earthworks of a mid-twelfth-century castle at Yelden, Bedford-shire, overlie the remains of earlier settlement. The earlier village is in the form of parallel strips representing former property boundaries

as a means of intimidating any potential unrest in the form of an unambiguous statement of Norman superiority.

The motte and bailey castle

One of the major areas of controversy in the development of the castle has been the question at what point in time did the motte and bailey castle evolve. Despite the fact that references to at least forty castles in pre-Conquest Normandy are known, authentic examples of mottes are rare, and their emergence as a regular feature of the Norman castle appears to have been a direct result of the Conquest of England.

What was required in England was a form of castle which would be defended by a small number of Normans against a large number of English, Welsh or Scots, and yet could be constructed with speed. For these purposes the motte bailey system was ideal. The motte (a Norman-French term

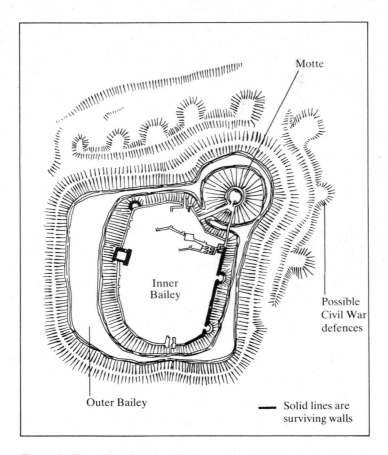

Figure 8 Plan of the motte and bailey castle at Berkhamsted, Hertfordshire. (It was from here that William I negotiated the surrender of London.) The typical early conical motte has a later shell keep built on top of it. It is probable that the earliest defences were built of earth and timber. The earthworks to the north of the main castle may have been civil war fortifications

for mound) was normally conical in shape, and could range in height from 3 to 30 metres. It was surrounded by a ditch from which the material making up the motte was extracted. There would have been a wooden bridge leading from the castle bailey to the motte, which was capped by a tower, normally constructed in timber. The bailey itself was surrounded by a ditch or ditches and a rampart on top of which a palisade was built. Inside there were various buildings, such as a hall, chapel, stable, a smithy, and buildings for storage.

Hundreds of motte and bailey castles of all shapes and sizes must have been built during the century and a half following the Norman Conquest in 1066. In terms of distribution their surviving earthworks are spread widely over England and Wales, lowland and eastern Scotland (the Highlands are virtually blank), and the eastern half of Ireland. Not all of these were built at the same time or for the same reasons; nor is the distribution even from area to area. A very large number of motte and bailey castles were built in the early days of the Conquest when Norman lords were establishing themselves in alien and hostile territory. But we should not underestimate the importance of fashion as a motive for building both earthen and stone castles.

Motte and bailey castles appear to have developed from the seigneurial enclosure with a tower gatehouse that was found in north-western Europe during the Carolingian period and, as we have already seen in England, during the late Anglo-Saxon period. In England the intermediate stage of private fortification appears to have had a tower, but no mound. It has been estimated that of the castles that are definitely known to have existed before 1215 some 198 were ringworks compared to 723 mottes and 141 other castles. The success of the practice of piling earth around the base of the tower to prevent it being burnt down easily may well be the reason why the motte became the principal feature of early Norman castles in England. The Bayeux Tapestry demonstrates that firing fortifications was an important part of siege warfare. The tradition of constructing ringworks continued into the twelfth century, however, and it has been suggested that in many cases the decision to build a ringwork rather than a motte seems to have reflected nothing more than the personal preference of the local lord or his castle builders. Perhaps speed of construction was also a consideration as many ringworks were built during the Anarchy.

The beauty of the motte and bailey, and indeed the ringwork, was that they were relatively easily and rapidly constructed using materials that were readily to hand. There were no problems in finding quarries or masons, and arranging for the transport of stone. All that would have been required were a number of carpenters and a force of men to dig the defences. In William's England this was not a problem as the Normans could command an endless supply of labour. Thus, in troubled areas, the Crown or its dependents could rapidly establish a formidable presence which was capable of withstanding cavalry attack. The chroniclers recorded that castles were thrown up in a few days (it has been suggested just fifteen days for Hastings), but although considerable scepticism has been expressed about the accuracy of these accounts, there seems little doubt that the basic structure could be constructed within a few weeks.

Apart from the advantage of speed in the construction of the castle, rapid rebuilding following destruction was also an important factor. At Hen Domen (Montgomeryshire) a motte and bailey castle was constructed between 1070 and 1074 as a base for an attack on Cardigan by Hugh, son of Roger de Montgomery. Incidentally the Domesday Book notes that the castle was built in an area of 'waste' used by three Saxon thegns as a hunting ground. During the next century and a half it was besieged on several occasions and changed hands frequently before a new stone castle was built at Montgomery after 1223. P. A. Barker has demonstrated that wooden buildings within the bailey which have left only ephemeral traces were repeatedly destroyed or dismantled, and rebuilt. Additionally, a succession of fine motte bridges has been identified, only the final-phase bridge being of the 'gang-plank' variety depicted on the Bayeux Tapestry. In the 1150s the Cistercians of Meaux (Yorkshire) built a bakehouse, a stable and some of their first conventional buildings from timber presented to them presumably from wooden buildings within the recently demolished castle at Mountferaunt, near Birdsall.

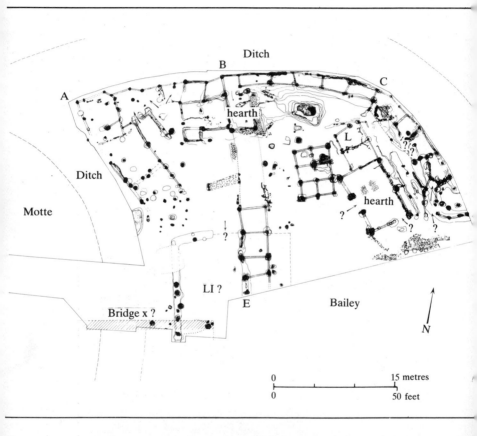

Figure 9 Plan of mid-twelfth-century buildings within the bailey of Hen Domen castle, Montgomery. The buildings, which were built entirely of timber, cob and thatch, have been identified by post-holes, timber slots and former floor areas using a technique of archaeological investigation developed and refined by the excavator Philip Barker

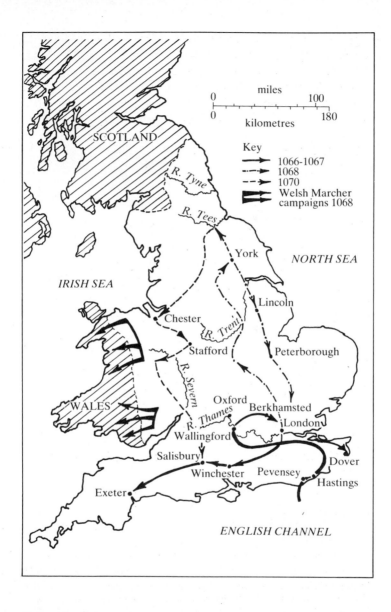

Figure 10 Diagram showing William's progress from Hastings to London and his campaigns immediately after the Conquest

71

18 A remarkable scene from the Bayeux Tapestry showing the actual construction of the motte at Hastings

If we trace William's circuitous campaign approach to London in 1066, by way of Hastings, Dover, Canterbury, Winchester, Wallingford, where he at last crossed the Thames, and Berkhamsted, where he negotiated London's surrender, we discover a sequence of mottes and re-used mounds. While this is not sufficient evidence in itself, as the dating of these earthworks cannot securely be attached to the political events associated with them, this, together with other evidence, indicates that mottes, some of them very substantial, were already being built in England in the late 1060s. Ordericus Vitalis records that in 1068 during the course of punitive expeditions, the Conqueror built castles at Exeter, Warwick, Nottingham, York, Lincoln, Huntingdon and Cambridge, and that all, except for Exeter which occupied an angle of the Roman wall, and Nottingham which was a cliff-top site, incorporated mottes.

In 1067 William returned to Normandy and castle build-ing continued in England under the vice-regents, William fitz Osbern and Bishop Odo of Bayeux. Fitz Osbern was killed in 1071 so that the castles attributed to him in the Domesday Book must have been started at least by 1070. Of these Berkeley, Clifford, Wigmore and the rebuilt Ewyas Harold all had mottes, while Chepstow and Monmouth were based on ringworks. Additionally there is the graphic if enigmatic evidence of the Bayeux Tapestry. During the course of this pictorial narrative of the Conquest, motte and bailey castles are plainly depicted at Dol, Dinan and Rennes in Brittany, and Bayeux in Normandy, and a motte actually in the course of construction is shown at Hastings. The importance of this evidence to the discussion depends on the dating of the tapestry. If, as is now generally held, the tapestry was completed in time for the consecration of Odo's new cathedral in Bayeux in 1077, we are confronted with clear evidence that the motte and bailey was already a familiar sight to the English embroiderers within a decade of the Conquest.

By far the densest concentration of earth and timber castles was in the borderlands between England and Wales, where the earthwork remains of several hundred such castles reflect the long struggle put up by the Welsh against the would-be Anglo-Norman conquerors. Many of the more permanent timber castles were later rebuilt in stone, to add to the range of stone castles already in existence. Recent excavations have suggested that early stone keeps were more common than previously thought, and a number of castle mounds which have been thought of as mottes are in reality overgrown collapsed stone towers. Mottes were not always easily converted to accommodate stone towers, and there are many records, such as those for Shrewsbury castle, which tell of the collapse or slippage of masonry following such an attempted conversion. A compromise solution was to ring the top of the motte with a roughly circular or polygonal curtain wall following the crest of the mound, forming what is generally known as a 'shell keep'.

At Carisbrooke (Isle of Wight), the shell was probably built by 1136 as Baldwin de Redvers is said to have had 'a stately castle built of hewn stone'. They were part of the apparatus of war and suppression and despite their apparent permanence in the landscape, this type of castle was relatively short-lived.

As the Normans were absorbed into England so the need for private defence on such a scale declined and those timber castles that were not rebuilt in stone fell into decay. Resident lords sometimes built themselves more comfortable manor houses close to the former castles, as at Middleton Stoney (Oxfordshire); while others used the opportunity to move out of the village altogether and build their homes on completely new sites, often maintaining a semblance of defence in the form of a moat. Whatever the origins of the motte and bailey castle it remains the most tangible and indelible element in the Norman contribution to the landscape. The sheer size of most mottes has ensured that although they lost their original function many centuries ago, they are not readily converted to alternative uses or eradicated from the landscape. With a few notable exceptions, such as Hereford, which was raised in the nineteenth century, mottes of all shapes and sizes have survived into the late twentieth century, into an age when they are protected for their historical importance. Like prehistoric hillforts their very presence in the landscape has influenced what has come after them, and the subsequent morphology of town and village alike has been affected by these great monuments to Norman confidence and energy.

Stone castles

The building of stone castles in Britain began a dozen or so years after 1066. As we have seen the stone castle already existed in Normandy and elsewhere on the continent, so that there was no question of it developing here from the wooden prototype. In part, also, the inspiration for their extensive use in Britain may have come from surviving Roman fortifications. We tend to forget that in the eleventh

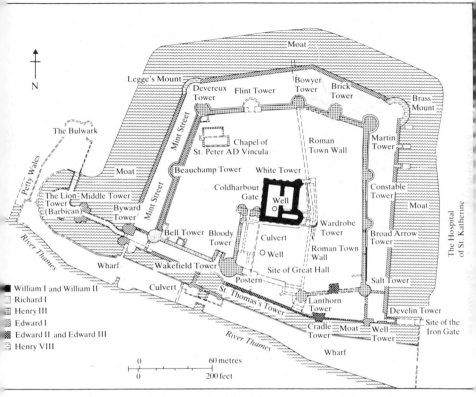

Figure 11 Plan of the Tower of London, showing phases of construction (after Colvin)

century many Roman fortifications, and public buildings must still have been standing both in England and Normandy. They supplied both a ready supply of worked stone and an architectural model for the Normans to imitate. It is significant to note just how many of the very early castles were built within existing Roman fortresses. Is it too fanciful to recall that one of the very first buildings that William and his men saw when they landed in England was the stone tower of the Roman lighthouse at Dover? They camped within the Roman fortifications there while recovering from an epidemic of dysentery and could well have been inspired

19 The early Norman hall at Chepstow castle

and influenced by their surroundings.

As soon as sufficient time was available, the important castles were translated from earth and timber into stone. The donjon replaced the motte as the primary element in the construction, housing stores, armaments and other equipment, and providing accommodation in a series of floors within a large square stone tower. In some instances, a stone castle was erected at the outset. The best known of all the great stone keeps is the White Tower of London. As originally built, *c*.1078, the castle consisted of the keep, with a bailey running down to the Thames in the south-east angle of the Roman city wall. The great three-storey square keep was built by William the Conqueror as a fortress, palace and seat of government (See Plate 13). This was then incorporated as the central feature of a much larger castle, the whole of which is now known as the Tower of London.

20 The tower keep of Rochester castle, Kent, built by Archbishop Gervase of Canterbury, soon after 1126

The designer of the White Tower, Gundulf, the Bishop of Rochester, was also responsible for the other great contemporary castle at Colchester (Essex) which was built at about the same time as the White Tower. The plans for Colchester Castle closely resembled those for the White Tower and a considerable volume of Roman material was used in its construction. Not one of the other authenticated eleventh-century keeps at palaces such as Chepstow, Oxford and Pevensey rivals these two in size, although some twelfth-century examples, such as Rochester (1126–39), and Dover (*c*.1180–90) are equally impressive. Both these great Kentish keeps are notable for the large buildings over the entrance

77

stairs, each of which incorporated a chapel. Rochester, which has four storeys, is the tallest stone keep in Britain, rising to a height of almost 40 metres, while the Norman

21 An aerial view of Dover castle showing the extent of the massive fortifications of many periods, and including the Roman lighthouse and Saxon church

keep at Dover now forms the centrepiece of a complex of later medieval fortifications.

The great keep at Norwich is noted chiefly for the architectural decoration of its exterior, most of which is, in fact, a refacing undertaken in 1834–9, but which faithfully followed the well-recorded original appearance. The keep stands high above the town on a mound which must be largely, if not entirely, natural. Other great rectangular keeps survive at Bamburgh and Norham (Northumberland), Bowes (Durham), Canterbury (Kent), Corfe (Dorset), Driffield (Derby – foundations only), Kenilworth (Warwick-

22 Norwich castle, built soon after the Conquest, was sufficiently defensible to withstand a siege in 1075. The keep was refaced in 1834–9, but follows the original design

24 The dramatic remains of Richmond castle seen from the south, showing the early hall (right). The castle was mentioned in the Domesday Book, and was believed to be the work of Alan Rufus. The keep is attributed to Earl Conan (1146–71)

shire), Middleham (Yorkshire), Castle Rising (Norfolk) and Trim (County Meath, Ireland), which has four great turrets, and wing-like projections in the middle of each side.

The large keeps are, however, only part of the whole group of rectangular stone keeps, most of which are of more modest dimensions, averaging around 15 metres square. Among the best preserved examples are the keeps at Richmond (Yorkshire), Porchester (Hampshire), and Hedingham (Essex). The keep at Richmond was built over an original gateway, which was then blocked, entry being made at first-floor (second-storey) level from the rampart walk of the surrounding curtain wall. The keep at Porchester is somewhat larger with an elaborate forebuilding to the

23 The imposing Norman keep at Castle Rising which sits within an unusual oval earthwork, which has a pair of outer enclosures attached to it

81

25 Porchester castle, Hampshire. The largely twelfth-century castle occupies the northwestern corner of a Saxon shore fort built during the third century AD. The church in the opposite corner of the Roman fort belonged to an Augustinian priory founded in 1133

east, and is preserved in part, to the top of the battlements on one side. The whole castle, keep and bailey, was built in one corner of the earlier Roman-Saxon shore fort. Hedingham is of similar dimensions to Porchester and still stands four storeys high, with two corner turrets rising another 6 metres. Many of these smaller keeps represent replacements for earlier mottes.

At the end of the twelfth century, new non-rectangular types of keep began to be built, possibly under the influence of ideas on fortification which reached Britain as a result of the Crusades. Although convenient internally for the disposition of rooms, the rectangular keep had certain external disadvantages: the corners were vulnerable to undermining by an attacker because they could be tackled from two sides and, moreover, it was difficult for a sentry on top of the keep to see exactly what was happening around the corners. Such disadvantages were largely, if not entirely, overcome in the later decades of the twelfth century, by building polygonal and circular keeps.

Castle building and repair continued into the later Middle Ages and indeed right up to the Civil War, particularly in Wales and Scotland. Castles continued to symbolize military and administrative power, but the first great age of castle building in England was over by 1216, and few new motte and baileys were built after this date. Most of the substantial sums paid by Henry III on castles was for repair and maintenance rather than new works. The idea of combining the main accommodation in one defensible structure, be it keep or motte, was brilliant, but made for extremely uncomfortable, inconvenient and expensive living conditions. Consequently many smaller castles were left to decay as soon as political conditions allowed. The great castles continued in use but gradually their functions changed: as their military and administrative role declined they first became residences and then, much later, some became prisons and arsenals.

To contemporary Englishmen, the physical presence of the castle and the feudal military implications that they carried were clear. The Norman castle was one of their most enduring and obvious legacies. For centuries after the end of Norman rule they symbolized the power of the conquerors over the conquered. They also reflected a strictly hierarchical society where Normans occupied all the dominant positions.

4 The English landscape at the time of the Conquest

When William set sail for England before the battle of Hastings he can only have had the most imperfect idea of the realm he was about to acquire. Indeed it was probably only after a decade of travelling throughout the kingdom that he fully realized how different England was to Normandy. It was, to begin with, far larger, and contained far more variety in its landscape. It was far wealthier, too, with considerable agrarian resources as well as minerals and building materials.

It was this cumulative wealth which in Norman hands was to be fully exploited and bring about far reaching changes. One contemporary chronicler, the Flemish monk Goscelin, was moved to eulogize on the glories of England: 'You must know that all earthly riches and delights, which in other places exist only individually, are here found gathered together.' Other contemporaries, such as William of Poitiers, commented more soberly on the abundance of grain and mineral supplies to be found.

So much we know, but the Norman Conquest comes at a curiously tantalizing time in the history of the English landscape. In order to reconstruct past landscapes it is necessary to amalgamate the evidence from a number of widely differing sources – contemporary documents, archaeological excavation and the analysis of surviving fossil elements in the landscape, including buildings. When it comes to detailed landscape reconstruction, the mid-eleventh century evidence in all these areas is weak. It does not enable us to draw up detailed maps conveying human settlement, human industry, and lines of communication with any degree of confidence.

It is particularly frustrating because by the thirteenth century there is an abundance of geographical detail in the archives, partly as a result of the centralization of administration instigated by the Normans. Added to which there is extensive topographical evidence for the high Middle Ages. This frustration has frequently led scholars into the twin traps of projecting the thirteenth century backwards into the eleventh and of marrying evidence from the two centuries in an unacceptable way. But however much we might wish it otherwise, only in the rarest of circumstances can we convincingly reconstruct the detailed local geography of England in 1066.

The administrative framework

The Normans operated largely within the framework of existing Anglo-Saxon administrative boundaries. The basic shire system was well established by the time of the Conquest and only Rutland, Lancashire and the few north-western counties were subsequent creations. Some represented older units such as the Anglo-Saxon kingdoms of Kent, Sussex, Surrey, Essex and Middlesex. Others were ancient administrative centres like the shires of Wessex. Some had developed around the headquarters of Danish armies as at Lincoln, Derby, Nottingham and Leicester, while many of the Midland counties had been artificially created in the early eleventh century, as the power of Wessex kings spread into Mercia, but even these shires were based on ancient territorial boundaries.

The smaller unit of jurisdiction was also already established, although these were re-arranged in some counties in the Middle Ages. The hundreds originally developed in varying shapes and sizes. In the south-east the hundred never replaced the more ancient units, known as 'lattes' and 'rapes', while in much of the Midlands the hundreds were created simultaneously with the shires to a fairly uniform size. The 'hide' was a much smaller land unit and traditionally it may have represented the area of land sufficient to support a family. But by the time of the Conquest it had become the basis of taxation and the Normans used it to fix feudal dues. The shires were divided into hundreds containing 100 hides, in the west Midland shires 200 or 300.

Perhaps the most confusing administrative unit was the 'manor'; strictly speaking it comes from the Latin term *manerium*, which is a version of the French *manoir* and was introduced into England by the Normans. The Domesday commissioners collected their description of England shire by shire, hundred by hundred, and village by village; that is to say, geographically. Their clerks rearranged the material within each shire into the holdings of each tenant-in-chief. The fundamental difficulty was that although many villages were the property of a single lord, many more were not. The manor was therefore the unit of holding of a feudal lord. The term is Norman, but in reality the concept probably dates back into the mid-Saxon period or even earlier. The Norman manor was an economic, a political and a judicial unit. The 'classic' manor consisted of a village, the lord's demesne land, the manor house (*heall* in English), the arable, pasture and meadow of the unfree and free tenants, common land, woodland and waste. However, manors varied considerably. Although most were compact and easily identifiable units, frequently co-extensive with the parish, others consisted of land in different villages or even counties. Some had no demesne or villeins or even manor house.

One set of Anglo-Saxon territorial units which was broken up following the Conquest was the earldoms. At the end of Edward's reign England had been divided into great earldoms, belonging to Harold, Leofwin, Gyrth, Waltheof, Edwin and Morcar. Next to the king the earls were the most powerful men in the kingdom, but the earldoms were not rigid geographical areas, they were indeed very fluid; and they were not ancient, but were effectively the creation of King Cnut (1016–35). The battle of Hastings itself was responsible for the immediate collapse in importance of the earldoms, since Harold's brothers, Earl Gyrth and Earl

Leofwin, fell with him. With the execution of the last of the English earls, Waltheof, in 1075, the political threat to the Crown disappeared, and, except for the Welsh Marcher earls, the titles became largely honorific.

The Domesday survey

At Christmas 1085, William was at Gloucester, where the Anglo-Saxon Chronicle reports he 'had much thorough and very deep discussion with his council about this country – how it was occupied, and with what sort of people'. As a result of these discussions he ordered his court to produce a *descriptio* of his new realm. By August of the following year, the best known, the most quoted, and the most misunderstood English historical document, the Domesday Book, had been compiled. The word 'Domesday' does not occur in the survey itself, but within a century it was widely known by that name. The Treasurer of England, writing in 1179 records: 'This book is called by the natives Domesday – that is metaphorically speaking, the day of judgement.' The inquiry appeared to contemporaries to be so thorough that its results could be compared to the bible, the book by which all would eventually be judged. Although there is some controversy over the use to which the survey was subsequently put, it was clearly not redundant after William's death, as some authorities have suggested, and was extensively referred to in the early Middle Ages. In some cases copies of the Domesday entries were used as title deeds to property.

The Anglo-Saxon Chronicle reported that William:

> sent his men over all England into every shire and had them find out how many hundred hides there were in the shire, or what land and cattle the king himself had in the country, or what dues he ought to have in twelve months from the shire. Also he had a record made of how much land his archbishops had and his bishops and his abbots and his earls . . . what or how much everybody had who was occupying land in England, in land or cattle, and how much money it was worth. So very narrowly did he have it investigated that there was no single hide nor virgate of land, nor one ox nor one cow nor one

pig which was there left out, and not put down in his record: and all these records were brought to him afterwards.

The country to the south of the river Tees and the Westmorland Fells was divided into seven circuits. A group of royal commissioners then progressed through each shire in their circuit holding formal meetings at the shire court after detailed preliminary inquiries had been made. The commissioners included some of the great men of the land, amongst whom were Remigius, Bishop of Lincoln, Walter Clifford and the Bishop of Durham. Within each circuit a full record of the inquiry was prepared and arranged shire by shire. Within each shire the information was tabulated in the order of royal lands, ecclesiastical lands, and then the lands of lay tenants-in-chief. The record incorporated elaborate statistics relating to the assessment of each estate, its population, its sources of wealth and its value. Attempts were made on some circuits to state the value of the estate, firstly before the Conquest in 1066, secondly at the time when the Norman lord took it over, and finally in 1086. Generally, however, only two values were stated: that in 1066, and that in 1086. Full surveys were then sent to Winchester and there, with the exception of the eastern circuit of Essex, Norfolk and Suffolk, they were abbreviated by scribes in the form that is now known as the Domesday Book Volume 1. The following entries relating to land held by the Bishop of Lisieux in Oxfordshire are typical of the way in which the information was presented.

(8. 1–4)
The Bishop of Lisieux holds 1 hide in (Little) TEW from the King. Land for 1 plough.
  2 villagers have it.
  Meadow, 11 acres.
The value is and was 30s.
  Leofwin, a free man, held it before 1066; Rotroc holds it now from the Bishop.

The Bishop also holds (Duns) TEW. 3 hides. Land for 4 ploughs. Now in lordship 1 plough; 2 slaves.
  5 villagers have 1 plough.

Meadow, 5 acres; pasture, 6 acres.
The value was 40s; now 60s.

The Bishop also holds 5 hides in DUNTHROP. Land for 8
ploughs. Now in lordship 1 plough; 3 slaves.
   3 villagers have 1 plough.
   Meadow, 15 acres.
The value is and was £3.

   The Bishop also holds (Westcot) BARTON and Rotroc from
him. 5 hides. Land for 8 ploughs. Now in lordship 3 ploughs;
5 slaves.
   10 villagers with 4 smallholders have 5 ploughs.
   Meadow, 3 acres; pasture 1 furlong long and ½ wide
The value is and was £7.
   Leofwin held these lands as he wishes. (See Plate 1.)

Volume 2 of the Domesday Book covers the counties in the
Eastern circuit in more detail than Volume 1 and is commonly known as the Little Domesday. In addition there is the
Cambridgeshire Survey, a copy of the verdict delivered by
the Cambridgeshire jurors, the *Inquisitio Eliensis*, which
consists of the accounts of the abbey of Ely in Cambridgeshire, Suffolk and elsewhere, and the Exon Domesday an account of Cornwall and Devonshire and certain
lands in Somerset and Dorset.

Generations of scholars have wrestled with the intricacies
of the survey arguing why and how it was produced, what
the various assessments mean in real terms and what it tells
us about contemporary society. It is a reflection of its
considerable importance that it has received more attention
than any other single English and probably European document. Despite this attention, however, it remains an
enigmatic and sometimes misleading source of information
about the society and landscape in the eleventh century.
Great caution must be exercised at every turn in the interpretation of Domesday information.

The details of the various scholarly arguments need not
concern us here, but the question of why it was compiled at
all has produced two main schools of thought. First those
held by the great Victorian Domesday scholar, F. W. Maitland, who believed that it was essentially a fiscal instru-

ment, a geld book to ascertain the taxable wealth of William's newly won kingdom; and second, others typified by V. H. Galbraith who believed that it was 'the formal written record of the introduction of feudal tenure and therefore feudal law into England'. Perhaps the fairest judgment was pronounced by D. C. Douglas when he wrote:

> He [William] desired, therefore, to know everything that men could tell him of his new kingdom, its inhabitants, its wealth, its provincial customs, its traditions, and its tax paying capacity. As a result, the record, so astonishing in its scope, escapes classification since it subserved so many needs.

Whatever its original function, such is the quantity and quality of the information in the Domesday Book that scholars have had to interpret it from many points of view, looking at all aspects of Norman administration, and their legal, military, economic, social, political and ecclesiastical organization.

We are interested in it here primarily as an indicator of the physical nature of early Norman England and for what it tells us about the landscape of the country taken over by William and his followers. Over the past three decades Professor H. C. Darby and others have attempted to map the Domesday statistics on a regional basis. The country has now been covered in a uniform plan, and the material has been published in regional geographies of Domesday England. The principal elements on the Domesday returns, including population, boroughs, plough teams, meadow, woodland and waste have been plotted on distribution maps on a county basis. The 'geographies' also note other miscellaneous material which Domesday presents in an erratic and inconsistent manner, such as references to salt making, fisheries, mills and churches. Each county is broken down into its geographical region and there is a commentary on the landscape as presented in 1086.

This has been a monumental work, pursued with considerable vigour. It is, however, not without its critics, some of whom maintain that the information in the Domesday Survey is far from complete, that its quality and content is erratic and that much, if not all of the information is actually presented in fiscal not geographical units, in which case, it would be virtually impossible to map realistically. Some scholars have suggested that it is only possible to use Domesday as an indicator of the landscape in association with other documentation and other forms of evidence. It is certainly true that the most effective work is done on a local and regional basis where it is possible to combine late Anglo-Saxon documentary evidence with the Domesday Book and other documentation. It has been claimed that it is possible to locate demesne land and field systems this way.

Given that these shortcomings do exist, nevertheless the work does have a considerable value in sketching out, in general terms, the character of the eleventh-century landscape, and one important factor is quite clear – the vast majority of English settlements were first recorded in this survey. About 13,000 places to the south of the Tees are mentioned. It has been demonstrated, however, that even this is not a comprehensive survey, probably representing only about 80 per cent of the settlements then in existence. These varied in types and size, from boroughs down to hamlets and even isolated farms, but as the Domesday Book is basically interested in estates and not individual settlements it is not usually possible to postulate what form of settlement the Domesday entries are referring to. Indeed there are numerous examples of composite entries where several settlements are covered by a single assessment.

Nevertheless the fundamental implication of the picture revealed by much of the Domesday Survey is that the Normans quite clearly inherited a landscape which was already largely settled and managed. Although there were to be far-reaching institutional changes in estates subsequent to the Conquest, they were to be carried out within the framework of an existing landscape of administrative and ecclesiastical boundaries which had evolved, not simply over the previous two or three centuries, but were the product of several millennia. The magnitude of the Domesday Book compared to earlier and indeed later documentation should not tempt us into believing that it necessarily signalled great innovations in the rural landscape.

Settlement and population

One of the most difficult tasks for historians is to estimate the size of past populations and to determine the nature of demographic trends. The Domesday Book would appear to offer a relatively simple means of assessing the population in 1086. However, just as it was not intended as a topographical gazetteer, nor was it intended as a census. Domesday incorporates references to some 275,000 people, including freemen, villeins, bordars, cottars and serfs. Conventionally this population figure is taken to refer only to heads of households, and in order to obtain an idea of the actual population, it is necessary to multiply it by a factor reflecting the average family unit size – normally taken to have been five. This gives an overall population of just over 1 million. Allowing for omissions this has been pushed up to 1½ million. Even this figure, however, is recognized as being on the low side and some authorities would put a more realistic estimate at nearer 2½ million. This figure is so far removed from the actual population recorded in Domesday, that the survey is virtually useless as a national indicator and has therefore to be used with extreme caution even on a local basis.

Settlement in England

By 1086 almost all the potentially good agricultural land appears to have been under cultivation, although there were still some notably blank areas, such as the forest lands of north Warwickshire, which were colonized during the following two centuries, and the dry sandy soil belt of Surrey, Berkshire and Hampshire, which was not brought into cultivation until the seventeenth and eighteenth centuries. Pockets of marsh and moor survived throughout the country until the post-medieval period, but they were deliberately preserved because they served the community as a whole, providing common rights of grazing and gathering. Generally speaking, however, there were no large expanses of 'wilderness' available for systematic colonization as could be found in parts of continental Europe at this time.

It is, therefore, clear that settlement was far more extensive than had been previously thought, and although most of our current village names are to be found for the first time within the folios of Domesday, we cannot always be certain whether these names are referring to a farmstead, a hamlet, a village, or even a group of villages. The Domesday Book appears to incorporate a high degree of artificiality in its assessment figures. It is not concerned with individual units of settlement, but the taxable estates. Hence there are frequently blanket assessments that can deceive us about the true settlement pattern. This discrepancy is well illustrated in Shropshire where, in addition to some 440 named places, a further 191 'berewicks' are mentioned, each of which represent a separate but administratively dependent village, hamlet or farm. In other manors in the same county, however, dependent settlements are not even mentioned as such, but are included within an overall assessment. Stoke St Milborough was assessed at twenty hides (units of five hides were commonly used) but later records show that apart from the mother settlement this also included five other hamlets within the manor.

Even manors assessed at only a modest hideage could conceal a large number of dependent settlements. In the case of Aldington (Kent) we can infer that the entry, consisting of an abnormally large number of peasant and plough teams, covers not only Aldington itself but the adjacent settlements which do not appear in the Domesday Survey. It has been suggested that some of these 'multiple estates' as they are known were of considerable antiquity, possibly dating back to the Roman period or earlier. This may be the case of Bottisham (Cambridgeshire), where the Domesday Book appears to record a single manor, village and parish, when in fact it consisted of a host of separate hamlets, whose origins are thought to be Roman.

Until very recently it was believed that the overall pattern of rural settlements that existed in the thirteenth century fairly faithfully reflected that found in the eleventh century. This consisted of a pattern of highly nucleated settlement in the Midlands, East Anglia and the north-east, grading into hamlets and isolated farms in the south-west, the Welsh border and the north-west. Recent work by field archaeologists, however, indicates that in the late Saxon period this model has to be modified. Intensive fieldwalking has revealed a wide variety of settlement types even within quite small areas, and that it is not possible to generalize in terms of nucleated or dispersed patterns of settlement. The largely nucleated pattern of settlement that is seen to be operating in the high Middle Ages appears to have developed out of scattered hamlets and farms of the mid-Saxon period, a process which seems to have begun in the late Saxon period and was still in progress during the eleventh century.

In fact, the dynamics of settlement geography are extremely complicated and as yet imperfectly understood. If we take a Cambridgeshire example, the process is admirably demonstrated. At Great Shelford, in the main Cam valley, the survey masks the fact that there were two separate hamlets almost a mile apart, but later documents indicate a substantial overall rise in population in the early Middle Ages. The recorded population in 1086 was apparently 34 while the number of tenants in 1279 is given as 137. Not only can we be certain that no new settlements in the parish accompanied this rise but we can still see on the ground where the increasing numbers of people were housed (see Figure 12). Of the two original hamlets of Great Shelford, one lay by the River Cam, near the shallow ford which gave the village its name, while the other lay on the edge of a small stream. Between the two lay a broad, roughly triangular area of meadow and pasture with the arable fields around it. As the population increased people from both hamlets built their houses on the edges of this meadow and gradually both hamlets merged to form one

95

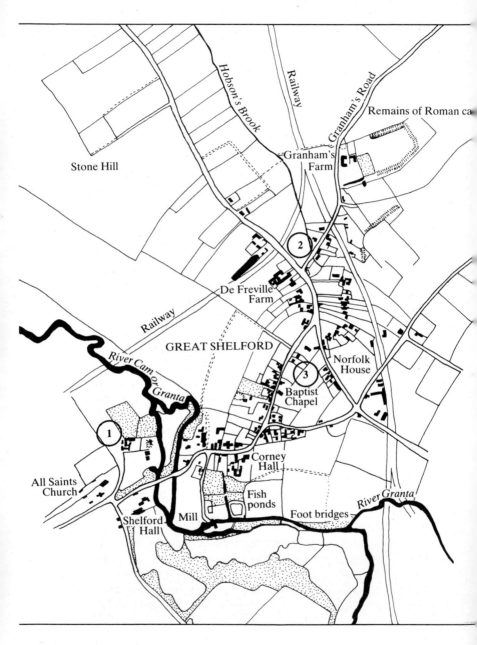

Stone Hill

Hobson's Brook

Railway

Granham's Road

Remains of Roman ca

Granham's Farm

②

De Freville Farm

Railway

GREAT SHELFORD

River Cam or Granta

Norfolk House

③

Baptist Chapel

①

River Granta

Corney Hall

All Saints Church

Fish ponds

Foot bridges

Shelford Hall

Mill

village. The resulting plan was a large triangular village 'green' known as High Green, which existed until the middle of the nineteenth century.

Such changes in village topography where change is gradual may be called organic, and in this case were associated with an increasingly centralized administration and a rising population in the twelfth and thirteenth centuries. There is also considerable evidence of more dramatic deliberate change in settlement forms. Some of the changes were the direct result of devastation caused by the political and military events associated with the quelling of the rebellions after 1066, where it was necessary to re-establish razed settlements. Others resulted from the exercise of strong seigneurial control which enabled settlements to be redesigned, normally for strategic or commercial reasons. A considerable number of nucleated rural communities were laid out afresh within the immediate vicinity of a castle or abbey.

One of the most intriguing categories of entry in the Domesday Book refers to 'waste land'. The term 'waste' found in many Domesday entries implies, not the natural wasteland of mountain, heath and marsh, but land that had gone out of cultivation mainly as a result of deliberate devastation. In the years before the Conquest there had been considerable disruption due to internal upheaval and Viking and Welsh raids. The Domesday folios for Cheshire, Shropshire and Herefordshire show that many villages lay waste in 1066 as the result of Welsh raiding. The Scots had also rendered waste extensive tracts of land along the northern border. In the account for eleven settlements on the Hereford-Radnor border, the scene of a frontier incident three decades earlier, the Domesday survey records: 'on these waste lands woods have grown up in which the said Osbern has the hunting and takes away what he can get.

Figure 12 Plan of Great Shelford, Cambridgeshire. The first settlement was at (1) by the river Cam; the early medieval development was sited by Hobson's Brook at (2); the final spurt of building took place between the two at (3), which became known as High Green

97

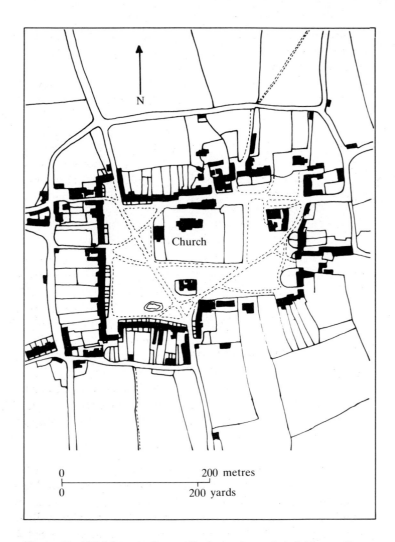

Church

0   200 metres

0   200 yards

Figure 13 Heighington, County Durham. A regularly laid out village, probably originating in the early Middle Ages. There has been some encroachment on to the green in the south-east corner, otherwise the plan can be seen clearly in the shape of the green, the parallel property boundaries, the central siting of the church and back-lane serving the back entrance to the plots. Such villages may have been created to replace settlements destroyed during the 'harrying of the North' following the Conquest and may have been inspired by contemporary town plantation

Nothing else.' And for the remote hamlet of Mynton sitting in the shadow of the Longmynd in Shropshire the survey starkly notes: 'waste it was and is.'

It has been argued that many of the regularly laid out villages found in northern England, particularly in County Durham were planted afresh subsequent to the 'harrying of the North'. To some extent the evidence for such planted settlements exists but in the vast majority of cases it is impossible to place a precise date upon the creation of a regularly laid out village. Although archaeological evidence for re-planning has been identified on a number of sites it has not been possible to relate it closely to political events. In the Welsh border there are examples of new villages being laid out next to strategically sited castles, in the form of an extended second bailey; often, too, there is evidence of a defended boundary. The plantation of such castle villages did not always lead to the abandonment of a previously existing settlement. Castle Pulverbatch (Shropshire) held by Earl Roger of Shrewsbury in 1086 is a classic example of this. The older settlement of Church Pulverbatch still sits high up a ridge overlooking the narrow Churton valley that runs south-westwards towards Wales. In the early Middle Ages a castle and village were created in the valley in order to control the route into Wales. The albeit decayed shape of the village today still tells of its deliberately planned origins.

Churches

Although we do have some archaeological evidence for early medieval house types (there are a few standing Norman town houses such as the Jew's House in Lincoln, see Plate 4), the Domesday Book is mostly silent on village buildings. The church, however, was one category of building which ostensibly at least was recorded, but even here Domesday is highly inconsistent. In some counties such as Suffolk, where churches are mentioned at 345 places (out of a total of approximately 639 named settlements), the record appears to be relatively complete, while in others, such as Cornwall, only collegiate churches are recorded and in

Oxfordshire the record is clearly incomplete as churches are recorded only for Oxford and Eynsham whereas at least eight of the counties' churches incorporate Anglo-Saxon architectural features. There is positive evidence that not only was the method of recording inconsistent in different counties but also in individual hundreds within a county. The discrepancy between the recorded number and the real number of churches can be demonstrated in the case of Kent where about 175 churches were recorded in 1086. Independent lists of the eleventh-century baptismal churches indicate that there were in fact over 400 in existence at the time the survey was being compiled. The truth is that the survey was only marginally interested in churches and if we look at various other sources available, such as place-names containing the 'church' elements such as *llan, eccles* and *circ*, other documentation, and architectural and archaeological evidence, we come up with a figure vastly inflated over those mentioned in Domesday. It has been estimated that by the late eleventh century there were at least 4,000 churches, of various categories, in existence in England as opposed to the few hundred recorded in Domesday.

The Domesday countryside

The Domesday Book contains a considerable amount of information about agriculture. Entry after entry states first the amount of land for which there were plough teams on each estate, and second the number of teams both required, and actually at work on the demesne and on the land of the peasants. Nevertheless because of the highly artificial nature of the assessments it is impossible to take this information at its face value. In an attempt to demonstrate the extent of arable land Professor Darby has mapped the distribution of the recorded plough teams but even this does not appear to be a satisfactory criterion with which to estimate the former. The information about plough teams is likely to be as erratic as that concerning the arable land and presumably more or less ploughs were required for different types of soil.

The survey is reticent about agricultural techniques and throws little light on the vexed question of the development of open-field strip agriculture. We know that the Normans were not directly responsible for any major agrarian developments, although during the eleventh century a heavier plough using more iron components appears to have spread across France into England. Only one solitary Domesday entry, that for Garsington (Oxfordshire), appears to refer to a strip system. So although we may infer from other sources of evidence, notably charters, that open-field agriculture was operating at least in parts of the country in 1086, the pages of Domesday are for the most part silent on detailed matters of agrarian practice.

There is still considerable controversy over the evolution of medieval field systems. To put it very simply the predominant system which was found in one form or another throughout England in the thirteenth century relied upon a division of land into strips – normally scattered throughout two, three or more open fields. The method of organizing the agricultural regime depended upon a wide variety of different customs and obligations. The question which has exercised historians, geographers and archaeologists, is at what date did this system supersede the Celtic system of square and rectangular enclosed fields that had operated for perhaps the previous 2,000 years? The view that the open-field system was brought in by Anglo-Saxon settlers has long been discarded, but there is no general measure of agreement about an alternative model.

One of the great difficulties in understanding field systems in the early Middle Ages is the necessity of distinguishing between the physical characteristics of the field divisions and the agrarian regime of customs and practices which were operated. We must also appreciate the degree of regional and local variation which clearly existed, and understand that, like settlements, field systems are rarely static for long. Such archaeological evidence that does exist demonstrates the existence of ridged fields in the early Norman period, and yet the documentary evidence points towards the evolution of the mature open-field system during the twelfth and thirteenth centuries. It seems probable that a considerable amount of arable was cultivated in strips at the time of the Norman Conquest, but that in the wake of the Conquest the system was gradually tightened within a framework of feudal control and perhaps in response to a growing population.

In its record of meadow and pasture land Domesday Book is equally tantalizing. The jurors in different counties used different units of measurement, while in Shropshire there is no reference to meadowland at all. This makes comparability between regions impossible. Occasionally, however, the record does hint at the organization of meadow – there are for instance scattered entries, notably for Devonshire, referring to 'common pasture', and it is recorded that the burgesses of Oxford held the pasture in common 'outside the wall', presumably in the area of Port Meadow. Sometimes it is noted when pasture had been converted to arable, as at Swyre (Dorset) where this was recorded on two occasions, and at Bourne (Kent) where there were 6 acres of pasture 'which men from elsewhere had ploughed up'.

The survey demonstrates that there were more sheep than all other livestock put together. At this time the sheep's main function was to provide milk to make cheese for winter food; wool, manure and meat were by-products in that order of importance. Some districts were clearly devoted to sheep farming. In Essex, for example, pasture for sheep is frequently mentioned, but the villages to which these pastures are assigned lay in 'a belt parallel with the coast', in fact coastal marshes. In the case of villages lying a few miles inland they formed detached portions of the manors to which they belonged. Elsewhere, coastal areas of East Anglia, and land adjoining salt marshes and fens, were used extensively for sheep rearing.

When it comes to plotting the distribution of woodland, which is extensively recorded in Domesday, we come across the problem of the application of different forms of measurement again. The commissioners variously recorded wood in terms of the number of swine it would support, or in terms of length and breadth, or leagues, furlongs and perches, or in the number of acres, as well as a number of other variants and idiosyncrasies, for example in terms of wood for fuel, for the repair of houses, or for the making of fences.

The conventional interpretation of Domesday woodland is that it reflects a countryside which was still fairly heavily wooded and into which settlers were still making inroads. Isolated references to *assarts* (land recently cleared for arable) in Herefordshire have in the past been regarded as only hinting at the scale of reclamation that was going on in the eleventh century. A recent reassessment of the Domesday evidence by Oliver Rackham questions this assumption. Rackham believes that far from being heavily wooded, England was relatively open in 1086, and that perhaps no more than 15 per cent of the countryside carried a woodland

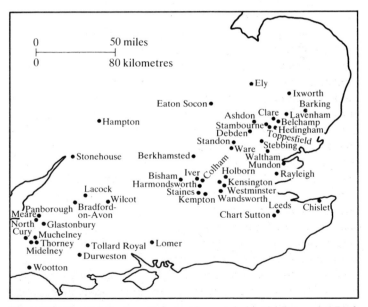

Figure 14 The distribution of vineyards recorded in the Domesday Book (after Darby)

cover. Huntingdonshire had about 7 per cent of its areas under woodland, while Lincolnshire had only 3½ per cent; Warwickshire, Worcestershire and Staffordshire had more woodland than the national average. It is ironic that many of the churches known to have been in existence in 1086 but missing from the Domesday folios for Kent are to be found in the Weald, this was an area that was for long thought to have been still under impenetrable forest in the Middle Ages.

About 50 per cent of settlements are recorded as having woodland, but there was considerable regional variation and some villages must have been as far as four miles from the nearest source of timber. Furthermore Rackham argues that there is evidence of woodland management in Domesday. Most notably that a distinction should be made between *silva minuta*, coppice woodland that was properly farmed, and *silva pastilis* or *pascualis*, pasture wood where there was no such management, only the regulation of the number of animals allowed in. The evidence from Domesday and other sources suggests that even in 1086 there was little natural or primary woodland left. It was a countryside which had been well organized before the coming of the Normans.

Other rural activities are noted in many manors, for instance the presence of fisheries. They are sometimes recorded in association with mills. As we might expect the majority of fisheries were located along the main rivers and their tributaries, the Thames, Severn, the Nene, Trent, Great Ouse, Dee, Medway, Avon and others, but the chief recorded assemblage was in and around the waterways of the Fenland. Here some of the north Cambridgeshire mills returned great numbers of eels to their lords, as many as 33,260 from Wisbech, 27,150 from Doddington and 17,000 from Littleport.

Sea fisheries, on the other hand, were hardly ever mentioned, although herring renders were recorded for a number of villages along or near the Suffolk coast, and there is a reference to a sea weir at South Wold and twenty-four fishermen at Yarmouth. Watermills were extensively recorded, but while some of these must have been associated with substantial engineering works enabling water to be carried a considerable distance, the location of many others suggests they were insubstantial structures.

Domesday Book also records vineyards for fifty-five places, the most northerly being Ely. J. H. Round argued that the culture of the vine was re-introduced by the Normans (since Roman times) on the basis that the Domesday vineyards were normally on holdings in the direct hands of Norman tenants-in-chief and that some had but lately been planted. This view has been modified due to references to vineyards in Anglo-Saxon England, but it is probably fair to assume that the Normans greatly extended the area of viniculture.

Eleventh-century urban life

The question of town creation and morphology is looked at more closely in Chapter 5, but some consideration of town life as reflected in the pages of Domesday Book should be included here. The Domesday survey affords an opportunity to assess, somewhat roughly, the degree of urban status possessed by those places to which the clerks gave their ambiguous title of 'borough' or in which burgesses were recorded. To have been favoured as the site of a fortified *burh* in Anglo-Saxon times was no guarantee of continued urban prosperity under Norman rule, as the subsequent history of places such as Burnham (Sussex) shows; several Domesday boroughs can no longer claim to be towns today. Yet the majority of the towns with the largest recorded populations in the poll tax of 1377 are those which Domesday shows as already being in existence in 1086 (See Appendix 2).

As with the countryside we encounter considerable difficulty when it comes to interpreting the town entries in the Domesday Book. Some towns, like Bristol, were dismissed with hardly a notice, yet were certainly already important in 1086. Neither London nor Winchester, two of the major urban centres in the kingdom before and after the Conquest, were recorded. Altogether some 112 places appear to have been classified as boroughs in 1086, but as we will see later the definition of such a settlement poses a major problem.

Some indications of prosperity and development are recorded in the survey. At Norwich, for instance, the presence of 125 French burgesses indicates significant colonization. Groups of Frenchmen or French burgesses were also recorded at Dunwich, Hereford, Shrewsbury, Southampton, Stanstead Abbots, Wallingford and York. A new borough had been established at Rye in Sussex and another at Rhudlan in North Wales. In the borough around the castle at Tutbury (Staffordshire) it was noted that there were forty-two men who devoted themselves wholly to trade, at Eye (Suffolk) there were twenty-five burgesses who lived in or around the market place, and there were thirty-five houses in or around the market place at Worcester. We hear of stalls in the provision market at York, trading ships at Chester and Suffolk, foreign merchants at Canterbury, and a guildhall at Dover as well as its harbour and shipping.

At Bury St Edmunds, a new planned town had been built beside the monastery, to the west of the Saxon town. The entry in Domesday is particularly revealing and worth quoting in full:

> Now the town (*villa*) is contained in a greater circule, including (*de*) land which then used to be ploughed and sown; whereon are 30 priests, deacons and clerks together (*inter*); 28 nuns and poor persons who daily utter prayers for the king and for all Christian people; 75 bakers, ale-brewers, tailors, washer-women, shoemakers, robe-makers (*parmentarii*), cooks, porters, stewards together. And all these daily wait upon the Saint, the abbot, and the brethren. Besides whom there are 13 reeves over the land who have their houses in the said town, and under them 5 bordars. Now, 34 knights, French and English together, and under them 22 bordars. Now altogether (there are) 342 houses in the demesne on the land of St Edmund which was under the plough in the time of King Edward.

The picture of this prosperous and much expanded community contrasts dramatically with the record of destruction preceding castle building seen in many other towns.

In 1065 310 people were recorded in the older *burh* which had arisen from a great expansion of the village of Boedericesworth, after the bones of St Edmund, king and martyr, had been brought here in 908 and a monastery founded. Both the stages of expansion have left their imprint on the town plan. Plate 26 shows how the abbey and its precinct intercept the straight route of Northgate Street and Southgate Street, forcing the main road to make a detour along the front, or west wall, of the precinct. At the north-west corner of the precinct lies the open market place on Angel Hill, just outside the great abbey gate.

The new borough consisted of five north-south streets all parallel to the west front of the precinct. The town was protected on the east by the river Lark, on the south by a town ditch, and on the north and west by a defensive wall built in the twelfth century. The arable land over which the new borough was spreading at the time the Domesday Book was compiled had originally been part of the West Field. The South Field came up to the town ditch, and the East Field lay over the river behind the abbey precinct. Contemporary accounts demonstrate that the process of urbanization was a profitable one. While the records show that the fields of Bury were not unprofitable to the abbey in yields of grain and stock, the sacrists' accounts make clear that the real importance of the urban property lay in house rents, market dues and tolls. One significant sign of the developing commercial basis of the town is the situation of the market place which was built in the new town to supplement or replace the earlier market place at the abbey gate. Now called the 'Butter Market', it can be seen, much encroached upon, in the northwestern corner of the street grid system, breaking the symmetry of the parallel roads of the town which Abbot Baldwin created.

There are fifty-eight markets specifically mentioned in the survey but only fourteen were recorded for boroughs. Thus

26 Bury St Edmunds. The abbey precinct and Saxon *burh* lie on the right and the new borough being laid out at the time the Domesday survey was being compiled takes the form of five north-south streets, all parallel to the west front of the precinct (see Figure 15)

Figure 15 Plan of Bury St Edmunds showing the relationship between the abbey and the town whose creation was recorded in the Domesday Book, based on a map by T. Warren dated 1747

109

of the four boroughs in Gloucestershire only Tewkesbury was said to have had a market recently established by William's wife, Queen Matilda, although there were three other places with markets, Thornbury, Cirencester and a new market at Berkley. There were other indications of mercantile activity: at Abingdon there were said to be ten traders dwelling in front of the door of the church, and similarly ten traders at Cheshunt. There are only two Domesday references to fairs, one at Aspall (Suffolk) and another annual fair at Methleigh (Cornwall). We must remember that markets and fairs were only of interest to the Domesday assessors if they yielded revenues. Most markets were probably held in churchyards and as they were not yet taxed they did not usually feature in the survey. During the twelfth century the Crown recognized that by licensing markets and fairs it could raise significant revenue. Thus the apparent growth in markets and facilities for trade, according to the number of charters surviving for the twelfth and thirteenth centuries may be something of an illusion. The charters may in many cases have been licensing a market or fair which was already in existence.

Industry

The Domesday Book is reticent and erratic in its recording of eleventh-century industrial activity. Where it is possible to augment the Domesday record with other documentary sources or archaeological evidence it is clear that the survey provides us with a very partial picture indeed. There are occasional hints of iron working, an iron mine is recorded in North Wales, and iron works are at East Grinstead in Sussex. Renders of iron in Gloucestershire probably reflect the presence of iron working in the Forest of Dean. The renders of Gloucester itself include: 'Iron rods for making nails for the king's ships'. It is questionable whether iron works recorded elsewhere reflect the presence of an iron industry, or in some cases simply the presence of forges. Archaeological evidence has, however, revealed that iron working in late Saxon England was extensive in those areas where iron ores were available for mining and furnaces have been excavated at West Runton (Norfolk), Stamford (Lincolnshire) and Lyveden (Northamptonshire).

Lead works are recorded in the Peak District of Derbyshire, but Domesday is silent about the other known lead working areas such as North Wales and the Cheviots, although we know that lead was used extensively in buildings and for the construction of brine vats in the salt-making process. Surprisingly, too, Domesday is silent on silver working, which appears to have been extensive in late Saxon England.

Considering the great volume of stone building that was going on at the time, references to quarries are equally rare. They are recorded at Taynton (Oxfordshire), well known for its great oolite stone, and those of Whatt (Nottinghamshire) and Bignor (Sussex) are recorded as producing millstones. E. M. Jope has shown that in fact there were three major stone-producing areas in Saxon England additional to Taynton; these were at Barnack in Northamptonshire, Box in Wiltshire, and Quarr on the Isle of Wight. Stone from these quarries has been identified, mainly in churches, throughout central and southern England. The Barnack quarries were particularly productive and supplied stone shipped down rivers throughout East Anglia. Millstones, too, were carried considerable distances, some from the continent and others from the English deposits of millstone grit, such as those in the Derbyshire Pennines.

Pottery production, always a poor relation to other industrial activity, receives scant attention in the Domesday folios as in other medieval documents. Potteries and potters are only entered for Bladon (Oxfordshire), Haresfield (Gloucestershire) and Westbury (Wiltshire). The archaeological record highlights the deficiency of the survey in this area: despite the fact that parts of Britain were still aceramic in 1086 there was demonstrably a thriving trade in pottery both within England and with mainland Europe. Recent archaeological evidence also points to the manufacture of floor tiles and bricks on a limited scale in England during the late Saxon period.

Salt making is one industry, however, about which information is relatively abundant. The chief areas of production of maritime salt were along the marshes and estuaries of the east and south coasts. The Domesday record usually states the number of salt pans on a holding, and sometimes also includes the render, either in money, in fish or in loads of salt. Caister in eastern Norfolk, for example, had as many as forty-five salt pans, and at Lyme (Dorset) some twenty-seven salt workers were recorded. The inland centres of production were in Worcestershire and Cheshire, based on brine springs. The centre of Worcestershire industry was at Droitwich for which numerous pits (*putei*) and salt pans (*salinae*) are recorded. Although there is no information about the process of manufacture, leaden pans or vat furnaces are recorded, and occasionally we hear of wood for the salt pans. References to the Droitwich salt pans are found in several other Midland counties, the furthest recorded trade is at Princes Risborough (Buckinghamshire). This suggests that the salt trade was of considerable importance by this date and was transacted by way of the saltways which radiated from the main centres of production. The Cheshire salt industry was centred at Northwich, Middlewich and Nantwich, but production here had suffered due to post-Conquest devastation.

The meagre record of industrial activity has led to a general feeling that manufacturing and processing were of little importance in eleventh-century England. Commonsense and evidence from other sources tells us, however, that a sophisticated economy such as that operating in late Saxon England must have incorporated a considerable amount of industrial specialization, far beyond the scale hinted at in the Domesday Book. Many trades such as charcoal burning and lime quarrying must have been carried out on a relatively small scale; while the building and construction industry, already active in 1066, must have operated on a much larger scale by the late eleventh century. Additionally the sheer scale and range of iron and

112

bronze artefacts points to a widespread working in these commodities as well as a more limited glass manufacturing industry.

When Reginald Lennard wrote *Rural England 1086–1135* (1959) he began in this way: 'when William the Conqueror seized the English Crown, he became the ruler of an ancient realm. England was already an old country.' Every page of the Domesday Book hints at this, yet it is unrealistic to believe that it enables us to reconstruct in detail English landscape in the late eleventh century. Domesday is a beguiling document yet it contains layers of ambiguity and uncertainty, some of which we can only guess at and some of which are no doubt unperceived. It is in itself a formidable Norman legacy. 'As an administrative achievement', writes Sir Frank Stenton, 'it has no parallel in Medieval history.' It moved some contemporaries to liken William, as the perpetrator, to a Roman emperor and it is undoubtedly true in administrative terms 'that there has been nothing like it since the days of Imperial Rome.'

5 The towns of the Conquest

One important difference in the pattern of urban settlement in Britain and that of mainland Europe, both of which had been part of the Roman Empire, is the survival in the latter of the basic distribution of Roman towns into the post-Roman period. In Europe, generally speaking, they survived as regional administrative and ecclesiastical centres, and the Roman town plan, with its street and defence alignments, often survived virtually intact into the Middle Ages: in France, for example, the medieval topography of the majority of regional towns has a sound Gallo-Roman base. In contrast the end of the Roman period in Britain was marked by an urban hiatus which accompanied the breakdown in the pattern of national communication. The collapse of urban institutions and topography which ensued in the fifth and sixth centuries was far more complete than in most other parts of the Roman Empire.

At the same time, however, it should be acknowledged that the actual density of medieval, in comparison to Romano-British, towns may be more apparent than real. There were probably far more small trading centres in Roman Britain than have yet been identified and these would have performed precisely the same function as the market towns of the Middle Ages. Differences in the siting of Roman and Anglo-Norman towns where they occur can be directly related to a new system of communications which developed during the middle and later Saxon period – a system which was more closely related to geographical and strategic reality than that created by the conquering Romans. Roman military and technological superiority was

27 Vertical view of Shrewsbury. The loop of the river Severn was fortified in the late Saxon period after Viroconium had been abandoned. The present complicated town plan represents a fusion of Saxon and medieval elements. The castle which lies on the extreme right of the picture at the neck of the loop was founded by Roger de Montgomery soon after the Conquest. The Domesday Book records that fifty-one houses were destroyed to make way for the castle

116

such that they were often able to ignore natural strategic considerations when siting towns.

The Anglo-Saxons and the Normans on the other hand were far more sensitive to the need of locating settlements on sites which enjoyed a degree of natural defence. In the Welsh Marches Chester was the only town which occupied the same site as its Roman predecessor. Shrewsbury had been developed as a late Saxon *burh* occupying a natural strongly fortified site within a loop of the river Severn, a few miles to the north of the deserted Roman-British town of *Viroconium*. Further south in Herefordshire, the Roman town at Kenchester had been abandoned in favour of a new defended *burh* by a fording point over the River Wye. While in the southern Marches there was no successor to Roman Caerleon until Newport was created in the twelfth century.

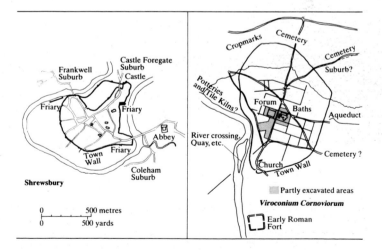

Figure 16 Plan showing the relative size of medieval Shrewsbury (left) and its Roman predecessor *Viroconium Cornoviorum* (right)

It is true that a number of towns emerged on Roman sites in central and southern England and that Roman elements survived in cities such as Winchester, Canterbury, Gloucester, Chichester, Exeter and Bath, where the sites of Roman gateways and the alignments of the principal highways can still be traced. But if we examine the late Saxon shire towns of England as a whole, such examples of continuity were in the minority, and looking at the existing English and Welsh towns today, the siting and original plans of the majority date to the Anglo-Norman period or later.

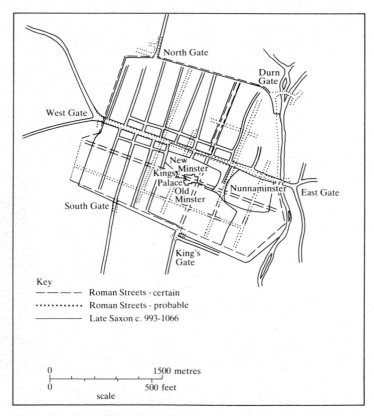

Figure 17 Plan of Winchester showing the Roman and Anglo-Saxon street patterns (after Biddle)

28 The Saxon *burh* at Wallingford, Oxfordshire. It was here that William the Conqueror at last crossed the Thames before moving eastwards to take London. The main outlines of the street plan are Anglo-Saxon but in the top right corner of the fortified area the extensive castle earthworks cover areas of former occupation (see Figure 18)

The renaissance of town life in Britain started in the eighth century, with both the revitalization of trading patterns and the threat from Scandinavian incursion. Ancient centres such as London, Leicester, Winchester and York were re-established at this time and new centres such as Oxford, Hereford and Shrewsbury had developed by the time of the Conquest. In Winchester, the dating of several streets, some of which were sealed beneath the Norman castle begun in 1067, indicates that the basic layout of the main streets was of tenth-century date within the framework of the re-inforced circuit of Roman defences. Similarly the plans of other *burhs* such as Hereford and Wallingford Berkshire indicate a considerable degree of regularity in their design. The emphasis within these late Saxon fortified towns was placed mainly upon the defences, and little attempt was made to provide special areas for commercial activity.

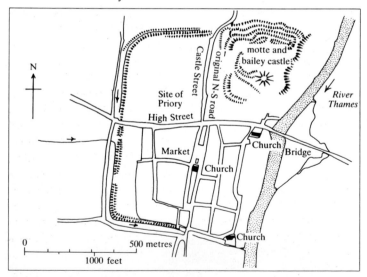

Figure 18 Plan of Wallingford showing the outline of the Saxon *burh* with its defences, street plan and bridging point. The castle was erected soon after the Conquest (William crossed the Thames here on his circuitous journey to London) and obliterated the north-eastern segment of the Saxon settlement

120

The increasing importance of market places can be illustrated through the examination of Anglo-Scandinavian town plans. In these settlements the market place was a late-comer to the plan, either being accommodated by internal demolition and alteration or as an added marginal feature outside the earliest line of the defences. At Hereford, Nottingham, Northampton and Stamford large open market places were developed outside the defences of the original *burhs* and effectively acted as new town centres which were subsequently included within the enlarged circuit of the medieval walls. In Oxford markets were held in the streets surrounding the central cross roads of the *burh* until the late eighteenth century. The very wide northern entry to the town in St Giles and Broad Street appear to have acted as extra-mural market places although in this case the markets were never actually incorporated within the city defences. At Buckingham the market place lies outside the *burh* defences forming the nucleus of the undefended medieval town. Elsewhere areas were cleared inside the defences to accommodate an intrusive market place as at Wallingford, Warwick, Worcester and Langport.

Defended Saxon towns differed in another important respect from their Norman successors. Saxon defended towns were conceived as communal centres, intended for the protection of the whole of the town's population as well as those living in the adjacent locality. In the early fortified Norman towns, defences, principally in the form of castles, were designed to protect the new Norman ruling classes, as well as proclaim their presence and their superiority. Apart from in Wales and the Marches communal town defences only became important again over much of the kingdom in the later twelfth century, when they served as much as a statement of civic status as for security.

The question of why towns developed defences after the political and strategic need for them had largely passed is one of considerable interest and complexity. It should be recognized that the walls performed a number of functions of which defence was only one. A circuit of town defences was an expression of urban status and was used to monitor and control trading access. The construction of town walls also had a fiscal function as murage grants were used to raise revenue and only a portion, sometimes a very small portion, was actually used for building or repair. Generally speaking of the 109 fortified medieval towns in England and Wales the majority were royal boroughs or shire towns. Most seigneurial towns, except for those in the Welsh and Scottish Marches, were unwalled.

Many of the institutional elements of the medieval town were present in the late Saxon period. Already in some late Saxon boroughs there were trade and craft associations and long before the Norman and Angevin kings issued borough charters tenth-century kings had tried to limit certain trading activities to within the borough boundaries. From this period onwards borough courts facilitated the establishment of special customs and tenures; when these first appear in writing they frequently contain archaic features indicating their antiquity. For example, York's first charter of 1154–8, largely confirmed already existing rights, while by 1066 there was already a guild of burgesses in Canterbury.

Trade associations were in existence even in small towns at an early date; for example, a merchant's guild was founded in the small wool town of Burford (Oxfordshire) between 1088 and 1107. This anticipated the pattern which was to become familiar throughout England in the twelfth and thirteenth centuries as the burgess members of the guilds and merchants took over the responsibilities for urban administration in most boroughs.

If urbanization was well advanced by the time of the Norman Conquest what was the Norman achievement in this area? Professor Carl Stephenson in his book *Borough and Town: A Study of Urban Origins in England*, published in 1933, clearly over-emphasized the impact of the Normans when he stated that town life did not restart in England until after 1066. Recent documentary research and archaeological investigation has demonstrated the high level of urbanization present in pre-Conquest England. It should also be recognized that the greatest period of medieval town and borough foundation dated from 1150–1250 and was therefore largely outside the Norman period proper. It could be argued, however, that this development was only made possible by the favourable climate created by the policies of the Norman kings, and the impact of the Normans in stimulating a significant acceleration in the rate of urbanization must be acknowledged.

The creation and expansion of towns was part of Norman strategy to control newly conquered territory. Towns had been used in Normandy as a means of centralizing political and economic control and the exercise was successfully repeated in England and Wales. The Norman kings saw the town and castle as basic instruments in the government of England. Not only was military control based on towns, but civil and ecclesiastical administration was also rapidly centralized. William transferred the seats of the bishops from rural areas to the protection of castle towns in places such as Lincoln and Norwich. In the 250 years following the Norman Conquest the urban geography of England and Wales was mapped out in a pattern which survived virtually unchanged until the Industrial Revolution, and, in parts of the country, survives today.

The general atmosphere of centralization that operated in the early Middle Ages encouraged seigneurial lords to try their hand at entrepreneurial activity by deliberately attracting trade and commerce through speculative urban plantations. Significantly there is important linguistic evidence which demonstrates a heavy reliance on French vocabulary for the language of commerce and borough affairs, reflecting the role played by the Normans and French in the creation of English town life. The impetus to urban growth was provided in part by the development of international luxury trade in commodities such as fine cloth and wine, which had largely been in abeyance since the collapse of the Roman economy in the West. An exclusive aristocracy with refined tastes had begun to shape itself and created the necessary lines of communication to satisfy them. The luxury trade in turn stimulated trade in more modest commodities. In some larger towns such as London, special areas or separate markets were set aside for different trades. For example in medieval Ipswich there were separate street markets for corn and bread, dairy products, apples and wine, meat, poultry, fish and pies, timber and cloth. Street names in many towns still indicate the location of the various occupations.

Another factor which it is generally agreed was a contributory factor to town development in the post-Conquest period was growth in population. The whole question of historic demographic trends is fraught with difficulties and it is impossible to quantify such trends with any degree of confidence. Certainly where documents exist they show a movement from rural areas to newly created urban settlements; against this, however, it should be remembered that most of the new market towns were relatively small, with average populations of perhaps less than 1,000. It is therefore possible that during the twelfth and thirteenth centuries there was more of a relocation of population than a massive increase in total numbers.

The early Norman castle boroughs
One of William's earliest tasks after the Conquest was to provide a secure political and military base in England. We have already observed that he chose the castle in conjunction with the town as the means of achieving this end. The earliest phases of the fortification between 1066 and 1071 followed a similar pattern to the early part of the Roman Conquest of Britain in the first century AD: castles being built along the south coast from Exeter to Dover, a scatter of fortifications in the Midlands stretching up as far as Lincoln and York, with a concentration in the west Midlands and the Welsh Borderland, with Chester forming the northwestern point of the attack and Chepstow the southern-most point in the Marches. The northwestern chain of defences roughly coincided with the line of Icknield Street which the

Romans originally saw as the northwestern boundary of their occupation.

The castles built in existing towns were normally sited on the highest ground available within the earlier *burhs* and often adjoining a river, which served both as a moat and a potential avenue for escape. We have already seen that the Domesday Book graphically records the impact of this process, whereby already existing property had to be destroyed to make room for the castle. In other cases topographical evidence demonstrates that the construction of a town castle must have caused considerable disruption. At Wallingford, for example, the plantation of the great motte within a quadrant of the Saxon *burh* must have destroyed a large built-up area (see Plate 28). This was subsequently compounded in the thirteenth century when a larger bailey was constructed. Recent excavations have demonstrated that the later defences covered a substantial area of town houses. The topography of other *burhs*, such as Wareham, Dorset, Worcester, Tamworth and Hereford, show a similar pattern, with the new castle being built either within the Saxon town or immediately adjacent to it.

Before 1100, in what Professor Beresford has aptly called 'the Conqueror's decades', Crown involvement in new foundations was at its height; subsequently the king played a significantly smaller role in creating boroughs. This reflected the importance the Norman Crown attached to the widespread distribution of royal boroughs, both to encourage allegiance, and to establish a political and strategic network throughout the country during the early years of the Conquest. At this time one in three planned towns was a royal foundation and some 80 per cent of the boroughs established were created in the immediate vicinity of royal castles. Early foundations, such as Windsor, Arundel and Launceston, were completely dominated by their castles.

During the early twelfth century, however, although more than half the borough plantations continued to be sheltered by castles the proportion of royal to seigneurial foundations changed in the favour of the latter. Already the emphasis on the town as an instrument of central government was declining. During the later twelfth century the majority of new towns were established without a castle and frequently without any form of town defence at all. For example amongst the second generation of town plantations, such as Kendal and Penrith, the town plan was divorced from the castle.

Of the first twenty-five Norman town plantations eighteen were located alongside a castle and one of them took its name from a new castle built on the River Tyne. At Windsor the Saxon settlement at Old Windsor was spurned and the castle was built on a chalk promontory which forms the only strong point in the Thames valley between London and Wallingford. New Windsor (the site of the present town) was grafted onto the castle.

In the case of Old Sarum (Wiltshire) the Normans chose a prehistoric hillfort, which now provides us with one of the most dramatic of monuments. The circular mound which formed the inner bailey of the Norman castle sits in the centre of the earthwork surrounded by a deep and wide ditch. The exceptional siting of the motte in relation to the outer defences is explained by the geography of the hill upon which it is placed. It occupied the highest ground within the area of the castle, in this case in the centre of the earthworks, which could not easily be made to conform to the standard plan of a Norman castle. They were therefore deepened and heightened in order to form what was in effect the outer bailey of a concentric castle. Within the bailey the ground was levelled-up with quantities of chalk from the enlarged ditch. Any structures which had formerly stood within the ramparts must have been destroyed in the process, and it would appear that the whole of the outer bailey was regarded as part of the castle. Bishop Osmund was, however, allowed to build his new cathedral church in the northwest segment when the see of Sherborne was transferred to Salisbury between 1075 and 1078, and the eastern limit of the cathedral precinct was defined by a bank. There appears to have been a borough here in the immediate post-Conquest period, but its precise location remains something of a mystery. Clearly there was not room within the fortifications, but there is little trace of urbanization adjacent to the castle and cathedral, which would have been the most natural site.

29   Old Sarum, Wiltshire. The predecessor to Salisbury is one of the great Norman monuments in England. The outer rampart was originally built in the Iron Age and re-fortified during the early Middle Ages. The castle and cathedral were built here following William I's transfer of the diocesan see here between 1075 and 1078. The Norman cathedral and borough were abandoned between 1220 and 1227 when Bishop Richard planted the town of New Sarum in the meadows of the Avon below

In another Wessex example, Devizes, the relationship between castle and town is far clearer. The original name, *burgus de devisis*, indicates that the borough was sited at the divide or boundary between two manors, Bishop's Cannings and Potterne, both incidentally owned by Bishop Roger of Salisbury (see Figure 19a). It is recorded that he built a

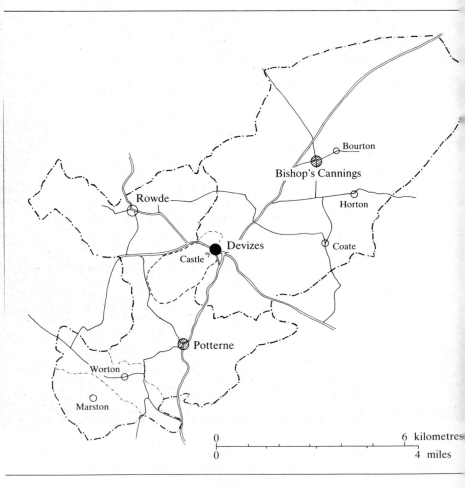

Figure 19a Site of Devizes, Wiltshire

30 Devizes, Wiltshire. A classic example of a castle town with the layout of the streets and markets following the pattern laid down by the castle. Note how the market close to the castle has been encroached upon, an indication of a successful trading centre

castle here c.1120 which replaced an earlier one destroyed in 1113. Devizes is one of the best examples of a town plan where the castle has played a dominant role in the layout. The streets are aligned with the castle defences in a distinctive semi-circular shape. There are two separate market

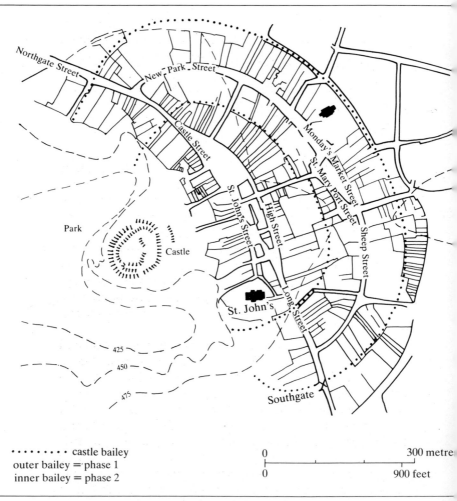

•••••••• castle bailey
outer bailey = phase 1
inner bailey = phase 2

0   300 metre
├────────┼────────┤
0   900 feet

Figure 19b Devizes castle town showing town laid out in two phases, first the outer bailey and then the inner bailey

places side by side, both curving slightly around the castle nucleus. The outer market place is the earlier, the inner one representing later colonization of the castle bailey.

The topography of Pleshey (Essex) demonstrates similar characteristics. In 1174 William de Mondeville obtained licence from Henry II to build a castle just off the upper Chelmer valley, seven miles north-west of the future site of Chelmsford. The name of this castle, Pless, was also taken for the town that grew up within an earthen wall which was built out in a loop from the castle, forming in fact a large second semi-circular bailey. Although no borough charter survives, thirteenth-century references to burgesses indicate that it had urban pretensions. The settlement never developed beyond its original design and today presents an obviously regular formation (see Plate 16). Apart from Devizes and Pleshey, Richmond (Yorkshire), Launceston (Cornwall), Wisbech (Cambridgeshire), Tutbury (Staffordshire) and Eye (Suffolk) also have semi-circular street plans dictated by the shape of the respective castle defences. In the case of Clare (Suffolk) only the layout of the area immediately adjacent to the castle has been influenced by the castle. While at New Buckenham (Norfolk) the town is laid out on a grid almost to the form of a second castle bailey. Such examples of urban topography being influenced by the presence of a castle are common and can almost always be dated to the early Middle Ages.

At Pontefract, the pre-Conquest settlement was a rural village called Tanshelf, whose site today is represented by the ruined church of All Saints, south-east of the castle. The establishment of the castle in the early twelfth century was closely followed by the layout of a small walled area with one central street axis, now represented by Micklegate and Horse Fair. The main street of this area, chartered in 1194, was just wide enough to serve as a market place, but its military derivation is clear. Beyond the west gate of the walled Anglo-Norman borough is a very different area, a large extra-mural market place, which received a separate charter in 1255–8 as the borough of West Cheap; a new

131

chapel, St Giles's, was built to serve it. Today the extra-mural market place, divided by infill into separate streets now known as Salter Row, Wool Market, Beast Fair, Shoe Market and Corn Market, forms the town centre of Ponte-fract. St Giles's chapel was elevated to become a rather shabby backwater. Kidwelly, Caernarvon and Cardiff are further post-Conquest military towns which developed extra-mural market places.

31 Eye, Suffolk. The outline of the perimeter road mirrors faithfully the layout of the castle which sits next to the church (top right). Unlike Devizes, however, the remainder of the street pattern has diverged from the original Norman form. The castle here was built by William Malet before 1086

Although the castle town was essentially a feature of the early years of the Conquest it was a tradition that persisted in the more unsettled areas well into the Middle Ages, most notably in Wales and the Marches. In such examples a

32 Clare, Suffolk. The impact of the massive earthworks of Clare castle have only incidentally influenced the development of the town plan in the form of a semi-circular street which echoes the alignment of the motte. A completely separate planned market unit lies in the centre of the picture, but the church forms an integral part of this development. Note here too the incidents of extensive encroachment between the church and castle

narrow single-street plan is commonly found with tenements on either side backing on to a lane running around
the inner perimeter of the defences linked to the castle.
Some of these towns were stillborn or enjoyed a life of only a
few generations. Today they are often only stunted settlements, like Richard's Castle or Kilpeck in Herefordshire.
Only a few houses remain, and the surviving earthworks
are the only indication of the line of the town walls and
internal tenements. In some places, of both English and
Welsh foundation, the borough amounted to little more
than an outer bailey of the castle, and some of the border
towns such as Cefnllys, Dryslwyn, Dolforway, Old
Dynevor, Bere, Skenfrith and Whitecastle, show little evidence today of their former urban functions.

33 New Buckenham, Norfolk. The castle here was built in the middle
years of the twelfth century by William de Albany. A regularly laid-out
new town was created outside the castle area but it was clearly influenced
by the topography of the fortification

French colonies

One of the interesting features of many early foundations was that French boroughs or colonies of French traders were often established alongside English settlements; sometimes these were already entrenched urban settlements, such as Stamford, Nottingham and Hereford. At

34 Kilpeck in Herefordshire is best known for its remarkable romanesque church built in the style of the Hereford school; however the church lies immediately to the east of extensive castle earthworks and at the centre of a fortification which represents the perimeter of a former borough. Earthworks in the centre of the picture indicate former buildings and tenement plots

Hereford French settlers were introduced by William fitz Osbern who granted them the fee customs of Breteuil Sur Iton (Eure), while the English community maintained their ancient burghal customs. The Breteuil customs were widely adopted by boroughs in western England and Wales. In the first instance there seems to have been a geographical separation of the two communities and their markets; gradually, however, English and French customs welded

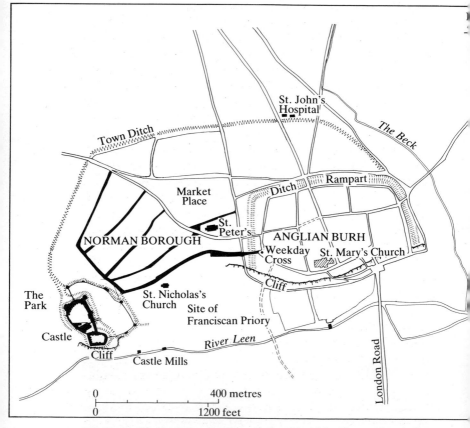

Figure 20 Nottingham, showing relationship of the Norman borough to the Anglian *burh*. Note the similarity in design between the Norman town plan here and that at Salisbury (see Figure 23b)

136

together. There were other 'French boroughs' at Pontefract, Ludlow and Richmond (Yorkshire).

Such was the success of Lynn in Norfolk that in 1135 a second town was laid out alongside the first on the river bank. At Nottingham, William the Conqueror established a castle and borough alongside an existing English borough. The French borough, as it continued to be called, was an appendage to the English borough with its own defences, streets and church. Within the new circuit of defences, encompassing some 120 acres, the northern and western walls of the Saxon *burh* were abandoned and by 1086 the ditch had been built over, but the distinction survived throughout the Middle Ages, each borough having its own sheriff and bailiff. The inheritance practices prevailing in both parts were quite distinctive, that in the English *burh* still being 'borough English' rather than the usual primogenitive. The situation in Nottingham underlines William's psychology and strategy: the area was one of royal interest, not least because of its close proximity to Sherwood Forest. First William was intent upon establishing a dominant Norman presence with a castle and a borough. Second although the Anglian city may have been detached and partially completed it was not entirely destroyed, thus William utilized the amenities already available. Third he was able to operate links that had existed prior to the Conquest, when Nottingham was the centre of a loose federation of five boroughs in an area with strong Scandinavian mercantile influence.

Planned towns

The question of 'planned' and 'organic' towns is one which has received considerable attention in recent years. The practice of deliberate plantation of whole or parts of settlements is now recognized as having been widespread during the Middle Ages. It was an activity begun by the Crown and rapidly imitated by lords, both religious and secular. One problem involved in the classification of planned towns is that although some were laid out completely afresh, many were tacked on to, or incorporated elements of already existing settlements. It was also possible for a town to be planned in several stages or in a series of separate units over a period of many years. A second problem which applied to all medieval towns is that the possession of urban functions was not always reflected in a settlement's legal status. Thus a highly successful early medieval plantation such as Ludlow did not acquire a borough charter until the fifteenth century. Conversely some settlements which were never towns in the commercial sense were granted charters from the outset. Thus because of the problems of definition the statistics used in this text should only be used as a guide to the real situation.

During the Middle Ages as a whole some 400 to 500 completely new towns were created in England and Wales, and an even greater number of rural settlements demonstrated urban ambitions through the acquisition of limited trading rights or the redesign of settlement layout. Professor Beresford in his pioneer work, *New Towns of the Middle Ages* (1967) has shown that there was a dramatic increase in town plantation immediately after the Conquest. The creation of new towns was quite common in Normandy before the Conquest, where at least twelve *bourgs* had been created in 1066. William himself had planted two *bourgs* at Caen close to the Ducal *bourg*, an operation he repeated when he added the new borough of Mancroft to Norwich. The term *novus burgus* is actually applied to Norwich in Domesday – the only other place where it is used is thought to be at Quatford in Shropshire. As there is no hint of any urbanization here, it may conceivably reflect an unfulfilled ambition, or it could refer instead to Bridgnorth which lies a few miles upstream on the river Severn.

Before 1100 twenty-one new towns had been established in England, with a further nineteen being added during the first three decades of the twelfth century. In Wales over the same period there were eighteen new town plantations. Although the rate of creation of new towns declined appreciably during the Anarchy, new foundations continued throughout the twelfth century, reaching a peak in the final decade. In all there were some forty-nine new town plantations in the years 1191 to 1230, after which numbers fell dramatically and the rate of failure of both new towns and well-established strategic boroughs began to rise.

Ludlow which lies towards the eastern edge of the Marches was one of the most successful of the medieval new towns, and since St John Hope's paper on the *'Ancient Topography of the Town of Ludlow'* was published in 1909 (*Archaeologia*, lxi) it has been recognized as a classic example of Norman town plantation. Built by Roger de Lacy on the edge of his extensive manor of Stanton Lacy at the time of its foundation at the beginning of the twelfth century, Ludlow presented one of the finest defensive sites in the Welsh Marches. The town is encircled on three sides by the river, and this natural defence is reinforced by a sandstone ridge that presents a precipitous cliff face of almost a hundred feet to the north and west. To the south and south-east, the land falls gently into the Teme valley and it was on these slopes that the streets of the medieval planned settlement were laid out. The castle which dominated the town was the greatest of the Norman castles in the Welsh border country and the key to the understanding of the town's creation and development. Within ten years between 1085 and 1095 the inner bailey and the great gatehouse keep had been constructed. Unlike many of the other early border castles, Ludlow did not reoccupy or replace a Roman site. The stone for the building of the castle came from the rock on which it stands, and much of the material for the semi-circular wall of the inner bailey must have been quarried in the making of the moat that was dug into the split rock alongside. The rough character of the medieval quarries can be seen along the slopes beneath the castle.

It seems most likely that the first streets were laid out in the decade of castle building between 1085 and 1095. A hundred years later, in 1199, there was certainly a large church on the site of the present parish church of St Lawrence, because a document of that date tells of sub-

35 Ludlow, Shropshire, is a classic example of a medieval planned town. The castle which lies in a loop of the river Teme occupies the highest point and the town streets and properties, which are laid out on a grid pattern interrupted by the medieval town wall, lie to the south and east (see Figure 21)

stantial alterations and enlargements. If the citizens of Ludlow had to extend their church in the last year of the twelfth century, it points to a prosperous and established town there at that time.

Although subsequently built upon, the key element in Ludlow's plan is the broad High Street that runs from west to east along the ridge-top from the castle gate to the Bull

140

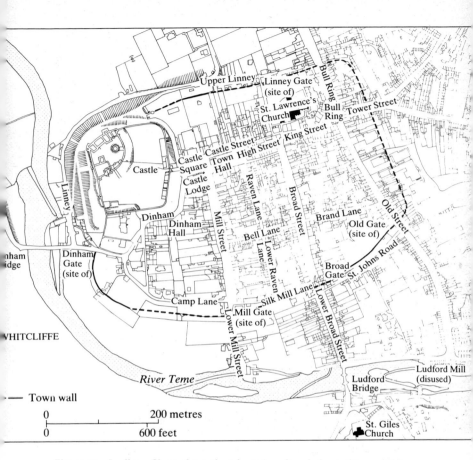

Figure 21 Ludlow, Shropshire, the 'classic' medieval planned town. The town walls are later than the street pattern. Note the redundant roads fossilized as property boundaries in the west of the town and how the majestic church of St Lawrence is hemmed in by later encroachment

Ring. The second part of Ludlow's medieval plan consisted of three broad streets, Old Street, Broad Street and Mill Street, that lead off from the High Street at right angles down the gently sloping plateau towards the Teme. Time has changed this central axis of Ludlow. At the eastern end closely packed buildings had been built on narrow islands in the former wide street by the close of the fifteenth

141

century. In fact, at the Butter Cross, medieval buildings converted the spacious High Street into four narrow lanes – Market Street, Harp Lane, Church Street, and the name of High Street still perpetuated in the axial road behind the Market Hall. The incongruous Victorian red-brick Market Hall occupies most of the original Norman High Street, and we can only appreciate the elementary grandeur of this urban core today in the wide Castle Square at its western end.

The plan was completed with a gridiron pattern of narrow lanes that divide the slopes south of the High Street into a chessboard design of rectangles. In turn, these rectangles were sub-divided into the long narrow plots owned by the burgesses of the medieval town, with a house or shop on the street front, sheds, workshops and gardens behind. But if Ludlow still retains some of the features of a medieval town, the centuries have not gone by without important changes to its topography. One of the greatest modifications to the plan of Ludlow resulted from the extension of the castle towards the end of the twelfth century. The huge curtain wall that encloses the outer bailey was built on the side, towards the town, encroaching on the western part of Ludlow so that part of the wide High Street disappeared under the open space of the outer bailey. It is probable, too, that this extension of the castle caused the disappearance of a street called Bell Lane that once ran down to the Teme to the west of, but parallel to, Mill Street. We can follow its line today at the bottom of the gardens of the burgage plots on the west side of Mill Street. Across this rectangle of land between Mill Street and the castle, now largely taken up with gardens, Bell Lane continued towards the little twelfth-century chapel of St Thomas of Canterbury. This chapel still stands and is used as a storehouse.

The importance of Ludlow as a town has been very closely linked with its castle. The descendants of Roger de Lacy ruled there until the first years of the fourteenth century. Gilbert de Lacy who died in 1160 built the Chapel of St Mary Magdalen in the inner bailey. With its circular nave, said to be in the very shape of the church of the Holy Sepulchre in Jerusalem, this style of Norman architecture is rare in England. It was Gilbert's son, Hugh de Lacy, who probably built the outer bailey and as a result extended the

36 The circular Norman nave of the chapel of Ludlow castle is one of only four such structures surviving in England

area of the castle fourfold.

A less successful but highly important border castle town lies a few miles to the north-west of Ludlow at Clun. The earliest part of Clun is represented by the church, isolated from the rest of the town and surrounded by a deep ditch on the south bank of the Clun river. There is no direct evidence

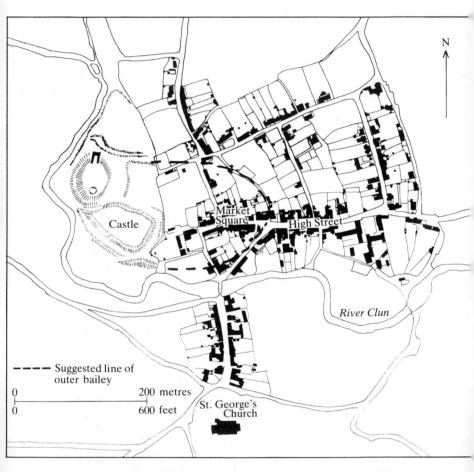

Figure 22 Clun, Shropshire, one of the less successful planned Marcher towns. The ancient centre lies around St George's church to the south of the river Clun

that the parish church of St Michael existed before the Norman Conquest, although the base of the huge square set tower and the west wall of the nave were certainly built about 1100, if not earlier. Clun's position, however, as the mother church of a large number of medieval chapels that are themselves separate parishes today suggests that there was a church there in pre-Conquest times. The chapels at Clunbury, Clunton, Hopton, Sibdon, Edgton and Llanfair Waterdine were all members of the vast primary parish of Clun in the Middle Ages. The manor of Clun as a political unit displayed a similar vastness of scale: at the Norman Conquest it was given to Picot de Say, one of Earl Roger of Montgomery's chief vassals, and was the greatest of Picot de Say's many estates. The Domesday Book records that there was land for sixty ploughs and that Welshmen were living in this scattered territory that stretched from the upper valley of the Teme towards the southern end of the Longmynd.

Clun's ancestry as a political unit, a focal point of territorial organizations, probably stretches far back in time beyond the settlement of this borderland by the Saxon state of Mercia in the eighth century. The complex structure of the manor, composed of several separate units, suggests that it formed a tribal core in Celtic society. Its very name has been identified by place-name historians as one of a small group of considerable antiquity – in fact, pre-celtic. Lost in a tree plantation to the north of Clun we may see the Iron Age forerunner of the Norman castle, the political centre of the twelfth-century Honour of Clun, in the huge hillfort of Bury Ditches.

Picot de Say and his successors as lords of Clun must have been responsible for the building of the castle and the laying out of the streets of the little borough on the north bank of the river. No documents survive that allow one to date with any precision these events and it is only by the beginning of the thirteenth century that we are made aware of a borough and a flourishing market centre at the gate of the castle when Clun acted as a meeting place for England and Wales

Figure 23a   Relative siting of Old Sarum, Salisbury and Wilton

where trade was transacted.

We can more often than not recognize the nature of the origins of planted towns through their plans. Two basic town types may be identified though within these categories there are wide variations: first, defended towns which are normally built within the shadow of a castle; second, market towns where the market function is emphasized in the form of large central open areas where trading was carried out. Such market areas varied enormously in shape and size. Both the defended borough and the market town could be grafted on to an original Roman or Saxon foundation. In some instances the two categories may be combined in one town and a fortified town may have had a later market area grafted onto it. An example of this is Alnwick in Northumberland, which originated as a fortress but took its final form from the triangular space later to become the market place created by the intersection of three important roads some way to the south of the castle. In other cases, such as Old Sarum and Salisbury, the original fortified nature of the town failed to meet the requirements of the emergent market centre and a completely new settlement was established some distance away on an entirely new site. The layout of Salisbury clearly demonstrates this difference, where the emphasis is much more on market functions than defence.

We have seen that the earliest group of foundations were dominated by royalist initiative and strategic considerations, most of them lying in close vicinity to a castle. Later on the towns which were primarily promoted by seigneurial interests were to be dominated by their market places. Battle, the first important unfortified Norman town, had neither town walls nor a castle, but consisted of a single main street running from the abbey gate to a triangular market place, in a pattern that was repeated in numerous other instances.

The common element in planned new towns was the burgage plot, representing individual burgess's property allotments. These normally took the form of long parallel

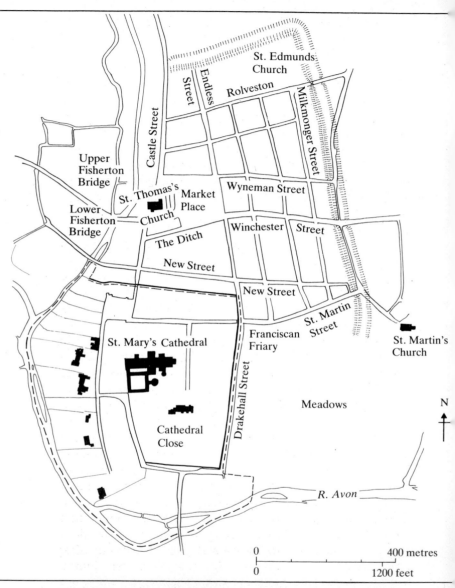

Figure 23b Salisbury, Wiltshire. Planned in the early thirteenth century to replace Old Sarum. The regular street pattern to the north of the new cathedral is a model of its kind

strips of land running at right-angles to the market place, with the other end delimited by a back lane which provided a rear access to the property. The width of the burgage plots varied considerably according to local conditions: at Stratford-upon-Avon, the Bishop of Worcester attracted burgesses with plots measuring 60 feet by 200 feet, while at Burton-on-Trent allotments were 70 feet by 400 feet, and in parts of the Midlands half-acre plots were not uncommon. In the cases of Stratford and Thame the burgage tenements appear to have been laid out over former arable strips and are characterized by a reversed 'S' plan, which probably reflects the aratral curve frequently found in ancient ridge and furrow.

Elsewhere the plot dimensions may have been dictated by medieval house construction. At Alnwick, for instance, almost half the burgages within the walls had frontages which were equal to, or a factor of, 28 feet. Another third were similarly related to a 32 feet width. The smallest widths recorded were 14 and 16 feet (exactly half the dominant units), which may represent the lower limits of bay widths. In 1155 the king determined that, at Scarborough: 'they shall pay me yearly for each house whose gable is turned towards the street four pence, and for those houses whose sides are turned towards the street, sixpence.'

In some cases the original property boundaries remained virtually intact, into the post-medieval period. For example in Westwick Street (Norwich) boundaries were unchanged from the twelfth to the eighteenth century and in Viking York they appear to have survived even longer. In other cases the town planners seem to have been over optimistic about the number of people they were catering for, and at Chelmsford, for example, excavations have shown that allotments which were originally laid out to a standard width were not built on immediately, and it was only after an interval of some twenty years that plots were joined together to create larger units, indicating that they had not succeeded in attracting sufficient people. In Lower Brook Street, part of Winchester's cloth-working area, there is

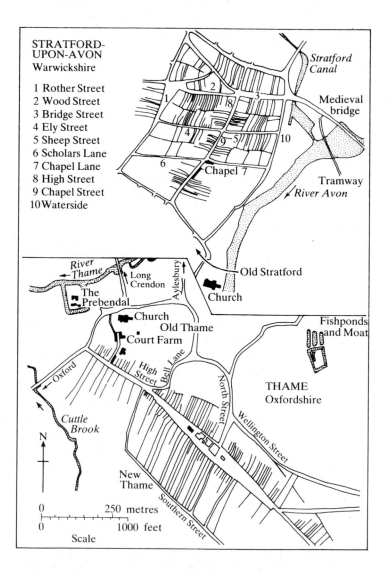

STRATFORD-
UPON-
AVON
Warwickshire

1 Rother Street
2 Wood Street
3 Bridge Street
4 Ely Street
5 Sheep Street
6 Scholars Lane
7 Chapel Lane
8 High Street
9 Chapel Street
10 Waterside

Stratford Canal

Medieval bridge

Chapel 7

Tramway
River Avon

River Thame

Long Crendon

Aylesbury

Old Stratford

The Prebendal

Church

Church

Old Thame

Court Farm

Fishponds and Moat

Oxford

High Street

Bell Lane

North Street

THAME
Oxfordshire

Cuttle Brook

N

Wellington Street

New Thame

Southern Street

0   250 metres
0   1000 feet
        Scale

Figure 24 Plans of Stratford-upon-Avon, Warwickshire and Thame, Oxfordshire showing different designs of early medieval planned towns. Both, however, appear to have been laid out over former agricultural land units as the individual tenement plots incorporate a distinctive curve of ten found in Midland strip farming

evidence of encroachment of some properties over their neighbours. Conversely in some towns the success of the plantation was such that subdivision of plots occurred at an early date. In Banbury, for instance, there was already considerable subdivision by 1225.

In the undefended market town tenements lying on either side of a single main street form by far the commonest medieval town plan. Single street towns were often swollen into a 'boat-shape' plan in order to accommodate the market. Good examples of this are to be seen at Thame (see Figure 24) Brackley, Chipping Campden and Ashford. These plans appear to have developed after 1100 when the advantages of market street frontages superseded defensive considerations. Usually the market access was related to a pre-existing route and clung closely to it. At Henley-in-Arden a new town was founded along the Stratford to Birmingham road late in the twelfth century by the lords of Beaudesert, which lies on the opposite side of the river. This followed an unsuccessful attempt to establish a market at Beaudesert Castle itself in 1141.

Sometimes roads were purposely diverted to pass through a market town. In 1219 the Bishop of Lincoln obtained permission to divert the Oxford to Aylesbury road into his new market town of Thame which lay along the axis between the ancient ecclesiastical centre of old Thame and the Cistercian abbey. The effect of this was to add a mile or so to the route. The plan of Thame also demonstrates another common element in these planned settlements: either end of the market is governed by a narrow entrance which enabled tolls to be levied and control imposed on anyone entering or leaving the settlement. The added advantage was that such an arrangement provided maximum burgage frontage with maximum market space. At Thame, however, we can see examples of encroachment on the centre of the market place. There are few early documented examples of this but in the majority of successful plantations we can be reasonably sure that it started almost as soon as the town was established. For instance in

Thame no sooner had the Bishop of Lincoln obtained his right to divert the road than he himself encroached on the market area.

37 Chipping Campden was created as a wool borough during the latter part of the twelfth century and demonstrates many of the features common to such plantations. The market square, which is 'boat-shaped' in order to accommodate a large market, has been encroached upon and the parallel property boundaries which mark the burgage plots are clearly identifiable on both sides of the street. Note, too, the way in which the church and manor are divorced from the main town indicating that they were not part of the medieval town design; almost certainly they were earlier foundations

Despite the excellent work of Beresford and others on planned medieval towns the full extent of medieval town planning has yet to be appreciated. Many small market towns demonstrate their planned origins through their layout. An excellent example of this can be seen at Eynsham in Oxfordshire. At first glance its plan seems confused, lacking any logic or regularity. If the plan is analysed, however, it is quite clear that the settlement has expanded by the addition of one new street after another. Although each unit has an internal plan, they are not all contemporary, and consequently the overall effect is irregular. The earliest access to Eynsham is on an east-west route via the early crossing point of the Thames at Swinford. The eastern part of this road is called High Street, but the western part, significantly, has long been known as Acre End, which makes it a candidate for the earliest agricultural nucleus of the community. The market place appears to be a later intrusion into the centre of the old east-west street alignment, and possibly required some buildings to be cleared away for it to be accommodated. It lies just outside the precinct of the Benedictine Abbey founded in 1005, adjacent to the parish church. King Stephen granted the right of the Sunday market to the abbey in 1139 as well as the privilege of burgage tenure.

Running northwards from the market square is Mill Street, whose western side is clearly lined with burgage tenements; this appears to have developed subsequent to the acquisition of a market. Moreover the Mill Street tenements are clearly later than the properties on the northern side of Acre End Street whose back lane and gardens continue through to Mill Street. The aptly named Newland Street leads off at an angle from Mill Street and its tenements lie not at right angles to Newland itself but parallel with Mill Street. This in turn suggests that Mill Street was in existence before the Newland tenement was developed. Newland dates from 1215 when a charter was acquired for a borough extension. The minor town of Eynsham thus displays several quite distinct phases of settlement growth. Similar

153

aggregations can be identified elsewhere even in new towns in which there appears to be only a single plan.

By 1200 the process of town creation and development was well advanced. Undoubtedly the overall level of European trading prosperity would have overflowed into England even without the Normans. It is difficult to believe, however, that the scale of urbanization would have been so great. The Norman town was an important instrument of political, strategic, administrative and economic control. The Normans found them flexible enough both to exert control over an area and to exploit it commercially. Thus towns, which the Normans originally created to dominate a region politically and strategically, were adapted to become the major economic force in the land.

6 The impact of the Conquest on the church

From the outset the Norman Conquest had deep religious connotations; quite apart from the powerful political and strategic support for the Conquest provided by European heads of state, including Emperor Henry III, William also received the seal of papal approval. Norman influence over the papacy was already strong, but it was still necessary for William's cause to be pleaded by the arch-deacon of Lisieux, on the grounds of Harold's alleged perjury. A conclave was held at which Harold was declared a usurper, and William the lawful successor to Edward the Confessor. Pope Alexander II, Anselm of Lucca, who had been educated by Lanfranc at Bec in Normandy, bestowed his blessing on the expedition, sending William a consecrated banner as a sign of St Peter's approval. In return, William agreed to reform the English church and when he was victorious he repaid the pope with the defeated Harold's banner. Such support brought immediate tactical advantage in that it gave a legitimacy to the Conquest, making it more difficult for English baronial revolt and virtually assuring English ecclesiastical compliance. In effect, by skilful preparation, William turned the expedition into a crusade. The concept of a holy war was not a new departure in Norman history; it was a cause that was repeatedly utilized in the process of Norman territorial expansion.

William also required financial support for the expedition from the well-endowed Norman church, and subsequently relied heavily upon political control of the church in England as an integral part of his administrative strategy. After the Conquest William used the church in England as in

Normandy as an instrument of government. Just as he insured that his political and military system was operated by loyal supporters, so, too, his nominees, such as Lanfranc, were to dominate the English church during the final part of the eleventh century and beyond.

The Anglo-Saxon church

Opinions on the state of the English church on the eve of the Conquest have varied considerably over time. William of Malmesbury attributed the revival of the rule of religion in England, 'which had there grown lifeless', to the Normans, while Dom David Knowles pessimistically noted: 'The [Saxon] church in England was reduced to little more than the performance, by an ill-educated, ill-found clergy, of the essential liturgical and sacramental services in the village churches and halls of the landowners.' Other historians have pointed to the wealth of learning and the artistic achievements of the late Saxon church. In truth it depends upon which area of the church's life is in question. It is, however, difficult to believe that taken as a whole the mid-eleventh-century English church was inferior to the church in Normandy in the early eleventh century before the influx of the reforming clerics from Burgundy and northern Italy.

Monasticism was well established and the influence of Cluny had already penetrated into England well before the Normans arrived. Partly as a result of this, by the end of the tenth century at least, twenty-five important new monasteries had been established at places such as Cerne, Eynsham and Abbotsbury, while many ancient centres such as Winchester, Abingdon and Muchelney had been rebuilt. Because of the great Norman rebuilding that was to follow, little of these establishments remains to be seen above ground level, but recent archaeological excavation at places such as Repton has demonstrated the impressive nature of the late Saxon foundations.

It has been argued that church reform was general in Europe in the 1050s and 1060s and that there is evidence of it in England before 1066. Edward the Confessor had installed foreigners in English dioceses and a few of these, such as William of London, maintained their positions after the Conquest. Any assessment of the state of the late Saxon church is complicated by the character of one of its leading personalities, Stigand. At the time of the Conquest pluralism was rife and he was typical of the political bishops against whom the reformers concentrated their attacks. As an associate of Godwin and his family, he took over Canterbury from the banished Norman archbishop Robert of Jumièges in 1052 – an event which was the cause of considerable scandal. He also held two cathedral monasteries, at Winchester and Canterbury, administered Gloucester abbey, and also for a time, Ely.

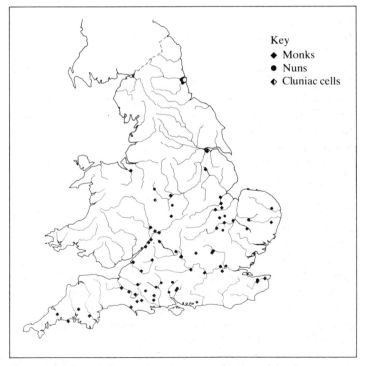

Figure 25   Monastic houses in existence at the time of the Conquest

If we turn our attention to the rural church it is clear that the changes following the Conquest were less profound. As far as parish churches were concerned by 1066 progress towards a thorough parochial organization was well advanced in parts of the country. At the close of Ethelred II's reign (c.1016) categories of churches were described as 'head minster, minster, lesser church with graveyard, field church or country chapel'. The head minsters were the cathedrals. The earliest churches to be established in any number were the minsters, mother churches with responsibility for very large territories. Such minsters were staffed by groups of clergy trained as part of the bishop's staff or *familia* who served the area over which the church had responsibility. The name minster is derived from *monasterium* which carries the implication that the clergy who once served them were monks. This was only partially true. In general, the minster clergy were priests living in communities, with the task of carrying religion to the ecclesiastically unorganized territories dependent on the minsters. They were authorized to baptize, marry, bury the dead and celebrate mass, and carry out all necessary pastoral work.

To begin with the early parishes served by the minsters were extremely large often covering tens of thousands of acres, but the process of subdivision was well advanced by the time of the Conquest, by which time the minster churches had already lost most of their importance and had been considerably reduced in number. This process was accelerated after the Conquest with many minsters falling into the hands of monastic communities. A documented example of this can be seen at St Gregory's, Morville (Shropshire). In 1066 the minster church possessed eight hides of land served by eight canons, but by 1086 there were only three priests here, and the church with five hides was held by Shrewsbury Abbey. In fact by 1200 something like a quarter of the parish churches of England had come into the hands of religious houses. To some extent the monastic financial involvement would explain the great phase of church rebuilding in the twelfth century which was imitated by lay patrons as well.

For several reasons it is difficult to obtain a true picture of the distribution of parish churches at the time of the Conquest. As already discussed the Domesday record of churches is notoriously imprecise and misleading, although a considerable number of churches do incorporate late Saxon architectural features and some well-known churches such as Earl's Barton (Northamptonshire) and Deerhurst (Gloucestershire), are largely of Saxon build. But the distribution of churches with Saxon features is also misleading, because clearly many late Saxon churches would have been built wholly or partly of wood and have long since perished, and many of those constructed in stone were demolished and rebuilt during the Middle Ages. In some cases, however, the original Saxon plan has survived into a later rebuild: for example, the cruciform plan of the fifteenth-century church of St Kenelm at Minster Lovell (Oxfordshire) is an indication of its earlier Saxon form, and 'ghost' Saxon elements of this type are probably far more common than is generally appreciated.

Looking at place-name evidence, the survival of the words, minster, *eccles* (north-eastern church) and *llan* (Welsh church) provide clear indications of the presence of a pre-Conquest church. We should bear in mind that in parts of the country – in the west particularly – Christianity had been practised uninterruptedly since the late Roman period. Thus many minsters, such as Leominster, were occupying sites which were ancient even in the tenth century. The degree of survival should show in dedications to early saints, but during the early Middle Ages there appears to have been a widespread process of rededication in this part of the country, often to saints such as St Catherine, whose cults were introduced into England at the time of the Crusades. Many of the early Celtic and English dedications were replaced in the two centuries following the Conquest by saints who were popular in Normandy, such as St Michael and St Stephen.

In general there were probably far more churches both in

town and country than we are able to identify. We know that Norwich, for example, had twenty churches and forty-three chapels in 1086. Minster churches serving large areas were still common in the west, but elsewhere England was clearly well served with parish churches. In areas such as Hampshire and Berkshire churches were normally created by local landlords, while in East Anglia and the northern Danelaw they were at times corporate institutions built by groups of freemen.

The new Norman church

Between 1070 and 1087, under the control of William, the English church experienced great changes, which largely repeated events that had previously taken place in the province of Rouen. Tangible links between the English and French church were immediately strengthened; the Conqueror paid his debt to Valéry, the Picard saint, for the favourable breeze that blew him to England before the battle of Hastings, by granting the manor of Tackley in Essex to the Valéry priory. The following year Hayling Island was granted to the monks of Jumièges to celebrate the consecration of their church. Altogether nearly thirty Norman monasteries received gifts of manors, estates, churches and tithes in England during the decade subsequent to the Conquest.

Although in general the Normans were awed by the English church and its traditions, they despised its customs and culture and they coveted its wealth. They disliked its archaic Roman liturgy, its buildings, constructed in what they regarded as an outmoded style, and its incomprehensible learning. Initially the Normans had little respect for the English saints, and Archbishop Lanfranc wrote: 'These Englishmen among whom we are living have set up for themselves certain saints whom they revere. But sometimes when I turn over in my mind their own accounts of whom they were, I cannot help having doubts about the quality of their sanctity.' With less circumspection Lanfranc's kinsman, Abbot Paul, broke up the tombs of the former abbots of St Albans, whom he referred to as 'uncultured idiots'. The new abbot of Abingdon tried to completely obliterate the memory of St Aethelwold whom he called 'an English rustic'. While at Evesham, Abbot Walter (1077–1104) put the saints' relics to the test by fire – only those that survived were deemed to be genuine. The hostility to the English saints did not, however, survive the first generation of Norman clerics: the writings of contemporary chroniclers did much to re-establish the reputation of the most famous saints and the church began to appreciate the financial importance of their relics in attracting pilgrims.

William needed bishops whom he could trust absolutely and who could serve as vice-regents in his newly won kingdom. He therefore delayed only a few years before instigating a radical re-staffing of the English church, and, prompted by clerical involvement in the northern risings, William set about the systematic replacement of the upper sections of the Anglo-Saxon church hierarchy. In 1069 Stigand, whom the Normans regarded as a usurper, was removed as Archbishop of Canterbury and replaced by William's friend and confidant, Lanfranc. So complete was the eventual foreign 'take over' that William of Malmesbury writing in about 1125 claimed that: 'England has become a residence for foreigners and the property of aliens. At the present time there is no English Earl, nor bishop nor abbot; strangers all, they pray upon the riches and vitals of England.' The semi-religious nature of the Conquest 'involved the Saxon church in ecclesiastical censure of the unfortunate Harold and contributed to render the Norman Conquest as complete intellectually as it was politically.' William and his immediate successors pursued a vigorous policy not only of appointing non-English archbishops and abbots, but also of radically restructuring the organization of the church.

Lanfranc, apart from being a resourceful politician, was also a sincere churchman and confirmed ecclesiastical reformer. He brought with him to England a group of pupils and associates from Bec and Caen mostly destined for promotion to high places, including his nephew, Paul, who be-

162

came the abbot of St Albans; Gundulf, subsequently Bishop of Rochester and surveyor of the king's works at the Tower of London; and Gilbert Crispin, abbot of Westminster. Within ten years of the Conquest all the English sees with the exception of Worcester, which was still held by the Saxon Weolfstan, were held by foreigners, mainly Normans.

William and Archbishop Lanfranc shared the concept of a sharp hierarchical structure and insisted that Canterbury had primacy not only over England, but over the whole British Isles. A council at Windsor, held in 1072, decreed that each rural see should be moved to a major town in its diocese. This manoeuvre had many implications, particularly as the ancient centres had largely been associated with Saints' relics. The see at Dorchester-on-Thames was transferred to Lincoln, Sherborne to Old Sarum, Selsey to Chichester and Elmham to Norwich by way of Thetford and the silted-up port of Dunwich, Wells to Bath and Lichfield to Chester. Although there were subsequent re-adjustments – Henry I created a new diocese in each province, Ely in Canterbury and Carlisle in York – those moves were to establish the diocesan framework in England for many centuries. Additionally bishops were ordered to appoint proper ecclesiastical officials, the dioceses were divided into archdeaconries and eventually these were subdivided into rural deaneries, thereby establishing the pattern of ecclesiastical territories until the Reformation and beyond. Whereas the Roman administrative centres served in Normandy up until the French Revolution, in England it was the Normans who created the basic ecclesiastical administrative network.

Despite the reorganization of the secular church, the essentially monastic character of the tenth-century reformation under St Dunstan survived the Conquest and gave rise to the peculiarly British custom of establishing a bishop's

38 St Mary the Virgin, Iffley, Oxford. A twelfth-century Norman romanesque parish church

163

39 This remarkable tympanum in the chapel at Aston Eyre, Shropshire, depicts Christ's entry into Jerusalem and is the work of the twelfth-century Hereford school of sculptors

see in a monastic church. In eight of the Norman dioceses the cathedral was a monastic church, the bishop being considered as the abbot and the prior the head of the working monastery. One immediate result of this reorganization, however, was that the secular church was able to build on the same scale as the great Benedictine monasteries. The cathedrals began to compete with the great monastic churches in their architectural achievements.

The foundation of parish churches
The processes of parish formation and parish definition continued at an accelerated rate after the Conquest, particularly in western Britain. A survey of Lancashire has demonstrated a doubling in the number of churches between Domesday and the mid-thirteenth century and there seems to have been a similar expansion in Staffordshire and Cheshire, each associated with the development of towns and Norman manorialization.

Morville in Shropshire provides us with an interesting

insight into parochial development in the twelfth century. The first stage appears to have been the creation of dependent chapelries, which eventually graduated into fully independent parishes. Following the acquisition of Morville by Shrewsbury Abbey a considerable number of chapels were planted in the parish in the following century. Apart from completing Tugford chapel, which was a parish church by the end of the twelfth century, other chapels in Morville parish were founded at Billingsley, Oldbury, Taselsey and Aston Eyre before 1140. This latter chapel contained a remarkable tympanum showing Christ's entry into Jerusalem, considered by many to be the finest example of Norman sculpture in Shropshire. Further chapels in Morville parish were later founded at Aldenham, Underton and Astley Abbots. Although all traces of the chapels at Underton and Aldenham have long since disappeared, along with the hamlets they served, the remainder all subsequently emerged as separate parishes.

In many other large parishes there was a similar burst of activity. St Mary's church at Shawbury founded chapels at Acton Reynald, Moreton Corbet, Grinshill and Great Wytheford. A certificate of Bishop Roger de Clinton dated 1140 tells of the time when these manors were without chapels and that he himself had consecrated three of them. This pattern of chapel foundation was repeated throughout the county. In the south-west of Shropshire there were extremely large parishes containing only scattered settlements; chapels tended to be planted in hamlets along the river valleys. A line of such chapels, later to become parish churches, follows the county boundary along the Teme Valley at Bedstone, Bucknell, Stove and Llanfair Waterdine. At Leominster (Herefordshire) there was a massive and ancient estate consisting of thirty-eight townships, which largely corresponded with later parishes. The estate was granted to Reading Abbey on its foundation in 1123. Most of the rural minsters ended up as parish churches by the twelfth century, although some were able to maintain rights over dependent villages well into the Middle Ages.

40 Priory church of St Peter and St Paul, Leominster. Work on the present building started soon after 1123 when the estate was granted to Reading Abbey by Henry I. The size of the church is a reflection of the importance of the immense late Saxon estate based on Leominster. Although much of the church is later the tower is basically Norman

The spread of monasticism

There were some fifty-two monastic institutions (all following the Benedictine rule) in England by 1066. They were essentially English in their origin although they drew many of their customs and observances from Cluniac and Lotharingian sources. New foundations in the immediate wake of the Conquest included Chester (direct from Bec) (1093), Selby (1068), Colchester (1095), Tewkesbury (1102) and

166

Shrewsbury (c. 1085). These creations were mostly grafted on to existing settlements, but unlike contemporary castles they were not responsible for large-scale disturbance to the existing town plans. Shrewsbury Abbey, for example, founded by Roger de Montgomery, lay outside the loop of the river Severn where the Saxon town sat. The most dramatic of the new foundations was Battle Abbey (Sussex) (1067) built at Senlac, the site of the battle of Hastings, a site which was reported as lying 'in a desert surrounded by swampy valleys and by forest out of which only a few homesteads had yet been carved.' William founded Battle as a thanks offering and a penance for his victory and treated it subsequently as his own parochial church. He insisted that the altar stone should occupy the very spot where Harold was killed. The abbey church was an excep-

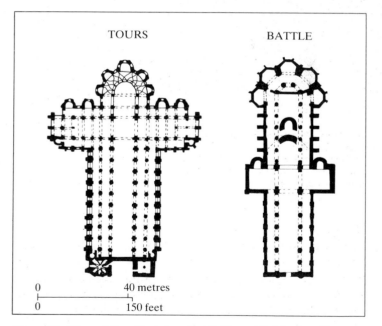

Figure 26 Plans of the abbey church at Battle and St Martin at Tours, to show relative size and design

167

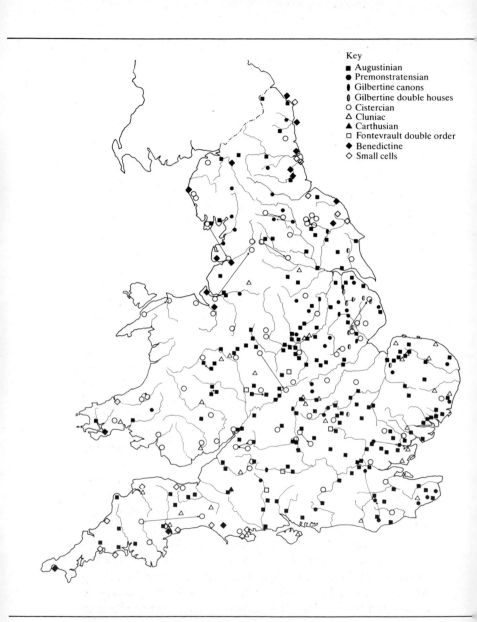

Key
- ■ Augustinian
- ● Premonstratensian
- ◗ Gilbertine canons
- ◑ Gilbertine double houses
- ○ Cistercian
- △ Cluniac
- ▲ Carthusian
- □ Fontevrault double order
- ◆ Benedictine
- ◇ Small cells

Figure 27 Distribution of monasteries and houses of regular canons by 1200

tional design for England, and its plan appears to have been based on the great tenth-century church of St Martin at Tours.

Four decades or so after the Conquest there began a great monastic invasion which continued almost without pause for a century and a half. In the words of the great ecclesiastical historian Dom David Knowles: 'successive orders like successive tribes and nations, crossed the frontiers as if they were impelled by those behind who had come from a greater distance.' The first to arrive were the Norman monks from the Conqueror's duchy, many of them were men who combined native energy and organizational ability with the zeal of a new and fervent religious movement. Some of them were carefully chosen to govern the existing monasteries, while others came to colonize the new foundations such as Chester and Battle from Bec and Marmoutier respectively. Some came to reinforce existing communities and their daughter-houses at Canterbury, Rochester and Colchester, or to man the small priories and cells which sprang up all over the great Norman fiefs, where lesser lords, unable to found an abbey, set up small communities in their castle or near their hall. The abbeys of Bec and Jumièges in Normandy were the most influential. It has been estimated that between 1066 and 1130 about forty abbots or priors of cathedral monasteries were recruited directly from one or other of the twenty-six Norman abbeys, and that fifteen of these came from Jumièges.

Norman monastic enterprise was particularly active to begin with in the prosperous areas of southern and eastern England, and in the more remote area around the Fens. Those few English clerics who remained in powerful positions, mostly in central and northern England, were influenced by the flurry of Norman activity. Wulfstan rebuilt the cathedral at Worcester, while at Evesham, abbot Aethelwig was expanding his community. These two also appear to have been the principal force behind the reintroduction of monastic observance into Northumbria. Paradoxically, however, Worcester, as well as Exeter and a few other monasteries, remained centres of Anglo-Saxon learning well into the twelfth century, but even these eventually succumbed to Latin and Anglo-Norman culture.

It would be impossible to exaggerate the regenerative power of the great Benedictine Norman abbots and priors of the first and second generation. They were soon followed by others. Foremost amongst these were the Cluniacs, who had already covered the rest of western Christendom with their network of dependencies. They were planted at Lewes (1078–82) by William de Warenne, and branched rapidly out into a family that was dependent upon the great Burgundian mother-house. However in general they failed to inspire to the same degree as their mother-houses on the continent: only Much Wenlock (*c.* 1080), Thetford (1107), and Lewes itself, out of the thirty-six Cluniac foundations established by 1160, were particularly impressive. Because of the strong monarchical constitution of the order, the offshoots from Cluny did not fit particularly well into the requirement of the Normans in England. Indeed they never really prospered in this country, and because of the fiscal links and loyalties between the dependencies and the mother-house in France, they were eventually alienated.

Following the monks came the regular canons, such as the Austin or 'black canons' who had the Rule of St Augustine as their code. But the greatest impact was made by the Cistercians, an austere order who aimed at following the Rule of St Benedict to the last letter (*ap apicem litterae*). Their founder was St Bernard who reacted against both the liturgical and architectural excesses of the early twelfth-century church. In 1125, in response to the increasingly confident flamboyance of the romanesque buildings, he pleaded: 'For God's sake, if men are not ashamed of these follies, why at least do they not shrink from the expense?'

The earliest Cistercian plantations were at Waverley (Surrey) (1128) and Rievaulx (Yorkshire) (1132). Thenceforward the movement spread with phenomenal rapidity over England and later over Wales. Normally their foundations were established on waste land in remote and uncultivated dis-

41 An aerial view of Sawley Abbey, Yorkshire. The ruins of the conventional buildings can be seen in the centre, but they are surrounded by earthworks representing agricultural and industrial enterprise, as well as fishponds and water courses. Sawley was a Cistercian house which moved from its original site because of the rain which 'almost every year drowned their crops'

tricts. In order to facilitate the tasks of clearing forests, draining marshes, overseeing flocks and crops in wild and desolate places, the Cistercians recruited cottars and small freeholders as lay brethren and in doing so they opened the religious life to classes hitherto excluded from it. Incidentally they created a labour force of great economic potential, that for a century did much to further the contemporary extension of the limits of cultivation. At Rievaulx, for exam-

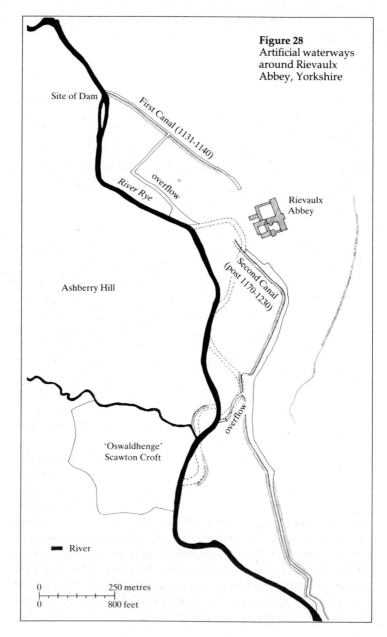

Figure 28
Artificial waterways around Rievaulx Abbey, Yorkshire

Site of Dam

First Canal (1131-1140)

overflow

River Rye

Rievaulx Abbey

Second Canal (post 1170-1230)

Ashberry Hill

'Oswaldhenge' Scawton Croft

overflow

▬▬ River

0   250 metres
0   800 feet

ple, under its third abbot, Ailred (1147–67), it is said that there were 140 monks and at least 500 lay brothers 'so that the church swarmed with them like a hive of bees.'

The sheer magnitude of the engineering feats undertaken by the Cistercians demonstrates their perseverance and a level of technological ability which is perhaps not generally appreciated. At Ryedale (Yorkshire) there were two twelfth-century foundations, Rievaulx (1131) on the lands of Walter L'Espec and close by, Byland (1142) on Roger de Mowbray's estates. They were so close that they could hear each other's bells, both by day and night, 'which was not fitting and could by no means be endured'. Thus in 1147 the newcomers at Byland moved to another site a little further away. At the same time negotiations about the boundaries between the two abbeys involved the re-direction of the river Rye, a process which meant the construction of artificial canals and was not completed until the early thirteenth century.

At Bordesley, Redditch (Worcestershire) the Cistercians founded an abbey in the valley of the river Arrow. The site was low lying and clearly subject to regular flooding, and consequently the Arrow was diverted for almost a mile in a channel dug for it in the northernmost part of the valley. At the same time the bed of the old channel was widened and deepened to accommodate a set of fishponds. The actual site of the abbey was better drained and an extensive area within the precinct was made available for fish rearing as well as agricultural and industrial activity.

The Cistercians are also commonly associated with the development of large scale commercial sheep farming, although recently some historians have questioned if there really was an expansion of sheep farming in the twelfth century. Certainly in parts of the country the Cistercians were responsible for a dramatic increase in the number of sheep. For example, Meaux Abbey went into sheep farming at an early date and soon after its foundation (1151) acquired pasture for 800 sheep in Myton, for 860 sheep at Warter, 300 sheep at Beeford and 200 at Hatfield. The sheep were reared presumably for the wool. By 1154–60 Meaux was making

42 An aerial view of one of the best-known and largest of the Cistercian houses in England – Fountains Abbey, Yorkshire

money from its wool sales and at the time of the collection of King Richard's ransom in 1193 the abbey was associated with the other Cistercian houses in giving up a year's wool.

Not all the engineering works of the Cistercians were simply for drainage, although clearly this would often have been an important consequence. Some were constructed to provide hygienic conditions for the abbeys, as can be seen with the impressive sewers and drains still surviving at sites such as Fountains Abbey (Yorkshire). The investigation of the remains of the early twelfth-century grange sites of Meaux (Yorkshire) show that dykes were used to divide the open fields from marshland or woodland. The other major motive for digging dykes in the Holderness region was to improve communications. Dykes made by the brothers at

Meaux Abbey were cut east-west across the line of the natural flow of water, and across a ridge of boulder clay to

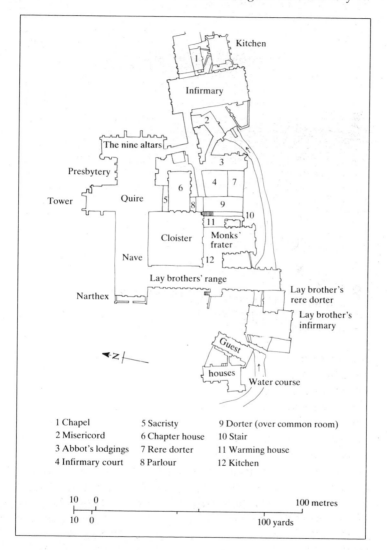

Figure 29 Plan of the Cistercian abbey at Fountains, Yorkshire. Effluent was discharged into the water course and carried away

1 Chapel
2 Misericord
3 Abbot's lodgings
4 Infirmary court
5 Sacristy
6 Chapter house
7 Rere dorter
8 Parlour
9 Dorter (over common room)
10 Stair
11 Warming house
12 Kitchen

connect the abbey with the river Hull and so with the Humber. The Foredyke was partially created to be a boundary between Sutton and Wawne, but from the first recorded agreement for establishing the dyke all parties concerned were to have boats on it.

In the Somerset Levels near Glastonbury there was similar drainage activity which served several needs. For an indication of the complexity of water transport in the Levels, it is most illuminating to look at some of the duties of Robert Malerbe, a tenant of Glastonbury in the early thirteenth century:

> he ought to provide a boat that can carry eight men, and be the steerman, and carry the lord abbot where he wishes . . . and all his men, and the cook, the hunter with his dog, and all those who can or ought to be carried by water. . . . He ought to be responsible for the abbot's wine at Pilton, after it has been put in the boat and until it has been brought to Glastonbury. . . . To look after all waters between Clewer and Street bridges, and between Mark Bridge and Glastonbury. And he ought to look after all the abbot's boat's in those waters and keep the waterways in Hearty Moor

While other monastic houses such as Bridlington and Aumale were acquiring cow and horse pastures, the Cistercians appear to have taken the lead in sheep farming. Meaux probably would have been guided by the example of the other Yorkshire Cistercian houses, and in the thirteenth century was continuing to add to its sheep pastures wherever possible. By 1250, if not earlier, Meaux was using former cow pastures for sheep farming.

The great Cistercian foundations of northern England were also involved in the repopulation process following the 'harrying of the North'. There is evidence to suggest new monastic granges were set up in 'waste' territory. Dr R. A. Donkin has shown that 44 per cent of all known twelfth-century granges (mainly Cistercian) were built on land that was completely or largely 'waste' in 1086. Conversely there are instances where monastic communities brought about the destruction or movement of settlements.

For example, the monks of Rufford Monastery (founded *c*.1145) destroyed two Nottinghamshire villages, one of which had ten villeins and the other eleven villeins and a church in 1086. At the southern end of the Lincolnshire Wolds the foundation of Revesby Abbey in 1142 uprooted three villages, while in Warwickshire, the village of Upper Smite was swept away by the foundation of Combe Abbey in 1150. In most cases a twelfth-century foundation in the more thickly settled areas of central and southern England resulted in disturbances in the local settlement pattern.

There is a rare reference to depopulation caused by civil war during the Anarchy in a charter for Unceby in the Lincolnshire Wolds. It was granted between 1163 and 1176, and it permitted Thornton Abbey to turn out sheep to graze in the fields of Unceby in a reasonable number until such times as the village should be repopulated and restored to life – '*donec ipsa rehabitata et restituta feurit.*' The depopulation must have taken place during the civil war, for in both the Domesday Book and the Lindsay Surveys of 1155–6 there is no sign that the village was razed at the time of the Conquest. The anticipated repopulation must have taken place, for Unceby is no longer a deserted village, but it is significant that the lord of Unceby assumed that the best garrison for a temporarily abandoned village was a flock of sheep.

In the wake of the Cistercians came the Premonstratensians, who had originated as an apostolic preaching institute, but, feeling the influence of St Bernard and the Cistercians, had become a semi-monastic order with houses in remote districts like the Cistercians, and similarly involved with sheep farming. Hitherto there had been little opportunity for women to join religious orders. The relatively few nunneries were old, selective, and often aristocratic Benedictine houses, almost all in Wessex or near London. A few had been added after the Conquest, but the real need was not met until a new order came into being. The Order of Sempringham, was in origin, and always remained (save for a single temporary exception) English in personnel,

177

though its codes and observances were all drawn from the continent. It was founded in a village of south Lincolnshire for women of the district, by Gulbert (of Norman origin), a small landowner turned priest. There were few other examples of such 'double orders', although Fontevrault did found a number of nunneries in England, notably at Amesbury.

There were several other orders, most of them small with only a few houses, including the order of Grandmont and the Carthusians, a strictly enclosed hermit group. Additionally military orders were founded as a direct consequence of the Crusades and although they may appear somewhat bizarre to us, they epitomized the piety of the age

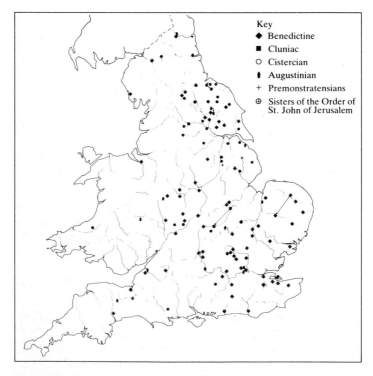

Key
◆ Benedictine
■ Cluniac
○ Cistercian
❘ Augustinian
+ Premonstratensians
⊕ Sisters of the Order of St. John of Jerusalem

Figure 30 Nunneries in England and Wales, *c.* 1200

by combining monastic and military ideals, uniting two divergent ways of life, each of which appealed powerfully to Norman society. The largest such order in England was the temple of St John of Jerusalem, or the Knights Templars as they were popularly known.

Another element of early medieval monasticism was the founding of the hospitals. There were certainly a number already in existence before 1066, for example at York and Worcester, but the great stimulus to the development of these establishments were the pilgrimages. After the first Crusade, pilgrimage in Europe to Jerusalem, Rome and Santiago de Compostela became increasingly important, and hospitals, which acted as hospice, almshouse and clinic, sprang up along the network of routes. Some were attached to existing institutions while others were specifically created by larger monasteries and other benefactors. A number of European routes began in England, notably from Reading Abbey which was closely associated with the cult of St James and hospitals were started in London and along routes leading to the ports. In the second half of the twelfth century the shrine of St Thomas of Canterbury became a particularly important goal for pious wayfarers, and hospitals at Canterbury and Southwark bearing the martyr's name were amongst the earliest. Within a very few years they proliferated. By the mid-thirteenth century there were almost 1,000 hospitals in England.

By the end of the twelfth century there were more than 600 monastic institutions of varying beliefs in England. Within a century they were in possession of a considerable amount of land and potential wealth of the country. In many respects their techniques and systems of land management were similar to that on other large estates. However they did possess one characteristic not guaranteed on other estates, namely assured continuity. This meant that they had the capacity of becoming far more powerful than their secular neighbours. The element of continuity and the wealth that it engendered, as we have seen, enabled the monasteries to undertake ambitious engineering schemes

179

during the twelfth century as well as to develop farming techniques to a high degree of competence.

Would the flood gates of monasticism have opened so wide in an Anglo-Scandinavian England? The answer is probably no. The cultural affinities between the Anglo-Norman ruling classes and the French homelands from whence the majority of the monastic institutions originated meant that there was an easy transition from mainland Europe to England. The radical redistribution of land after 1066 provided fertile ground for the spread of monasticism. The Conquest resulted in the concentration both of land and of wealth within the hands of a very small group of Normans. Overnight it had turned many of them from being simple manorial lords into great magnates and they found they had a considerable surplus, to their accustomed requirements of wealth and land. Traditionally and diplomatically pious by nature, they spent a percentage of this surplus on the endowment of churches and cathedrals, and some of the surplus land, most frequently that which was of marginal agricultural value at the time of endowment, was painlessly given to the newly founded monasteries in order to buy a place in heaven.

Church architecture

'Norman architecture' is probably the best known of all building styles in Britain. Yet how Norman in design were the buildings erected in the century following the Conquest? And how much was the style which developed in England in the twelfth century the result of the marriage between English and Norman and other general European developments? Indeed, would the vigorous romanesque architecture of the eleventh and twelfth centuries which is still universally known as Norman in England and 'Roman' in France, have developed irrespective of the Norman Conquest? As with all such historical speculation there can be no definitive answer.

During the decades following the Conquest Anglo-Saxon masons appear to have been employed in building churches in a hybrid style often called Anglo-Norman. Both Anglo-Saxon churches and Norman churches were built in a style generally known as 'romanesque'. They used round arches for arcades, doors and windows, and columns with capitals which were based, sometimes remotely, on classical models, particularly the Corinthian capital, which was simplified by the Normans. Doorways, chancel arches, corbel tables, and other surfaces were eventually covered with a profusion of ornament. In some cases this was a wild mixture of abstract, Christian and pagan ornament: some of which, such as the dragons and beak heads, betray the Norman's ultimately Norse origins.

It is clear that the distinctive style of early Norman architecture on the continent can be traced back to 1002 when Duke Richard 11 invited the Italian St William of Volpiano, abbot of St Benigne at Dijon, to Normandy. With him came a colony of Benedictines who settled at Fécamp and brought with them the newly developed Burgundian and Mâconaise traditions of architecture and blended it with Norse ornamentation. One of the principal architectural features of true Norman romanesque, not seen in earlier building in northern France, was the application of genuine stone vaulting. This was first applied in Normandy in the choir of La Trinity (Caen), 1062–1166 and at Notre Dame sur L'eau at Domfront 1150–60. The majority of the true Norman buildings were, however, constructed after the Conquest and the flourishing period of the romanesque style took place simultaneously in Normandy and England.

It was in Westminster Abbey that William the Conqueror was crowned King of England on Christmas Day 1066. The two English archbishops Ealred of York and the controversial Stigand of Canterbury officiated at the ceremony. Although it was an English building constructed by an English king – Edward the Confessor, who had been buried there just a year earlier – the structure was in fact the first example of the Norman romanesque to be built in England: it was modelled closely on contemporary Norman churches, notably Jumièges (1040–67), but was larger than all of them.

181

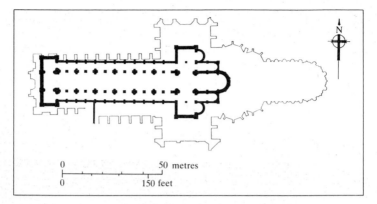

Figure 31 Plan of Westminster Abbey showing Edward the Confessor's church in relationship to the existing Abbey church

In consequence, almost alone among the greater English churches, it was spared after the Norman Conquest, and was not rebuilt until the thirteenth century. Thus the architectural style which was so closely associated with the Normans, preceded the Normans themselves into England.

The new Norman prelates, drawn largely from flourishing Norman monasteries, hastened to reform both the practices and architecture of the English cathedrals, and the most tangible result of the Conquest was the almost immediate rebuilding of the majority of them. Based on the Norman model their reconstruction started within a few years of the Conquest. The Saxon cathedral at Canterbury was damaged and partly destroyed by fire in 1067. Lanfranc built a new one between 1071 and 1077, which led William of Malmesbury to remark: 'you do not know which to admire more, the beauty or the speed.' The design was based upon that of St Étienne, Caen: both had elaborate western faces, and a spacious nave to match the intended function of the church – to accommodate crowds on the great festivals and to manifest the prestige of the community.

Lincoln cathedral was begun by Bishop Remi of Fécamp in 1072–3 and consecrated in 1092. Work on the cathedral of Old Sarum was started by Bishop Hermann between 1075

182

43 Durham cathedral and castle from the south. Naturally fortified by the river Wear, Durham grew in importance after 995 when the body of St Cuthbert was brought here for safety. After the Conquest the church became a Benedictine monastery and work began on the new cathedral in 1093 and was completed by 1133

and 1078. The abbey church of St Albans was begun by Abbot Paul between 1077 and 1088, although it was not consecrated until 1115. Rochester cathedral was begun by Bishop Gundulph shortly after his consecration in 1077 and completed within a few years. Durham cathedral was not begun until 1083.

Although Worcester was one of the very few cathedrals to retain an English prelate and some of its English customs, the story of its rebuilding is worth repeating, because it is particularly well documented. Wulfstan had survived the political upheavals and ecclesiastical reforms associated with the Norman Conquest, and had been bishop for over twenty years before he turned his attention to any major building work. The *Worcester Annals* (compiled in the early fourteenth century) state: '1084 The beginning of the work of Worcester Minster by St Wulfstan'.

The circumstances surrounding the new work are detailed in a charter issued by the bishop in 1089. It reads:

I Wulfstan, by the grace of God, pontiff of the church of Worcester, desiring to enlarge the monastery of the holy Mother of God, Mary, built in the episcopal see by my predecessor of pious memory, that is by blessed Oswald – to enlarge it with greater honour and dignity, not only in the building and adoring of the church, but indeed also of the monks serving God there, I have sought to enrich it by an augmentation of property. Both of which things the mercy of Almighty God has designed to fulfill in part through me His Servant. For since few more than twelve brethren were found by me, up to fifty have been gathered by me there in the same monastery, given up to the service of God. Whence it has come about that we have taken possession of land to augment as much the number of the brethren as also their appropriate work. Therefore, having taken council with my leading men, I have acquired – with great labour and with money from the gift of King William the Elder – a certain estate of 15 hides, which is called *Alfestun* by the locals; and having acquired it have given it for the food of those brethren, serving God in the same monastery, and have offered it devoutly on the altar of the holy Mother of God, Mary for the benefit of my soul, and that of the same King, and of his son William likewise king having as witnesses both his and my leading men, and also the whole people; in the year of our Lords's incarnation 1089, the 12th incidation, moreover the third year of the reign of King William the younger, the twenty-seventh of my episcopate, the first of our entrance into the new monastery, which I have constructed in honour of the same Mother of God, on the day of Pentecost.

The charter indicates that Wulfstan on his appointment to the see in 1062 had founded a small community for whom the old cathedral buildings were probably quite adequate. Subsequently he had set about its reform, within the context of Lanfranc's wider reform movement after 1070. The size of the community had increased to nearly fifty monks, and this must have made the old buildings practically unusable – quite apart from what may have seemed the desirability of replacing them for liturgical reasons. It was St Oswald's church of St Mary that was to be replaced by the new building, to which the dedication was transferred. By May of 1089, the new building was sufficiently far advanced for the monks to move into it. This must indicate that, within a space of only five years from the start of the works, the area of the liturgical choir together with the presbytery were virtually complete.

William of Malmesbury gives further historical information about the state of the works around 1089 and, perhaps more interestingly provides an insight into Wulfstan's own views about what he was doing. This information he derived as he says from Nicholas who was an eyewitness at the time, and who became prior of Worcester *c*.1113. William says that: 'When the work of the main church, which he had begun from the foundations, had advanced to that stage of growth that now the monks might move into it, the old church which blessed Oswald had built was ordered to be unroofed and destroyed.' The move of 1089 thus was definitive and the old monastic church was destroyed as it was no longer needed. Possibly the progress of the works meant that the site of the old building was then required for the continuance of the new, which could indicate that it may be in the area of the present nave.

William of Malmesbury paraphrases Wulfstan's sentiments on the occasion of this demolition:

> We miserable people have destroyed the work of saints, that we may provide praise for ourselves. The age of that most happy man did not know how to build pompous buildings, but knew how to offer themselves to God under any sort of roof, and to attract to their examples their subordinates. We on the contrary strive that, neglecting our souls, we may pile up stones.

Despite these reservations William goes on to record that Wulfstan: 'Yet then completed the new church, and you could not easily find the ornament that did not decorate it, so marvellous was it in single details and singular in all parts.'

The move into the new church in 1089 must have been accompanied by a removal of the relics from the old church of St Mary and their re-enshrining in the new. The most important of these relics were those of St Oswald, and William of Malmesbury says that Wulfstan contributed 72 marks of silver towards embellishing the shrine which contained them and also many other relics. The subsequent history of building is not so well recorded and it is not certain if William's account of when Wulfstan saw the finished cathedral can be believed. There is no reason to believe that there was any significant delay in its completion and Wulfstan who died in June 1095 was buried in the cathedral.

Worcester, which was started in 1084 was the earliest major church undertaken after the Conquest in the south-west Midlands, and can hardly have had significant local romanesque traditions upon which to draw. In a recently published survey Richard Gem has pointed out that the main direct source of inspiration for the new cathedral at Worcester lies in what had been happening in the previous decade at Canterbury, at Christchurch and St Augustine's. The influence of St Étienne, Caen, at Christchurch has, however, already been mentioned, so the cross-channel link is still clearly present, if only indirectly: St Étienne was only begun in the early 1060s.

The plans for rebuilding St Augustine's were formulated in the years 1070 to 1073 and the work was largely com-

44 Worcester cathedral seen from the river Severn. Only the south aisle and transept on this photograph are part of Wulfstan's building, but the remains of the monastic buildings in the foreground are in part early Norman

pleted up to the east bays of the nave by 1087. The east arm, therefore, must have been well enough advanced by 1084 to serve as a model for Worcester. Gem points out that the influence of Worcester itself may also be seen in later buildings in the area as it formed the doyen of romanesque designs in its region and clearly influenced buildings such as Great Malvern Priory (founded c.1085), the abbey church at Gloucester (begun 1089) and the abbey church at Tewkesbury founded in the early twelfth century. As we have seen the transfusion of architectural ideals had already begun under Edward the Confessor whose Westminster Abbey church borrowed freely from several contemporary Norman Benedictine monasteries, notably Jumièges, but under the early Norman kings this process was considerably accelerated.

In the post-Conquest period there was a great surge of military and church building. The policy of appointing Norman bishops and abbots in England, and drafting monks from Normandy naturally led to a strong Norman influence on English architecture. Despite the fact that several major English churches had been rebuilt in the tenth or early eleventh century the Normans considered Anglo-Saxon architecture as inferior and missed no opportunity to erect new buildings. As soon as a Norman prelate had taken charge of an English see or monastery a new church was begun. Such was the scale of rebuilding that it prompted a contemporary to write: 'one would have thought that the world was shaking itself to cast off its old age and was clothing itself in a white robe of churches.' (Raoul Glaber). The Conquest, therefore, presented an opportunity to start afresh, and with the arrival of the new school of Norman romanesque, these elements combined to produce one of the great periods of architectural history.

While many of the newly applied ideas came via Normandy from Burgundy, the majority of masons and craftsmen used in the construction of the new buildings were English. The distinctive Anglo-Norman school which developed soon came to dominate the homeland, and subsequently

45 Tympanum of Samson and the lion, at Stretton Sugwas, Hereford-shire; the work of the Hereford school, *c.* 1150

spread back to Normandy and other parts of Europe. The Anglo-Norman achievement is a landmark in architectural history for western Europe in which Durham cathedral, being the first building to be roofed with ribbed vaulting, represents the apotheosis. This technique of vaulting spread back to Normandy and thence to the Ile de France where it laid the foundations for Gothic architecture.

The influence of the Anglo-Saxon decorative tradition is more clearly seen in the eleventh-century parish churches than the cathedrals of the same date. Although the earliest Norman parish churches in England, such as Blythe, Last-ingham and Winchester, were very similar to contemporary buildings in Normandy, gradually the survival of the Eng-lish emphasis upon surface enrichment resulted in a growing divide. The blending of the English decorative tradition with Norman architectural skills, led to a form of architecture which was very different from its austere Norman counterpart. The early Norman architects used plain surface decoration such as *opus reticulatum*, which was borrowed directly from Romano-Gallic temples and aqueducts still standing in France. Later they were to adopt many of the richer and freer surface embellishments found in England. Some architectural devices, such as the use of cushion capitals and the beak-head ornament found principally in northern parish churches, were taken from England back to Normandy. In the words of Zarnecki: 'The Normans were not totally unfriendly to local achievements and once they adopted a feature from Anglo-Saxon buildings they used it widely.' Because of the austerity of the eleventh-century Norman architecture it has been suggested that certain repeated geometric features such as the chevron, or 'dog-tooth' decoration, were English in inspiration, but this does not in fact appear to be true. There is no known geometric decoration of any significance in pre-Conquest England, and its sudden popularity after 1066 seems more likely to be due to the influence of the duchy.

In the twelfth century there was a fresh burst of architectural inspiration. The growing prosperity of monasteries meant that recently built monastic churches needed to be enlarged. Lanfranc's cathedral at Canterbury, for instance, which had been built in the 1070s, was enlarged with a new 'glorious choir' and dedicated in the presence of Henry I in 1130. The few Anglo-Saxon churches which had escaped the first great rebuilding campaigns, such as Lichfield and Peterborough, were levelled and new buildings erected. Many new churches were started at this time, such as Reading Abbey in 1121. The principal characteristic of these churches distinguishing them from their eleventh-century equivalents was the extensive use of decoration. The original inspiration may have been Cluniac, but as we have seen there was already a strong English decorative tradition prevailing on a more local level in the parish

46 A twelfth-century font showing a primitive carving of Sagittarius at Hook Norton, Oxfordshire

churches. The work was executed by native masons, and by the mid-twelfth century the work of several local schools, such as those based in Herefordshire, Northamptonshire, Canterbury and East Anglia, can be identified.

English romanesque architecture of the twelfth century was an exuberant blend of classical, Scandinavian, Anglo-Saxon and even Moslem elements. Generally speaking it was far more inventive and less stylized than contemporary French work. The combination of geometric design and colour played a vital part in Moslem architecture, which was seen by the Normans during their crusades, and in Sicily and North Africa. The prevalence of geometric motifs in Islamic art may well have been the inspiration for much

191

47 This well-preserved north doorway at Barford St Michael, Oxfordshire, incorporates several common features of Norman sculpture, in particular the two orders of roll moulding overset with beak-heads. The tympanum is filled with an abstract design of beaded interlace

subsequent romanesque decoration. And it is worth commenting that although the decorative motifs of romanesque sculpture have been much studied and debated the fact that colour, which was extensively applied but which rarely survives, also played a vital part and is now often ignored.

The sources of inspiration, however, were not only architectural. Clearly the double quality of decoration and colour also seen in contemporary manuscripts, both in England and on the continent, was extremely influential. This may be seen most clearly in the development of romanesque sculpture, which relied heavily on the figurative depictions seen in manuscripts. At Kilpeck (Hereford-

192

48 Kilpeck, Herefordshire. The figure on the shaft of the south doorway is a fine example of the work of the Hereford school. The school derived inspiration from the churches along the pilgrimage route to Santiago de Compostella

shire) the influence of Anglo-Saxon manuscript decoration is writ large around the doorway, where the entwined creatures are extremely well preserved. The development of

49 Melbourne, Derbyshire. The interior of a fine Norman romanesque parish church

human figurative sculpture, for example the depiction of saints, is more likely to have come from manuscripts from the continent.

Finally we should dwell on the sheer scale of the Norman achievement. Virtually every cathedral was built afresh, hundreds of completely new monasteries were erected and perhaps thousands of parish churches were built or rebuilt before 1200. The twelfth century, in particular, saw a massive rebuilding in all spheres in England on a scale which was not paralleled until the Victorian era. The magnitude of the achievement in logistical and architectural terms is breathtaking and without doubt forms the most impressive artistic legacy of the Normans in England.

7 Forest, park and woodland

One of the charges levelled against the Norman kings, both by contemporary chroniclers and later historians, was that they imposed a draconian system of Forest Law over much of England. The Anglo-Saxon Chronicle for 1087 bemoans that: 'The King, William, set up great protection for deer and legislated to that intent that who so ever should slay hart or hind should be blinded. . . . He loved the high deer as if he were their father.' At one stage in the twelfth century up to a third of England was Royal Forest and subject to the Norman Forest Law which was quite distinct from the Anglo-Norman common law prevalent on land not designated as Royal Forest. One of the most immediate effects of the Conquest was the introduction of a new Forest Law which was gradually tightened up during the twelfth century and only began to weaken in the first half of the thirteenth century: after 1216 the Crown could no longer withstand the antagonism which the Forest Law and its officials caused among their subjects. It is, however, doubtful whether the Forest Laws were ever as harsh as contemporaries described them, certainly by the thirteenth century a considerable degree of lassitude had crept into their implementation. Many of the fines for encroachment were no more than an annual rental, and fines imposed for tree felling in reality represented a form of trading.

Pre-Domesday kings hunted and created game reserves for the purpose, but these were not forests in the legal sense, even though a twelfth century forgery attributing the Forest Laws to the Saxon king, Cnut, was used to imply their respectable antiquity. Although the Saxons actually

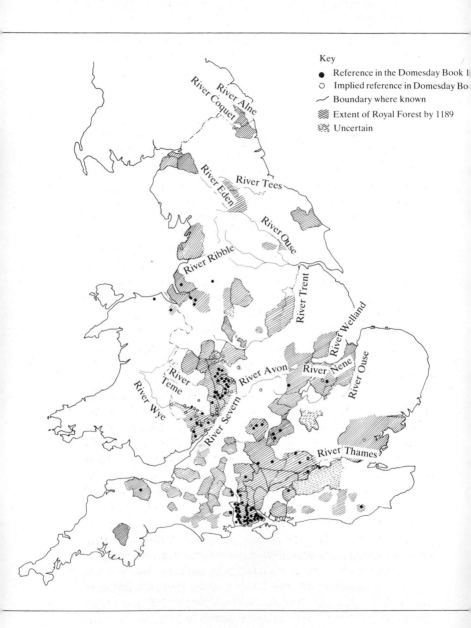

Figure 32 The distribution of Royal Forests 1066–1200

had no word for forest, the concept of the king's wood was not a new one. Kingswood in the Weald of Kent was so called from the mid-Saxon period, and specific areas such as Woodstock Chase in Oxfordshire and the Brown Clee Hill in Shropshire appear to have been associated with the hunting activities of the Saxon monarchy. Under Edward the Confessor it is recorded that three thegns held land in Dene (Forest of Dean) free from geld in return for the services of guarding the woodland. Certain of the early Norman forests appear to be strategically positioned in the centre of their respective counties, for example, Dartmoor in Devon, Shirelett in Shropshire and a group of forests in central Huntingdonshire. Paradoxically the whole county often had common rights in these centrally placed forests and it is possible that they represented very ancient areas of common land. Perhaps it was simply a geographical coincidence that the areas of ancient common were also found to be attractive for hunting by the Norman kings.

The Forest Law and forest courts of Normandy, which were originally derived from Carolingian imperial law, were introduced into England after the Conquest to service the rapid, and at times possibly violent, extension of forest land. Along with their love of horses the Norman kings reputedly had a passionate love for the chase. At the same time, however, the king's deer were an extremely important source of food for the itinerant court, and in the twelfth century the movement of the court seems to have been directly related to the geographical distribution of forests. Significantly the Forest Law represented the one major legal innovation which the Normans introduced into England.

The word 'forest' was originally a purely legal term applied to a tract of land governed by special laws with their own administrative machinery, ostensibly concerned with the protection of deer. It was not until 1184 that the first act of legislation relating to the forest was passed (see Appendix 3). It is generally known as the Assize of Woodstock, since Henry II is known to have made legislation dealing with the forest at a council held there at that date. These laws are composite in character and include restatements or modifications of early decrees, together with some additions made at Woodstock. During the reign of William I the enforcement of the rights of the king's forest was undertaken by shire courts and it was probably Henry I who officially formulated the Forest Law in England.

Forest rights, that is the right to keep deer, to appoint forest officials, to hold forest courts, and to levy fines therein, were not necessarily synonymous with the ownership of the land. Whereas in Hatfield Forest (Essex) the king happened to own the land on which he kept his deer, in Epping Forest he kept deer and had forest rights on other people's land although he had no right to cut down trees or

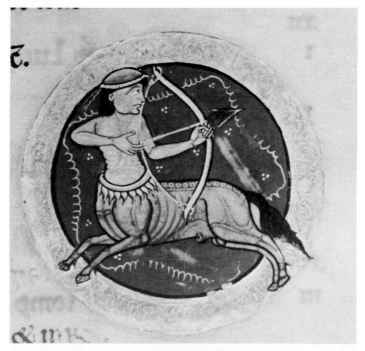

50 A twelfth-century centaur hunting. Such illustrations of hunting activities are common in twelfth-century manuscripts and underline the important role played by hunting in early medieval England

graze any other animals. When in 1238 the king disposed of his Hatfield estate he retained his forest rights and continued to keep deer there.

Although some scholars have claimed that the full forest system was operating by the Conqueror's death it would appear that it was only in its infancy by 1087. Only about a quarter of the eventual Royal Forests had been created. The Domesday record of only twenty-five forests, although incomplete, clearly indicates that the process had far to go. Many forests such as Sherwood (1154) and Epping (1130), are not heard of until the twelfth century and there appears to have been a third phase of afforestation under Richard I which probably includes the Neroche Forest (Somerset) which was not mentioned until 1221.

Each forest normally contained a tract of uncultivated land in which the deer lived and to which the forest name eventually became transferred. The remainder of the forest consisted of ordinary farm land, private woodland, villages and even towns, such as Colchester in Essex Forest. It is important not to confuse the legal term with the physical area of forest. The legal jurisdiction included not only the land in which the deer lived but any land on to which they might stray. Land could be afforested or disafforested for political reasons without any visible effect on the ground. Normally there were no physical boundaries to the Royal Forests, although there are some exceptions such as Dartmoor where the boundaries can still be identified in the form of linear earthworks today. Generally, however, such administrative changes were an important political and fiscal device but would have made little impact on the landscape. It has been estimated that normally the legal forest covered at least five times the area of the physical forest and confusion about the terminology, the physical difference between the two areas, and the meaning of the word 'disafforestation' is largely responsible for the popular myth that the woodland was continually shrinking.

There are no early medieval records indicating how a forest was first declared in England. At first Forest Laws were confined to large estates over which the Crown had complete control, such as the king's demesne forest in Oxfordshire, but later in his reign William began to impose forest jurisdiction over other men's lands. The New Forest was so called because it represented an unprecedented extension of forest jurisdiction. It is also possible that an area was depopulated for the benefit of the newly introduced deer, but this has been disputed by modern scholars. Besides defining the boundaries and appointing the forest officials, such as justices and wardens, it would have been necessary to introduce the game. There are plenty of accounts of the stocking of new parks throughout the Middle Ages, normally by transferring animals from areas which were already emparked. For example at Middleton Stoney (Oxfordshire) in 1203 deer were brought from Woodstock and Kirtlington. We can trace the extension of Windsor Forest from the time of the Conquest, when it appears to have been limited to the Windsor area. By 1086 William had considerably extended the bounds as can be seen from a variety of Domesday entries. By the middle of the twelfth century not only did it cover most of Berkshire, but it extended into the neighbouring counties of Buckinghamshire, Oxfordshire, Middlesex, Surrey and, in the early thirteenth century, it even extended into Hampshire. As a result of a forest perambulation held in 1225 to decide which parts should be disafforested, only the original area in the immediate vicinity of Windsor remained as forest.

Decisions to disafforest were not taken entirely as a result of pressure from local inhabitants, as in some instances it was clearly a means of raising revenue for the Crown. Enormous sums were raised by associations of knights and freeholders and by religious houses in order to procure the release of large stretches of land and even whole counties from restraints on assarting or indeed full forest regulations. In 1204 the men of Devon paid 5,000 marks for freeing their county, with the exception of Dartmoor and Exmoor, and in the 1170's Waverley Abbey (Hampshire) rendered

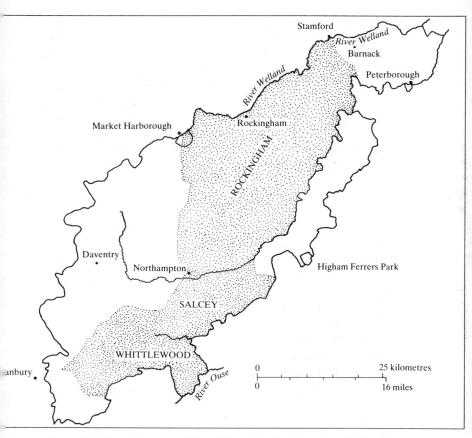

Figure 33 The full extent of Royal Forest in Northamptonshire in the twelfth century

£882 for 'pleas of the forest, assarts, waste and purpasture'.

The legal forests did not necessarily closely relate to existing woodland. There were comparatively few of them in the largest concentrations of surviving woodland, i.e. the Weald, the Chilterns and Arden, and they appeared to be most numerous in moderately wooded counties such as Hampshire, Wiltshire and Shropshire. There were, in addition mountain and moorland forests such as Dartmoor, Exmoor and a number in the Pennines and Lake District which were almost woodless. Some forests consisted of fenland such as Kesteven (Lincolnshire) and Hatfield Chase near Doncaster, while others consisted of heath, like Woolmer (Hampshire) and Rudheath (Cheshire), and still others appeared to have consisted largely of arable land in places such as the Wirral (Cheshire) and Corfe (Dorset). Although the choice of forest areas seems to have been somewhat random, in some cases incorporating whole counties, in general they tended to be based on large Crown-held estates which included well-wooded or mountainous areas.

The largest physical forests which were not moorland were the New Forest, with about 80,000 acres of heath and woodland, and Sherwood with about 50,000 acres of woodland. Several, such as Weybridge (Huntingdonshire) or Hatfield (Essex), had as little as 1,000 acres of woodland pasture, while others such as Chute (Wiltshire) appear to have been merely fragmented patches of woodland with no identifiable nucleus. At a rough estimate at its fullest extent the legal forest jurisdiction, royal and private, covered a third of the country, compared to the physical woodland forest which probably covered little more than 15 per cent of the whole of England in the twelfth century.

In a recent major review of early medieval forest land, Oliver Rackham has recorded 142 forests in England, some of which, such as the Forest of Arden (Warwickshire), are recorded only fleetingly. The Crown controlled eighty-six of these. The forest was the supreme status symbol for the noblest of families, such as the Earls of Richmond, and amongst churchmen only the bishops of Durham and Winchester achieved proprietorial rights. In Cheshire the forests of Wirral, Delamere, Mondrem and Macclesfield were all in the hands of earls. We should perhaps note that the term 'chase' is inconsistently used to distinguish the forest of a subject from that of the Crown.

It has been convincingly argued by Dr Clifford Owen that William the Conqueror saw deer not merely as a royal hobby but as a business, a form of subsistence farming to support the court and consequently he introduced special laws to protect the deer. The early medieval kings and their courts lived largely on venison and were prepared to devote much of their territory to its protection. The itineraries of the court demonstrates that their main concern was to remain close to the principal supplies of royal venison. Despite the Norman kings reputed love of the chase references to the king hunting in person are surprisingly few, and normally the task of killing the deer was undertaken by professional huntsmen. From the middle of the twelfth century the Pipe Rolls contain references to large quantities of venison killed, the preservation of meat by salting and its transportation. For example, Henry III's Christmas dinner in 1251 consisted of 180 harts, 250 hinds, 200 fallow bucks, 100 roe deer, 200 wild swine, 1,300 hares, 395 swans and 115 cranes.

It is certain that although the Anglo-Saxons and Welsh knew the high or red deer and roe deer, the fallow deer was an exotic species not found in Britain before the Conquest. The Normans introduced fallow deer from the Levant or Near East as a means of producing meat from poor agricultural land. The rabbit and pheasant which have comparable histories are other relics of Norman enterprise in seeing alternatives to agriculture and cattle breeding in otherwise unprofitable areas. Fallow deer are not mentioned as one of William the Conqueror's favourite animals in the Anglo-Saxon Chronicle's obituary in 1087, and it has been surmised that it was first introduced in the early twelfth century as part of the second phase of making parks and forests. A conceivable source would have been via the Sicilian connection; the conquest of Sicily after 1060 brought the Normans into contact with the classical and Islamic traditions of emparking and the keeping of beasts. Whatever their country of origin the fallow deer were an immediate success in England.

The Crown's interest in the forests was not limited to deer alone (incidentally, wild pigs were normally classed as deer, as in some cases, were hares). They included other resources and sources of revenue such as timber, underwood and, in the case of the Forest of Dean, minerals. In 1237 the constable of St Briavel's was ordered to 'cause to be erected 9 mobile underwood forges [*forgias itinerantes ad subboscum*]' and 'to sustain those forges . . . with thorn, maple, hazel and other underwood; so that no oak, chestnut or beech be cut down; and to cause the area felled and allocated . . . to be well and sufficiently fenced lest any deer or other beast be able to get in to browse there.' By the early thirteenth century references to other industrial activity within the forests are common, for instance in 1228 the king ordered a forester in Hainault Forest 'to make a certain limekiln [*roqun*] for the works of the said Tower of London'.

In addition there was the income provided by fines levied throughout the forest courts, although much of the revenue from the forests must have been absorbed in administrative costs on the forest bureaucracy. They also provided an inexpensive source of perquisites and bounties which were dispersed by medieval kings out of piety, self-interest, or reasons of state. These included gifts of venison, of live deer for starting parks, of timber in various forms, of assarting rights, and appointments to offices in the forest hierarchy.

The Royal Forests were most extensive in the late twelfth century and by the mid-thirteenth century when records of individual forests become plentiful they were already in decline. Although the process of disafforestation was a protracted one extending over several centuries into the nineteenth century and many of the legal and administrative trappings survived throughout the Middle Ages, the true Royal Forests were a relatively short-lived feature in the landscape. Only the Norman kings at the very height of their authority could have imposed and maintained such a system and thus the forest should be seen very much as a phenomenon of Norman England.

Early medieval parks
Various references in the Domesday Book indicate that there were already enclosures for the retention of animals in the Anglo-Saxon period; some thirty-five 'parks of wood-

land beasts' are mentioned. In addition there were some seventy *hayes*, chiefly along the Welsh border. It has been suggested that the occasional explanatory note 'Haye for taking roe deer' indicates that these were not parks but corrals or other devices for catching wild deer. However, at Ongar (Essex) a will of 1045 refers to 'the wood . . . outside the deer haye' in the very place that Domesday records a *parcas*. Almost the whole park perimeter survived until recently as field boundaries. It was a rectangle with rounded corners enclosing about 1,200 acres: a very large park in which red deer might well have been kept before fallow were available. Its antiquity is corroborated by the manner in which the settlement pattern and the parishes have

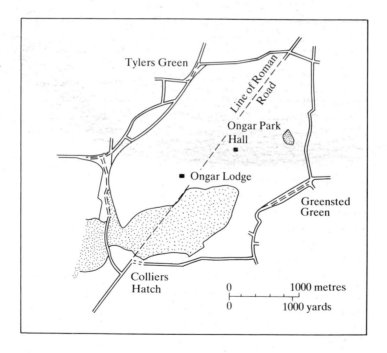

Figure 34 Ongar Great Park, Essex, *c*. 1950. A pre-Conquest deer park, whose boundaries have determined the parish boundaries (after Rackham)

developed round it. Some of the surrounding greens abut against it but none intrudes and much of the perimeter has been used as a parish boundary. The park interrupts the Roman road from London to Great Dunmow. Evidently the emparking took place before the local settlement and land ownership had fully crystallized: even by 1086 it would have been difficult to acquire so large and regular a piece of land in this well-settled area of Essex.

The *haye* of Earnstrey on the Brown Clee hill in Shropshire appears as a well-defined land unit in the early twelfth century and other circumstantial evidence suggests that this, too, may have been an example of a late Saxon park. There was a 'park of woodland beasts' in 1086 at Borough Green (Cambridgeshire) whose massive earthwork remains still exist in Burrough Green Park Wood. Some of these parks clearly pre-date the creation of parish boundaries. In general, however, park creation appears to have been very much a feature of post-Saxon feudal England.

As the Royal Forests went into a gradual decline parks became increasingly fashionable. To some extent the forest can be viewed as a dramatic, but relatively temporary interval in the story of the management of wild animals. The park was a far more effective means of controlling animals, although the creation of medieval parkland could involve considerable capital outlay. Although strictly speaking the zenith of the medieval park falls outside the chronological scope of this book a considerable number of parks were created in the twelfth century. Just as the greatest nobles aspired to the ownership of forests so, too, the acquisition of a park became a status symbol of considerable importance which permeated to much lower levels of the social strata. The speed at which such ideas spread is demonstrated by looking at the considerable number of mid-twelfth-century deer parks found in Scotland. They were introduced north of the border by King David, who, as Earl of Huntingdon, would have been well acquainted with the hunting reserves of the English Midlands.

The medieval park differed from the forest in that it was

normally demarcated by a boundary consisting of a ditch and wooden pale, or in certain areas a stone wall. Parks

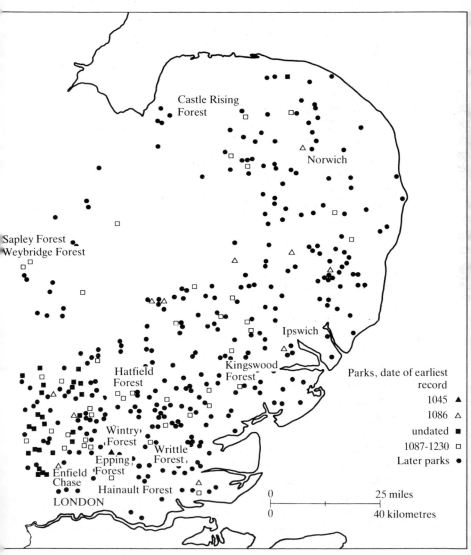

Figure 35 Medieval deer parks in eastern England (after Rackham)

varied in size considerably from just a few acres to well over 1,000 acres. Most of the medieval parks have subsequently been cleared and enclosed for agriculture but their curving linear earthworks survive as modern boundaries, and place names such as Park Farm, Park End or Lodge are often found indicating the site of a former park long since departed. Although the Crown could and did own parks of its own, by the late thirteenth century the vast majority were in the hands of private individuals. The parks were essentially for the retention of deer, at first roe and red deer, but later exclusively fallow.

To begin with parks were attached to palaces and castles. Both Nottingham and Guildford had parks in the twelfth century and in the case of royal parks we hear something about their creation. For instance at Clipston in Sherwood Forest, which appears to have superseded Mansfield as the site of the principal hunting lodge in the forest, between 1176 and 1180 over £500 was spent on works included the building of a chamber and chapel, the construction of a fishpond and the formation of a deer park. Later they were also found in association with manor houses and monastic institutions. Normally parks were carved out of woodland or moor, but in some instances their creation involved the expropriation of agricultural land. The incidence of ridge and furrow within the confines of a medieval deer park is a clear indication that arable land had been enclosed. In the mid-twelfth century in the North Riding of Yorkshire County William le Gros destroyed several villages to create a 'chase'. Conversely in 1151 he granted part of his demesne intended as a park to the monks of Meaux Abbey. He had already started work on enclosing the west side with a bank and ditch which is still called Park Dyke.

The counties near to London appear to have had the earliest parks, for instance, five parks in Sussex are mentioned in the Domesday Book and by 1145 the lords of all the Sussex rapes held parks, many of which were adjacent to motte and bailey castles. By the thirteenth century the Honour of Arundel had ten parks and the Archbishop of

Canterbury nine within the county. However by 1200 Dorset only had one recorded park out of its eventual tally of thirty-eight and Staffordshire two out of eighty-eight.

Much of the evidence for the creation of parks comes during the thirteenth century when it was necessary to obtain a licence to empark or enlarge parks. Prior to this the creation of a park appears not to have required any special permission. Because of the absence of control, documentary references in the twelfth century are uncommon, although we can be quite sure that deer parks, both large and small, were being created throughout the country.

At Woodstock (Oxfordshire) we have slightly more information about the park which appears to have been in existence before the Conquest. Ethelred II (979–1016) held a council 'at Woodstock in the land of the Mercians', and a brief reference in Domesday to the extent of the king's demesne forests of Woodstock, Cornbury, and Wychwood indicates the reason why both Saxon and Norman kings visited this area. It is recorded that Henry I came here on many occasions and that it was 'the favourite seat of his retirement and privacy'. The Hundred Rolls of 1279 were more candid: 'King Henry II visited the manor house of Woodstock for love of a certain woman called Rosamund'; and they go on to record the creation of a new town at Woodstock probably in the years 1174–6: 'and there was a waste place without the said park and manor, and because men lodged too far, the King gave places to divers men to build hostelries there for the use of the King's men.' A grant to Abingdon Abbey which is dated 1110 was signed 'at Woodstock in the park' and according to later accounts it was in this or the following year that Henry I enclosed the park with a stone wall. There are frequent references during the twelfth century to work on the wall: £30 was spent in 1164–5 and its maintenance was to be a regular and heavy item of expenditure throughout the Middle Ages.

Henry of Huntingdon refers to it as 'the celebrated place which Henry had made for the habitation of men and beasts', and William of Malmesbury elaborated on this by describing 'a park called Woodstock' in which the king kept wild animals obtained from abroad including a porcupine sent to him by William of Montpellier. Within the park there appears to have been a menagerie as well as gardens, fishponds and later pavilions. It is clear from thirteenth-century and later documents that Woodstock park represented something much more exotic than the average deer park. It had a royal palace and gardens, some of which, in the Moorish style, used water as a principal design element. The water gardens were centred around a spring known as Evenswell (later called Rosamund's Bower). It has been suggested that the gardens here might have been inspired by the twelfth-century romance of Tristan and Isolde, a version of which was probably written for Henry II himself. The most likely source of inspiration, however, was Sicily where the Norman kings had a series of rural pavilions within easy each of their capital at Palermo, and one of these, the Palace of La Zisa, had a central court across which water from a spring ran through a series of basins set in the floor. This was an oriental feature which the Normans had learnt from the Arabs, and it recurs in the Alhambra Palace in Muslim Spain. Evenswell now lies under the lake which formed one of the principal features of Capability Brown's landscaping for Blenheim Palace.

Woodstock Park was to remain an inspiration for other great landowners in the vicinity for many centuries and accounts for the dense distribution of parks still to be found in central and northern Oxfordshire. In the twelfth century it was largely the very wealthy and the very powerful who were able to create parks. The earliest reference to Beckley Park (Oxfordshire), owned by the lords of St Valéry, was 1175–6 and between 1192–7 it was enclosed by a stone wall in the fashion of Woodstock.

Table 1 shows the preponderance of royal parks in Nottinghamshire during the twelfth century. It is true, however, that the very fact that they were royal makes them much more likely to have been recorded and we should be wary of taking this information purely at its face value.

Table 1   Parks in twelfth-century Nottinghamshire

Earliest reference	Owner
Bestwood	Crown
Clipston	Crown
Laxton	Earl of Lincoln
Nottingham	Crown
Scrooby	Archbishop of York
Serlby	Matilda de Mules
South Muskham	Hugh de Muskham
Worksop	Crown

Some of the earliest references to the creation of non-royal parks are those associated with monasteries in one form or another. The park at Lavendon (Buckinghamshire) is first heard of in the mid-twelfth century as part of the original endowment of Lavendon Abbey; while in the same county Gervaise de Pagnell granted the tithe of the venison of Newport Pagnell Park to Tickford Priory in 1187.

In the case of Hugh de Muskham's park at South Muskham a charter of 1148–53 indicates a Cistercian grange was built within the park. Hugh's park is in the present Muskham wood which forms the western tip of the parish. In the south-western corner of the wood there is a small triangular area occupied by Park Leys farm adjacent to which are the earthworks of the grange. In another chapter reference is made to 'the new ditch which the monks made from the corner of Bugwang to Wardecroft'. This ditch is still identifiable on the ground and represents the shifting of the park boundary north-eastwards to accommodate the new farm and to prevent the deer from straying into the monks' yards. At Fountains Abbey traces of the Monk Wall around the park can still be clearly identified on the ground today.

During the thirteenth and fourteenth centuries the number of deer parks increased significantly, particularly in those areas that had formerly been Royal Forest. With the licensing of parks the Crown had discovered yet another means of raising revenue. Were the deer parks part of the

Norman legacy? Strictly speaking the answer must be no, as there were already parks in England in 1066. However the seigneurial monopolies that developed from the imposition of Norman feudalism created precisely the conditions under which lords of manors could create restricted hunting areas for deer. They were another demonstration of Norman superiority in the words of Professor Beresford: 'if the seigneur of Devizes looked westward from his ramparts he saw his palisaded deer park, and if eastward, the burgage plots market place and church of his castle-borough.'

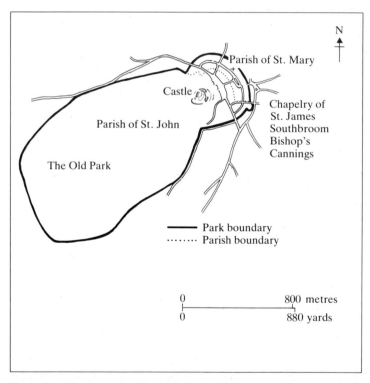

Figure 36 Devizes castle town with its attached deer park was the work of the Bishop of Salisbury and forms a classic example of Norman seigneurial landscape design. There were many such parks attached to Norman castles, but they have rarely left such a distinct imprint

Interest in hunting was not restricted to deer in the early Middle Ages. The rabbit, a Norman introduction into England was encouraged and rabbit warrens were deliberately created, often within deer parks. The 'pillow mounds' found on Dartmoor and other moorland areas were deliberately built up for rabbits and hares and were in use in some areas until relatively recently. Tavistock Abbey in Devon, for example, had a charter issued by Henry I authorizing the abbot to maintain warrens. The Domesday Book even includes some references to hawks' nests, mainly in the Welsh Marches, confirming that falconry, like hunting, was a favourite sport in Anglo-Norman England.

8 The Norman impact on Wales and the Welsh borderlands

The Normans and the Welsh

It is arguable that in the long term the Norman impact on Wales and the Welsh people was greater than upon England and the English. By 1200 the conquest of Wales was still far from complete, but the Normans had left their imprint both on the society and on the landscape. The Norman occupation had introduced into Wales certain features that were entirely new to the country, notably feudal methods of land tenure, large-scale agricultural organization, towns and trade, and a church organized on diocesan lines.

The castle, the manor and the borough represented the essentially imported elements in the lordship. They were most common in the more lowland parts which, as the area of Anglo-Norman settlement, formed the 'Englishry' of the lordship, where knights and freemen held their land direct from the lord. Here the lord granted estates to his knightly followers in return for military service in the field or on guard at the castle as in England. In this way the lord was able to provide a military force for the defence of his lordship. Like the chief lord, each knight built his own castle and established his manor, holding the courts and receiving the dues of his own tenants.

The remainder of the lordship, usually the more hilly parts, and commonly known as the 'Welshry', continued to be held by the Welsh, living their own mode of life in scattered farmsteads and paying to the Norman lord the tribute they were accustomed to make in the past to the Welsh ruler.

The story of the Norman occupation of Wales and the March is a very particular one whose beginning can be traced back to before the Norman Conquest of England. From rather hazy sources we learn that upon returning to England from Normandy in 1042 Edward was accompanied by a number of Norman followers, including his brother-in-law, Ralf, who later became Earl of Hereford, and settled then in the borderlands. Reference had already been made to the acquisition of castles here by the Normans as well as their disruptive activities. Two decades before the Conquest, therefore, Normans had had the opportunity to get to know the Marches.

It is not difficult to understand why the Normans acquired a strong taste for this region – Normandy itself had started life as a marcher duchy. There were geographical as well as political similarities: gently undulating country with plentiful natural stone and timber for buildings, and politically a frontier zone with potentially rich pickings, in this case, beyond the Welsh border. Additionally Wales was a hilly, misty, Celtic country, reminiscent of Brittany, a kingdom over which the Normans also claimed control. It was a region tailor-made for the Normans, and it is no accident that they were so attracted to it, and that in their ambitions and their feuding they left behind such a deep impression on the landscape.

However the apparent similarities between Wales and Brittany were to be dangerously deceptive. Brittany was a kingdom which had more in common with Cornwall than Wales. The Breton landscape of weathered granite, rarely reaches above 1,000 feet, and in comparison with Welsh mountain geography it is gentle. Brittany had been a far more prosperous and integrated region in Roman Gaul than Wales had ever been in Roman Britain, and despite the legendary Celtic links between the two peoples, the Bretons shared more of a cultural and a political heritage with the rest of France than did the Welsh with Anglo-Saxon England. It is perhaps a measure of Anglo-Norman arrogance that the lessons which should have been learnt in Wales were not subsequently applied to Ireland, and that in the later twelfth century they could subdue a kingdom that had not known the Romans at all, with repercussions that have resounded down the centuries to us today.

Whereas the complete conquest of England was accomplished in less than twenty years, the conquest of Wales was only partially achieved in a piecemeal fashion over a span of a hundred years after the battle of Hastings and even then was far from total. The risings of 1068–70 must have first alerted William to the political and military problems of the Welsh. The geography of Wales made it a difficult country to control, but the divided and relatively weak nature of the independent princedoms in 1070 meant that at first the Normans had little difficulty in defeating or intimidating the Welsh. The main problem, however, was in maintaining political control after military victory, and there followed marcher revolts in 1075, 1088 and 1100.

The parts of Wales conquered by the Normans came to be known collectively as 'the Welsh Marches' (*Marchia Wallia*) to distinguish them from the unconquered parts, which were known collectively either as 'Wales' (*Wallia*) or 'Wales proper' (*pura Wallia*). The term 'march' comes from the old English *mearc*, which simply means boundary. The distinction was not simply geographical, but also legal and constitutional; 'Wales proper' lived under what was then conventionally called 'the law of Howel', i.e. the indigenous Welsh law; while 'the March of Wales' lived under what were called 'the customs of the March', under which the Norman marcher barons were allowed a considerable degree of independence.

There was a real distinction between Normanized England and the Normanized March of Wales. The lords of the Welsh March were allowed by Norman kings to exercise high and exclusive judicial powers in return for conquering the March. They had jurisdiction over all cases, high and low, civil and criminal, with the exception of crimes of high treason. They established their own courts to try these offences, executed sentences, and collected fines. They possessed all of the royal perquisites – salvage, treasure-trove, plunder and royal fish. They could establish forests

Figure 37 The early stage of the conquest of Wales (after Rees)

MON
Gt. Orme's Hd.
(Aberlleiniog)
Prestatyn
Degannwy
Rhuddlan
(Bangor)
GWYNEDD
RHOS
St
Asaph
TEGEINGL
Cheste
(Caernarvon)
Conway
RHUFONIOG
Howarden
EAR
CHES
•M
ARFON
EDEYRNION
IAL
MAELOR
NANHEUDWY
CYNLLAITH
•Oswestry
EAR
SHREW
MEIRIONYDD
POWYS
Shrew
Otta's Dyke
CORBET
•Caus
Chirbury
CYDEWAIN
Montgomery
ARWYSTLI
CERI
SAI
MORTIME
•Knighton
Wigmore•
Radnor•
Rich
Cas
LACY
Weobley•
Clifforde
EA
HER
TONI
Her
EWYAS
LACY
•Ewyas
Harolc
Monmouth•
BADERON
GWENT
Caerleon
Striguil•
FITZROLF

0 —— scale —— 60 kilometres
0 —————————— 40 miles

MORTIMER - Marcher Family   ⫙ Anglo-Norman Occupation

220

and forest law, declare and wage war, establish boroughs, and grant extensive charters of liberties. Their unique rights of unlicensed castle-building and of waging what was conventionally called 'private war' were a reflection of their vulnerable position on the border, where they inevitably bore the brunt of any Welsh attack. It was, therefore, under the Normans that the geographical and political entity, 'the Marche of Wales' came into being.

The early stages of the Conquest

William did not play a major role in the conquest of Wales; he delegated the problem to trusted border barons. In 1071 arrangements were made for the administration of the lowlands of the rivers Dee, Severn and Wye to be divided between three earldoms: Chester, Shrewsbury and Hereford respectively. These three great territories were to be defended by castles both internally and, where possible, westwards into Wales. Hugh d'Avranches (made Earl of Chester in 1070) was based in the north with a forward defence against the Welsh at Rhuddlan, which was under the control of his cousin Robert. In the centre Roger de Montgomery, Earl of Shrewsbury, built an outpost on the Welsh side of Offa's Dyke in the region of Montgomery. In the south, the Normans headed by the Conqueror's friend, William fitz Osbern, Earl of Hereford, defended the Wye basin with castles at Wigmore, Clifford and Ewyas Harold, and invaded Gwent, establishing the Lordship of Striguil around Chepstow.

When Earl William returned to Normandy in 1070 he had pacified his section of the border and completed the organization of the March from Ludlow to Chepstow. He was killed in Flanders the following year, leaving as his monument in England, a chain of Norman strong points on the Welsh border and a number of boroughs which he had created in order to organize urban centres. The particular franchises and the laws of his boroughs, such as Hereford, were based on those of Breteuil which served as models for many newly created towns in the rest of England and

51 Rhuddlan castle. The site of the earliest Norman occupation in Wales and the site of a pre-Conquest town

Wales.

By 1086 the Normans held Caerleon and the line of the Usk, and in 1093 following the defeat of Rhys ap Tedwr, they extended their control over South Wales with the establishment of the lordships of Brecon and Glamorgan. The sequence of events was reminiscent of the Roman conquest of Wales. While from Montgomery, the Earl of Shrewsbury attacked Wales along the Severn Valley to gain control of the cantrefs of Cydewain and Arwystli, thus imposing border power on the waist of Wales. From Oswestry the Normans pressed north-westwards into Welsh lands beyond Offa's Dyke, and in the far north, moved quickly along the coastal plain, establishing castles at Degannwy, Conway and Caernarvon.

The details of the process by which the Norman lords took over from their Saxon predecessors in England are curiously murky, but they are less so in Wales where annexation and conquest beyond Offa's Dyke was well advanced by the time the Domesday Book was compiled. By 1086 there had been considerable penetration into north-east and south-east Wales. Entries concerning Welsh land in Norman hands are given in a different form than those concerning English land. Upon the defeat of the Welsh ruler, the new Norman lord took over the government of the lordship he had seized, collecting the former Welsh dues and setting up his own system of law and private courts. He was thus in the position of a petty king, exercising both royal and lordship rights. In this respect, a lord of the March of Wales differed from a lord of an estate in England, for the latter enjoyed none of the royal privileges but held his lordship as a direct grant from the king.

The Marcher lord took responsibility for the defence of his lordship, and though he regarded the king as his suzerain, the king had little right to interfere in the lordship except on the death of the lord, when he had right of entry to conduct an inquiry as to the legal heir and to arrange for the succession. He could not, however, interfere with the succession, which normally passed by the custom of primogeniture from eldest son to eldest son, except in the absence of male heirs, when the lordship was divided equally among the daughters. If, however, the lord abandoned his territory, or if he were guilty of treason or felony, the king could then confiscate the estates.

It is clear that in the conquest of Wales the Normans adopted the basic Welsh administrative unit the 'commote' and the Domesday entries for Shropshire and Cheshire demonstrate the process of colonization. According to the Domesday evidence the Normans penetrated into Wales, and created the March of Wales, not merely by acquiring Welsh lands, but by also acquiring Welsh commotes or

Figure 38 Wales in the early thirteenth century (after Rees)

YNYS MON

Beaumaris

Aberffraw

Aberconway

Rhuddlan

Basingwerk

TEGEINGL

Flint

Che

Aber

RHOS

St. Asaph

Bangor

Conway

Caernarvon

Denbigh

Hawarder

RHUFONIOG

DYFFRYN CLWYD

Ruthin (GREY)

YALE

Dolwyddelan

GWYNEDD

Chirk (MORTIMER)

BROMF

Criccieth

Oswestry (FITZALAN)

Harlech

R. Dee

ARDUDWY

Cymmer

POWYS

Bere

MEIRIONYDD

Maes × Moydog (1295)

Shrewsbury

Caus (COR)

Montgomery

ARWYSTLI

R. Severn

IRISH SEA

Aberystwyth

Cym Hir

R. Teme

Wigmo (MORT)

CEREDIGION

Strata Florida

MAELIENYDD

Radnor (BRIOUZE)

Cardigan

R. Teifi

Irfon × Bridge (1282)

Builth

ELFAEL

R. Wye

Herefo (BOHU)

St. Dogmael's

EMLYN

YSTRAD

Llandeilo (1282) ×

Llandovery

EWYAS LACY

St. David's

DYFED

Drwslwyn

Dynevor

BRYCHEINIOG

Llandaff

Haverford

R. Tywi

Carreg Cennen

(BOHUN)

Abergavenny

Monmo

Carmarthen

TYWI

R. Usk

GWENT

Whitland

Kidwelly (CHADWORTH)

GLAMORGAN (CLARE)

Chepstow (BIGOD)

Pembroke (VALENCE)

GOWER (BRIOUZE)

Neath

Caerphilly

Margam

Llandaff

Cardiff

BRISTOL CHANN

0   80 kilometres

0   50 miles

(CLARE) – Important Anglo- Norman Marcher Family   ■ – Religious House   + – Episcopal S

224

groups of commotes known as 'cantrefs'. In turn the cantrefs were grouped to form the unit known as a 'country' (*gwlad*). Each 'country' consisted of varying numbers of cantrefs: thus the 'country' lying between Gwynedd and Powys and called in Welsh Perfeddwlad (i.e. Middle Country), consisted of four cantrefs, and came to be known in English by the name 'The Four Cantrefs'. The aggregate of the 'countries' was Wales itself. Thus the commote was the basic subdivision in an hierarchical pyramid and was as distinct an institution in Wales as was the hundred in England.

It is worth examining one relatively well-documented area in more detail in order to illustrate the process of acquisition and the link between castles and commotes. The castle was the seat of the administrative offices of the lord – the exchequer and the chancery. Here, too, were held the lord's courts for the trial of offenders, the castle also functioning as a jail. Before the Conquest the court-house or *llys* of the Welsh ruler was undefended, but the Norman, as an alien ruler among a hostile population, guarded his court against attack. A castle was a fortified centre of government, from the security of which the lord maintained his hold over the lordship. There was, therefore, only one main castle in each lordship although there would usually be subordinate castles, each the centre of a sub-lordship.

One of the best recorded invasions of Wales of the period was that of Ceredigion, the 'country' extending northwards along Cardigan Bay from the mouth of the Teifi to the estuary of the Dyfi, because a Welsh chronicler writing at that time happened to live at Llanbadarn near Aberystwyth. This invasion was begun in 1093 under Earl Roger of Shrewsbury, but after the treason of Roger's son, Robert of Bellême, in 1102, the leadership in Ceredigion passed to the house of Clare. The struggle was at its height between 1110 and 1137, first under Gilbert fitz Richard and, after his death in 1117, under his son Richard fitz Gilbert, who was ultimately killed in 1136. Eventually the Welsh prevailed in 1165 and the house of Clare was driven out. It was only after many further vicissitudes, and not finally until 1241, that the lordship of Cardigan was definitively acquired by the Crown, and even then the bulk of Ceredigion remained in the hands of Welsh princes until the Edwardian conquest.

Sir John Lloyd has commented that 'to no quarter of Wales did the title "land of castles" more truly appertain than to Ceredigion during the quarter of a century (i.e. the years 1110–36) which followed its conquest by Gilbert fitz Richard.' In the course of his account of the fighting of those years, the chronicler specifically mentions eleven castles in Ceredigion, and with the exception only of that of Richard de la Mare's castle, all their sites are known. Ceredigion was a 'country' made up of ten commotes. It has been pointed out that the coincidence of eleven castles and ten commotes is sufficiently close to demand attention, especially as the 'castle of Caerwedros' and the commote of Caerwedros in which the castle stands, share the same name. It would appear that the castles built by the 'Flemings', as the Welsh chronicler calls the Normans, were evenly spread over the commotes, and it is possible to assign them to their respective commotes in the following way:

Castle	Commote
Dingeraint	Iscoed
Aberystwyth	On border of Mefnydd and Creuddyn
Blaen Porth	Iscoed
Ystrad Meurig	Mefenydd
Dineirth	Anhuniog
Castell Caerwedros	Caerwedros
Razo's Castle	Perfedd
Walter's Castle	Geneu'r Glyn
Richard de la Mare's Castle	(Pennardd)
Stephen's Castle	Mabwinion
Humphrey's Castle	Hwinionydd

The process of building a stronghold in each basic unit of administration almost certainly occurred in England to the west of the river Severn and perhaps even further eastwards, using the vill or manor as the basic unit of administration, instead of the commote. This probably accounts for the profusion of motte and bailey castles found in virtually every hamlet in western Herefordshire and Shropshire.

The making of towns
Prior to the Conquest the normal unit of settlement in Wales was the isolated family homestead or small hamlets which sometimes huddled around the courts of local chieftains. Groups tended to be self-sufficient, and there was little inter-community trade to stimulate the growth of market centres. The conditions necessary for urbanization were therefore not present. The coming of the Normans changed this situation drastically. As we have seen both in Normandy and England it was soon found that the combination of a castle and a borough formed an economic unit of great vitality. The castle attracted merchants with its promise of protection and guarantee of a local monopoly of trade.

In Wales trade in each lordship was confined to boroughs, being the monopoly of the burgesses who paid the lord a fixed sum annually in return for the right to collect the town dues and to elect their own officers. These privileges were set out in the town charter under which the town was governed. At the weekly market the country folk of the locality were permitted, on payment of toll, to trade their produce in the street, and on the occasion of the town fair, held for several days once or twice a year, itinerant traders, offered their wares for sale.

At the same time the garrison of the castle provided the merchants and artisans of the borough with a minimal market. Eventually the borough provided for the material needs of the castle, and brought the lord a substantial revenue. The burgesses often produced enough in the way of agricultural goods to provide an adequate food supply for the entire community, and also constituting an additional defence force in time of attack. The castle-plus-borough possessed a strength and unity which the combination of castle-and-manor had never exhibited.

52 An aerial view of Pembroke, a typical early Welsh castle town. Gilbert de Clare was made first Earl of Pembroke by Henry I and built the castle which dominates the western end of the narrow peninsula on which the walled town stood

Thus the second motive for the foundation of boroughs emerged. It was soon recognized that the borough, and its attendant fortification, formed a suitable unit for the settlement of uninhabited areas. It was but a small step to realize that such communities were the most effective method of attracting settlers to occupy and control newly conquered or disputed areas. To some extent the scope of town creation, unparalleled since the Roman period in Britain, reflected what was going on at the same time in the rest of England and indeed many parts of Western Europe. In the Marchlands, however, the movement towards the creation of new towns and market centres was more feverish than elsewhere. The fragmented political condition of the Welsh border country, a jigsaw of almost 150 different baronies, lordships and earldoms, provided fertile ground for the establishment of new towns. Each unit of the new political order needed central places where trade and government could be carried on and the logical focal point where these functions could be safely encouraged lay in the shadow of the walls of scores of new castles founded between 1066 and 1300. The new towns were largely inhabited by people from the surrounding districts but there is some evidence to suggest that in the first instance Normans or Frenchmen were brought in; the Domesday Book indicates that the greatest concentration of Frenchmen in 1086 was in the border countries of Cheshire, Shropshire and Herefordshire.

The early penetration of the northern coastlands of Wales was the work of the earls of Mercia, but the English were then expelled by Griffth ap Llewelyn who was able to live in his palace at Rhuddlan and have his ships unmolested at the river mouth, until in 1063 the English recaptured the town and began to invade Snowdonia. Harold was then called away to meet the Norman Conquest of his own country. Subsequently borough creation was undertaken by the Norman lords.

Initially all boroughs except Rhuddlan were the property of Marcher lords. William I went through South Wales to St

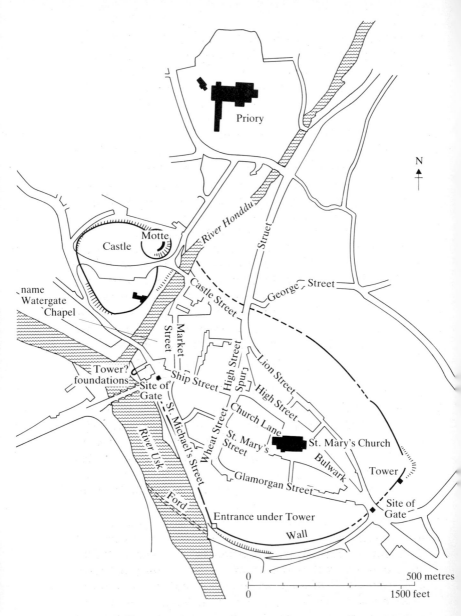

Figure 39 Plan of Brecon, showing castle separated from the rest of the town by the river Honddu

230

David's in 1081, but no royal castles or boroughs were established. William II was in Wales in 1096 and again in 1097, but neither expedition was successful. Although the baronial conquests were part of the Crown's successful schemes, successive kings saw the threat of independent power. The second earl of Hereford revolted in 1075, and in 1102, soon after Henry I's accession, the earl of Shrewsbury and his brother Arnulf of Pembroke took part in a revolt. Their lands were confiscated and from this time royal boroughs were created to counteract the power of the magnates. The rural estates of Pembroke were developed for the Crown in 1105 with the importation of Flemish immigrants, and by 1109 Henry had also acquired Carmarthen where he built a new castle to the west of the Roman fort and created a new borough between the two. At his death in 1135 dependent English lords had been established in Kidwelly, Swansea, Llandovery, Nevern (near Newport, Pembrokeshire) and Llanbadarn. Boroughs were certainly to be found at the first two, and the others provided the base for later foundations. At this stage, only fifty years after the Conquest of England, the speed and degree of penetration by the Normans is striking and the multiplication of towns a major part of their achievement.

The creation of the towns of the Welsh Marches was closely related to the westward expansion of the territories of the Marcher lords. Of the many towns in the region created in the late eleventh and early twelfth centuries Brecon illustrates, perhaps more clearly than most, the relationship between the westward advance of the Norman frontier and the planting of towns.

By 1110 the army of Bernard de Newmarche had overrun the whole of the Dark Age Welsh princedom of Brycheiniog. In his wake three new towns, Brecon, Builth and Hay were created. Brecon was planted at the junction of the river Usk with its tributary, the Honddu, draining in from the north. The first element of the Norman settlement appeared on a steep western bluff overlooking the two rivers in the form of a motte and bailey castle constructed in

1092. Outside the north walls of the castle the foundations of the church of St John were laid, a church which later became a priory and is today a cathedral. Facing the site of the castle on the east bank of the Honddu the new town of Brecon appears to have been implanted at the same time as the building of the castle. Traditionally it is believed to have been created by Bernard de Newmarche who was also the benefactor of the monks at Battle Abbey to whom he gave St John's church as well as lands in the town. Bernard himself came from Neufmarche in Normandy, a name whose literal meaning is Newmarket.

We can still see today the elements of the Norman town engraved on the townscape. The centre piece is the market place, in the form of a triangle which, as so often with successful new towns, has been encroached upon by later buildings. The oval shaped defences of the walled borough, once crowned by ten equally spaced towers, can also be traced. It is believed that stone for the Norman defences was obtained from the Roman fort at Brecon Gaer, which lies three miles west of the town. Today minor changes of level and a curving street pattern that follows the inner line of the walk betray the presence of the former ditch. In the then parallel backyards of the backstreets of Brecon the shapes of the original burgage plots can still be identified. Both Builth and Hay also retain clear indications of their Norman origins in their street plans, and it is reasonable to assume in all three cases that they were laid out within a few years of the building of their castles.

The outbreak of civil war in England in 1135, however, gave the Welsh an opportunity to re-establish themselves in west Wales. Henry II came to terms with Rhys ap Griffith (the Lord Rhys) who ruled from the Dovey to Haverford and Llanelly. It is not surprising that in this period of Welsh ascendancy the new Anglo-Norman towns were mainly created in south-east Wales and Monmouthshire. Of the new western towns, the creation of Newport (Pembrokeshire) below the older castle at Nevern may date from after the death of the Lord Rhys in 1197.

Despite the fact that the urban geography of the border-land can largely be dated to the early Middle Ages, there were some failures: some towns which refused to grow and some which declined as they outlived their original strategic function. Scattered throughout the border there are failed towns, places such as Caus in Shropshire and Richard's Castle and Huntingdon in Herefordshire. In general the earliest foundations such as Chepstow and Ludlow were the most successful. They had the opportunity of occupying the prime sites and of attracting and monopolizing trade, and as the threat of conflict moved further westwards they were left in peace to prosper.

Today the landscape of the Marches is littered with places that were once granted market charters, the rights of boroughs, and are places that have since failed completely. Their rectangular shaped fields may be the sole visual evidence of former market place, narrow high-hedged fields mark the plots that attracted burgages to a newly found borough eight centuries ago. Deep lanes and foot-paths indicate the lines of former streets and the castle of forgotten founding Marcher lords is no more than a mis-shapen overgrown mound.

A number of towns occupied former Iron Age hillforts and many of these did not succeed for although well de-fended they were poorly sited to exploit local trade. An example of this is Caus near Westbury, on the southern foothills of the Long mountain. The place-name of the new town echoes the name of the homeland from which the founder, Roger Corbet, came – Pays de Caux which lies to the north of the Seine estuary. Sited on a high ridge it commanded the valley road from Shrewsbury to Montgom-ery. The ruins of a massive earthwork and stone castle with outer fortifications now have to be disentangled from the undergrowth; nothing except earthworks remains of the borough. The town appears to have been created by Roger Corbet in 1198 and it is recorded that by 1349 there were fifty-eight burgesses living here. In the mid-fifteenth cen-tury much of the town appears to have been burnt down

53 Caus castle, Shropshire. The site of a failed medieval town – the wooded area is the centre and hides a massive Norman motte and bailey. The town declined along with its strategic function in the later Middle Ages; there is now a single farm here

during the rebellion of Sir Griffith Vaughan. By the time a survey was made of the site in 1521 the castle was being recorded as being in 'grete ruyne and decay'; thus the borough of Caus faded away in the later Middle Ages and is remembered now by its earthworks, its place-name and a single farm. In the words of Professor Maurice Beresford Caus was like 'a prehistoric monster crushed beneath the weight of its own armour', and was unable to adjust to the new economic conditions of the later Middle Ages.

Another town with a rather similar history lies further into Wales beyond New Radnor; this is Cefnllys. The site of Cefnllys stands on a rocky spur 100 metres above the

234

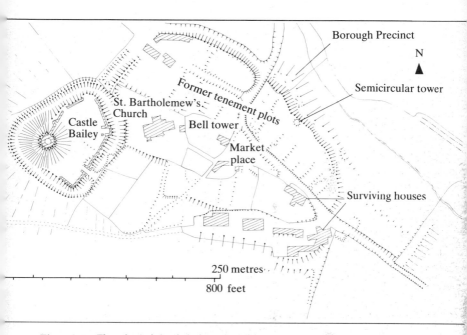

Figure 40 The plan of the failed medieval borough of Richard's Castle, Herefordshire, shows the town precinct bank attached to the castle. Traces of former property boundaries and roads can be seen within the compound. As early as 1086, fifty-one persons were recorded within the *castellaria* in addition to another twenty-three in the castle itself. It is possible that there was a castle on this site before the Conquest built by a Norman favourite of Edward the Confessor

wooded gorge of the river Ithon. The Mortimer family built a castle here between 1240 and 1246, at the same time as other outposts at New Montgomery and Painscastle. It is recorded that in 1332 Cefnllys had twenty burgesses and a survey of 1360 records it as a borough. But it would appear that this highly exposed settlement had little chance of subsequent success and was already in decline by the time that Edward I led his attack on Wales. A document of 1383 mentions only ten burgesses here. Like other border boroughs of its type the earthworks of the actual town are difficult to disentangle. Only a short stretch of street with possible burgage plots can be identified with the rampart of

235

the Iron Age fort, and like so many of its colleagues it has been fairly extensively robbed by stone quarrying. Like Wigmore and Richard's Castle it is dominated by a massive motte and castle defence. At the close of the sixteenth century the antiquary Camden described Cefnllys as a lonely ruin, but surprisingly it survived as a 'rotten borough' into the early nineteenth century. In 1832 the parliamentary boundary commissioners' report showed that there were sixteen burgesses there who had the right to return a member of parliament, but they were living in three farms and one cottage.

Moving eastwards we come to Huntingdon where the borough was created in the late twelfth century as part of a policy of political reprisal. In 1173 after a rebellion against the king the honour of Kington, a planted borough close by, was suppressed and absorbed into the new Marcher kingdom of Huntingdon. This was granted to William de Braos and as a result Kington Castle was abandoned sometime before 1230 and the government of the lordship was settled at Huntingdon. The outlines of the new borough were sketched out between the castle mound and the church. Ironically Huntingdon failed to make any real progress and the successful town in the area was Kington-in-the-Fields which had been laid out in a valley bottom some distance away from the old borough of Kington and its church and castle. Huntingdon is today perhaps one of the most spectacular of the failed border boroughs occupying as it still does a little territorial enclave which projects into Wales; the boundary of the borough is still marked in an indentation in the border. The earthworks are in the form of an extended outer bailey marking the town precinct and the lumps and bumps of the medieval settlement indicate former town houses. Its situation, however, is so rural that it is difficult to imagine that the settlement ever harboured urban ambitions.

Another site where it today is difficult to imagine there ever having been a town, so rural is the environment, is Richard's Castle near Ludlow. This site was important

54 More, Shropshire. All that remains of a Norman castle village are the earthworks of the ringwork castle and traces of house platforms. The church (off picture right) occupies the easternmost point of the settlement and has a squat Norman tower typical of such plantations

because, before the Conquest, Richard le Scrob, a Norman, was given land at Orleton and had built a castle here before William arrived. By the beginning of the next century a small town had developed here known as Richard's Castle. For although no trace of the borough charter survives here there is little doubt that an urban community flourished here for some three centuries after the Norman Conquest; a document of 1304 records some 103 burgesses. However like Huntingdon and Caus and Cefnllys, Richard's Castle went into a decline in the later Middle Ages. Today the ancient town survives only through the church of St Bartholomew, noted because of its detached tower and the out-lines of the borough still surviving in earthwork form, providing one of the best examples of such earthworks in the borderland. The reasons for its failure appear to be largely commercial; sitting on a high bluff looking east-wards it was to some extent rather uncomfortably situated and as Ludlow thrived in the later Middle Ages so the commercial fortunes of Richard's Castle must have declined. A little to the south, Wigmore occupies a very similar situation and although a village survives here only the enormous earthworks of the castle and former borough give an indication that this was the capital of the great medieval Mortimer kingdom.

The castle dominated settlement was not limited to just urban or proto-urban centres, but was to be seen in small villages; for instance, Kilpeck in Herefordshire, renowned for its famous romanesque church, lies within the shadow of a considerable Marcher castle and at the apex of a rec-tangular shaped fortified enclosure, now identifiable only in earthwork form (see Plate 34). Similarly at More, near Bishop's Castle a defended deserted village lies immediately to the west of a ringwork castle. There is evidence to sug-gest that the settlement here was a post-Conquest creation contemporary with the castle and church. More, which was carved out of the great Saxon manor of Lydham, was granted by Grand Serjeantry in the reign of Henry I; this service is described by the antiquary Rev. R. W. Eyton in the following words: 'The Lord of More, as a Constable of the King's host, to assume the command of two hundred foot-soldiers whenever the King of England crossed the Welsh Border in hostile array. The said Constable was to march in the vanguard of the army, and with his own hands to carry the King's standard.' The topography of the surviving settlement, with the earthworks of the castle at the western end and the church at the east demonstrates clearly its planned origins. The church has a squat Norman tower, typical of the Clun region, and found in other settlements where similar plantation is suspected.

238

The Welsh church

The other major area of life affected by the Norman Conquest was the Welsh church. Welsh religious organization was dominated by the *clas* or community churches, originally based upon Welsh tribal structure. The organization was decentralized and the enforcement of discipline was virtually nonexistent. This led to a wide variety of practices, ranging from excessive asceticism of holy hermits to the secularism and corruption of monks scarcely distinguishable from the lay members of the community around them. As we have seen in England the Norman church could hardly have been more different, being more centralized, having a much more complex hierarchy and observing the Roman liturgy.

The church in Wales was quickly Normanized by the early conquerors, however, and used as a means of strengthening Crown authority. The *clas* system was replaced by an episcopal structure which, as in England, was soon staffed with Norman prelates. This had the double effect of destroying one of the structural elements of Welsh tribal life, and of placing the church in Wales under the direct royal domination. The Norman bishops of Wales were responsible to the Archbishop of Canterbury, who was, in turn, responsive to the needs and desires of the Crown. Thus the church in Wales became closely linked to the interests of the conquerors. So close was this identification that in some areas the distinction between the Norman cleric and the Norman conqueror disappeared. Several bishops were also Marcher lords. The bishop of St David's, for instance, maintained a military force at his disposal, and exercised the right of erecting fortifications within his diocese.

However, in the north in particular, the changes were slow to be implemented. Theoretically at least there was an Anglo-Norman bishopric founded at Bangor from 1092 and St Asaph from 1143; these sees corresponded roughly with the kingdoms of Gwynedd and Powys. But their tenure was uncertain and until the early thirteenth century there were long vacancies and periods when the bishops wandered in exile.

The effect of the Norman Conquest was not confined to the secular church with the creation of bishopric and parishes. Its influence was equally revolutionary in the case of the monastic orders. These monastic communities, modelled on those of England and of Western Europe and introduced for the first time into Wales by the Normans, differed fundamentally from the preaching monks of the early Welsh Church in that their numbers dwelt in the seclusion of the monastery, following the religious life in accordance with the rule of the order to which they belonged. The early Norman foundations were mainly Benedictine priories attached to castles such as Chepstow, Monmouth, Abergavenny, Brecon and Ewyas Harold. But it was in the mid-twelfth century that the most successful of the monastic orders in Wales came along – the Cistercians, whose main foundations were Neath (1130), Margam (1147), Strata Florida (1164) and Strata Marcella (1170).

There was little love lost between the Normans and the Welsh, although they did co-operate and collaborate from time to time. Whereas Anglo-Saxon society did have some features in common with the conquering Normans the same could not be said of the Welsh. Virtually every aspect of Norman life was alien to the Welsh and although as usual the Normans tailored their institutions to what they found, in Wales this did not make them any more palatable. The stark differences in culture means that it is difficult to talk of Cambro-Norman in the same way as Anglo-Norman. On the whole the Normans remained as occupiers in a hostile country; this is clearly demonstrated by the impressive legacy of castles and fortifications both in Wales and along the border.

Geoffrey of Monmouth (d. 1151), although probably not Welsh but Breton, sums up the Welsh attitude towards the Normans in his *Life of Merlin*:

Normans depart and cease to bear weapons through our native
realm with your cruel soldiery. There is nothing left with
which to feed your greed for you have consumed everything
that creative nature has produced in her happy fertility. Christ,

aid thy people!, restrain the lions and give to the country quiet peace and the cessation of wars.

9 The Norman heritage

There are only rare moments in history when the actions of a particular king can be seen to have affected every single member of his kingdom. Perhaps the dissolution of the monasteries by Henry VIII was one of these occasions. The conquest of England by William I most certainly was. Both in the manner in which he acquired the Crown and the way in which he organized and ran his feudal monarchy ensured that every one in the country would have been affected to a greater or lesser degree. Although William maintained and perhaps believed that he was the direct and rightful successor of Edward the Confessor his actions were truly that of a 'conqueror'. Unlike another earlier invader, Cnut, he did not intend to leave England in the same state he found it, nor did he.

On one level it is easy to catalogue the results of the Conquest. On the negative side there were the brutal reprisals following the abortive risings in the decade after 1066. While on the more positive side everyone would have seen the castles and cathedrals, and slightly later, the new abbeys and parish churches that resulted from the Norman Conquest. Although many who were forcibly involved in the quarrying of stone and the erection of the buildings and fortifications would not necessarily have viewed them favourably. These were the immediate and obvious results of the Norman victory. It is far more difficult to determine the effects of the less tangible consequences resulting from the redistribution of power and wealth, church reform and the infusion of Norman culture. In other areas of everyday life such as agriculture and industry it is virtually impossible to detect which developments were influenced by the coming of the Normans, and which would have occurred irrespective of the Normans. It is fair to say, however, that the archaeological record shows no dramatic changes in the life style of the vast majority of English people in the eleventh and twelfth centuries.

By the time of the death of the last of the Norman kings in 1154 the Norman presence in England was in any case beginning to diminish. The conquerors were being absorbed into English society and although a French connection was maintained through the Angevin kings and persisted throughout the Middle Ages it was no longer Norman either in name or character. While the Normans were the key by which England acquired its French possessions there was never any question of it being part of a Norman empire after the mid-twelfth century.

The Normans and the English language

We should remind ourselves that the Norman Conquest did not involve a folk movement as had been the case with the previous Scandinavian invasions of England. In terms of population movement it basically involved a radical transposition of the lay and ecclesiastical aristocracy. It has been estimated that perhaps no more than 10,000 Normans entered England in the wake of the Conquest, and some recent place-name studies even suggest some movement of English-speaking settlers across the Channel to northern France and the Low Countries at this time.

Whatever estimate of the total population of England at that time, 1½ or 2½ million, the Normans must have formed an insignificant percentage of the whole. It is therefore not surprising that the basic language did not change. Although the French language had a considerable influence on the development of English it did not replace it, and eventually the descendants of the Norman aristocracy spoke English. The Dialogue of the Exchequer written late in the twelfth century declared that English and Norman were so intermingled that: 'it can scarcely be discerned at the present day

– I speak of free men alone – who is English and who is Norman by race.'

The areas covered by 'borrowed' words from French in the English language tells much of the social pattern imposed by the Conquest. There was heavy borrowing in administration, government and law, and the legal vocabulary became almost exclusively French. There was also considerable influence in matters concerning the social organization of the upper classes. In literary, architectural and cultural fields the terminology is also predominantly French. It is not surprising that the language of commerce and of town life should, too, have become mainly French. It must, however, be emphasized that these changes were not sudden and some of the transference did not take place until the twelfth and thirteenth centuries when by way of Angevins, French survived as the courtly language. In striking contrast to this strong permeation in the language of the upper echelons of society there was relatively little influence in the more mundane activities where the vast majority of the population worked. There was very little borrowing of agricultural, industrial or fishing terms. This reinforces the view that the Normans brought little new in the way of technology, or even organizational change in contrast to commerce, trade and administration.

As French was a language spoken mainly by the ruling class it had relatively little impact on place-names, compared to a new language introduced by peasant settlers such as the Saxons and Scandinavians. Very few agrarian based settlements of the twelfth century carried French names and hardly any changed from an Anglo-Saxon or Scandinavian name to a French one. The exceptions were in places where a completely new settlement was laid out, for example, the place-name Sheene was replaced by Richmond (strong hill), Biscopestone by Montacute (pointed hill), and Tattershall by Pontefract (broken bridge). Pontefract is in early records sometimes *Pontfreit*, the Old French form, which is no doubt original, and sometimes *Pons fractus*, the Latinized form. The spelling represents the Latin form, but the pronunciation pŭmfrĭt, which goes back to Old French, is still used locally. Montacute is from French *Montaigu*, but the present form is a Latinization of the French name. Sarum, the Latinized form of Salisbury, is preserved in the name Old Sarum.

Apart from the very limited number of French settlement names the striking feature is their stereotyped nature. The majority contain the adjective *beau* or *bel*, in names like Belasize of Bellsize (beautiful sea), or Beaulieu or Bewley (beautiful place), Beaumont (beautiful hill), Beaudesert (beautiful wilderness). Such names were normally applied to completely new settlement sites, abbeys or castles. One exception was Beaumont in Essex, which replaced the old Saxon name of *Fulanpettae* (OE foul pit)! A much smaller number of places were given names incorporating the element *mal* (poor or bad). Macegarth (Yorkshire) was earlier Melasart (bad clearing), Malpas which occurs at least eight times in England and Wales usually refers to marshy ground. Such derogatory names are, however, rare compared to the complimentary. Haltemprice (Yorkshire), the site of a priory of Augustinian canons, comes from the French *haut emprise* (great undertaking) and Dieulacres (Staffordshire) means 'may god increase it'. Other descriptive names are more neutral, often incorporating environmental references; Boulge (Suffolk) means 'uncultivated land covered with heather'. Breura (Cheshire), Temple Bruer (Leicestershire) and Bruern (Oxfordshire) all refer to 'heath'; Kearsney (Kent) 'place where cress grows', and Salcey (Northamptonshire) 'a place abounding in willows'.

After the Norman Conquest radical changes took place in the types of personal names used in England. Though Old English names continued in use for some time, indeed one or two have had a continuous history to the present day, for the most part they gradually fell into disuse. The Normans introduced their own personal names, chiefly French or continental German in origin, and a little later biblical names, which are hardly ever found in Anglo-Saxon England. We have already noted the changes in fashion in the use of saints names after the Conquest.

Norman personal names were sometimes attached to an earlier Anglo-Saxon place-name element. The largest single group is that compounded with Old English *tun* 'farmstead, village' and later also 'manor'; such as Williamston (Northumberland) from William, Howton (Herefordshire) from Hugh, Rowlstone (Herefordshire) and Rolleston (Wiltshire) from Rolf, Walterstone (Herefordshire) from Walter, and Botcheston (Leicestershire) from Bochard. They also occur occasionally in the central south: Marlston (Berkshire) from Martel, and Mainstone (Hampshire) from Matthew; more so in Wiltshire where they include Faulston from Fallard, Flamston from Flambard, and Richardson from Richard, while Dorset has Bryanston from Brian (a Norman name of Breton origin), Ranston from Randulf, and Waterston from Walter. In the south-west there are also places which use a family-name as the first element, while the former contains the largest concentration of place-names with a post-Conquest personal name. These include Drewston from Drew, Johnstone from John, Jurston from Jordan, Penson and Penstone from Pain, and Stevenstone from Stephen. Post-Conquest personal names are only rarely compounded with other English elements for habitations, as in Painswick (Gloucestershire) 'Pain's Farm'.

There are, of course, a considerable number of village names where an aristocratic French family name has been attached to an old English settlement name, thus providing us with some of our more exotic and bizarre place-names; for example, Stoke Mandeville, Bury Pomery, Ashby-de-la-Zouch, Croome d'Abitot and Shepton Mallet. Occasionally the names have coalesced as in the case of Stokesay (Shropshire), which comes from Stoke-de-Say. Other combined names of interest are Chapel-en-le-Frith and Haughton-le-Skerne. One uniquely exotic place-name that dates from this period is Baldock (Hertfordshire) which comes from the Old French name for Bagdad – *Baldac*. The name which clearly comes to England by way of the Crusades was given by the Knights Templar who held the manor in the twelfth century.

Place-name scholars have recently pointed out ways in which the coming of the Normans considerably modified the spelling of a large number of English place-names. It is possible to compare the earlier English spelling of place-names with the French equivalent as seen in the Domesday Book. The place-name spellings must to some extent represent an attempt by French speaking clerks to render the pronunciation of English country people. In general, the influence of Norman scribes is very strong in the Domesday Book, and in official records of the Twelfth century. When they came across sounds or combinations of sounds which were absent from French or Latin, they would tend to substitute for them the nearest sounds in those languages. The names most affected appeared to be those of important towns, or places situated near to or belonging to a monastery.

Many earlier Old English or Scandinavian names were affected by this process. For example the simplification of 'ch' to 'c' has resulted in many names which might have ended in 'chester' finishing in 'cester' as in Gloucester, Cirencester, Worcester, and is the reason for Cer in Cerne and Cerney. Similarly Old English names beginning with 's' followed by a consonant were liable to be affected by this process: sometimes the 's' was dropped thus Snottingham becomes Nottingham and Studbury becomes Tudbury. The combination 'shr' as in Shrewsbury was particularly difficult for French speakers which the scribes contorted into Salop, an alternative name which it has retained to this day. 'Cn' was made easier by the insertion of a vowel, and Cnock became Cannock. The initial sounds of place-names beginning with 'y' did not exist in Norman French, place-names such as Jarrow and Jesmond would have been Yarrow and Yesmond if they had not been subject to French influence. The initial sound 'the' was also unknown to the Normans, this they replaced by 't' or 'ch'; thus French pronunciation has survived in some names such as Chilsworth and Tingrith which otherwise would have been Thilsworth and

248

Thingrith. It has recently been pointed out that a concentration of Anglo-Norman pronunciation in the Durham area, for example Durham itself, Whorlton, Lintz and Jarrow, could indicate a concentration of French-speaking population in that area in the twelfth century.

In a few cases a part of the earlier names has apparently been replaced by a French word, usually one related, whether in sound or meaning, to the element which it replaces. French *eau*, Old French *ewe*, 'water' has replaced Old English *ěa* 'river, stream'; for instance Caldew (Cumberland) 'cold river', recorded as *Caldeu* in 1189. Similarly, *mond* 'hill' has replaced various Old English and Old Norse words: Old English *mūoa* in Jesmond (Northumberland), formerly *Gesemuthe* 'mouth of Ouse Burn'; Old Norse *mot* in Beckermonds (Yorkshire) 'confluence of the streams', and Old English *mōt* in Eamont (Cumberland) also 'junction of the streams'. The commonest alternation is that of French *ville* with Old English *feld* 'open land', especially in the south and west. Surviving examples include Clanville (Hampshire, Somerset) 'clean open land', Enville (Staffordshire) 'level open land', Longville (Shropshire) 'long open land', as contrasted with Tovil (Kent) 'sticky open land'.

Thus the introduction of French as the language of the ruling class and of Latin as the language of written administration after the Conquest had a significant if somewhat discreet effect upon the English language and place-names. The nature and extent of these changes was to some extent compounded by the introduction of a cadre of French scribes, largely recruited from Norman monasteries.

The countryside in the late twelfth century

We have already seen the impact on certain parts of the countryside with the imposition of Forest Laws and the spread of royal and seigneurial deer parks. It is unlikely that either of these developments would have taken place on the scale that they did without the Normans. Indeed the Forest Laws represented the only major Norman departure from Saxon legal practice. Many of the changes that can be detected in the countryside in the early Middle Ages, such as the increased use of stone in both ecclesiastical and lay buildings, can at best be only loosely connected with the change of dynasty: with other changes, such as the movement towards a mature open-field system over parts of the country, it is virtually impossible to assess what role the Norman presence played.

When we come to examine the countryside in the late twelfth century there are a number of points that need to be taken into consideration. The main one concerns the nature of the evidence. The twelfth century can boast no Domesday Book, and although the quantity and quality of documentation surviving begins to improve by 1200, there is surprisingly little in the way of documentary evidence which would enable us to accurately reconstruct the geography of the time. Although the great estates, notably the monasteries, were beginning to keep accounts and to record disputes, the surviving evidence still tends to be largely of the charter type, dispassionately recording boundaries and only rarely hinting at physical characteristics, forms and customs. It is true that central government was beginning to keep consistent records and this enables us to reconstruct certain activities such as repair work on castles and other crown buildings with a degree of confidence, but they are normally sadly inadequate for detailed topographical analysis. Nevertheless there are sufficient indications and hints from a variety of sources to make certain assumptions about the mid-twelfth century, even though we cannot be absolutely certain that all of these are unique to the twelfth century – some were continuing long established processes while others persisted into the later Middle Ages.

It is only the painstaking local studies, each constituting part of the jigsaw, that enable us to obtain a clear picture of what was happening region by region. Let us take a sample area which has recently been examined in detail by Dr B. English – Holderness. The village house, tofts, crofts and sometimes gardens and orchards of the villagers lay at the centre of the rural community, inside the circle of common fields, meadows and pastures. The parish church and the priest's house were features of many Holderness villages, as well as the lord's hall.

The toft was the site at which a house and its outbuildings stood. So insubstantial were twelfth-and thirteenth-century houses in an area like Holderness, which has no natural building stone, that in the surviving charters it is almost always the toft that is transferred from one man to another, and the buildings on the toft are rarely mentioned. One Holderness medieval village has been excavated: Wawne, where from the sites of twelfth- to fourteenth-century village houses no building materials were recovered except the squared corner stones *in situ*. These flimsy houses, probably built of turf or earth, appear to have lasted little more than a generation, being repeatedly rebuilt on new foundations and often on new alignments.

There was no standard area of toft, and some of the tofts were large for building plots, amounting to smallholdings. Tofts of ½, 1, 2, 3 and 4 acres are recorded in the twelfth century. The size of the toft was not fixed permanently, for in the thirteenth century one toft was subdivided by Meaux Abbey into seven tofts. Only on rare occasions are the buildings on the tofts mentioned in the documents: such as a toft with buildings at Rough next to the manor house, and a toft with a hall at Wyke on Hull.

Behind the tofts lay the crofts, small enclosed areas behind the houses which could be used for gardens or to pen in animals. The crofts of deserted medieval villages can be seen as rectangles on many aerial photographs. In many villages the croft ran back from the house as far as the edge of the open fields, and at the meeting place of croft and open field there was often a back land, with walls or ditches to prevent the animals straying from croft to field and vice versa. The boundary walls where the crofts met the open fields still form prominent earthworks on many deserted medieval village sites.

There is considerable circumstantial evidence to indicate that many settlements were redesigned during the twelfth century. In some cases archaeological evidence confirms this; at Wharram Percy (Yorkshire), excavations have clearly demonstrated the antiquity of settlement in the area and shown that the landscape framework within which post-Conquest developments occurred was created over a thousand years earlier. The Anglian settlement probably lay in the bottom of the deep Wolds valley where the church still stands and where springs fed a stream supplying the village with water. On either side of the valley, at the top of the slope, is a bank and ditch, which may have marked the boundary of the village. In the twelfth-century a group of houses was built on the shoulder of the valley above the church and beyond the boundary bank, where there was more space than in the confined valley bottom. Thorough excavation of part of this area has revealed a succession of peasant houses dating from the twelfth century to the fifteenth century, but none earlier. A short distance beyond this group of houses stood the twelfth-century manor house. Further expansion took place in the thirteenth century, when a row of tofts and crofts was laid out beyond the earlier manor house, and again excavation has revealed a series of houses finishing in the late fifteenth century shortly before Wharram Percy was depopulated. A new manor house was also built, standing as before just beyond the row of peasant houses.

In addition to these large-scale changes in the layout of the village there were also detailed changes in the position of houses and even in the boundaries of the tofts. For example in the thirteenth century, the twelfth-century house site was occupied by two houses in separate tofts, both side-on to the street but one set back from it; in the fourteenth century a house lying obliquely to the street occupied a single toft; and in the fifteenth century the house was rebuilt end-on to the street.

In other parts of the country redesign was common and a similar realignment of a village on a regular plan has been noted at the deserted village of Seacourt (Oxfordshire). Part of the impetus for such changes may have come from the creation of new towns, regularly laid out around central market squares. Indeed urban aspirations seem to have seeped through to a considerable number of settlements that never had any real chance of succeeding as towns. This is not to say that all planned villages of the early Middle Ages were putative towns. In many cases lords may have encouraged rebuilding as an opportunity to create a more manageable community or even to redesign the field system.

In a typical medieval village in Holderness the cluster of houses and garths, the tofts and crofts, the house of the lord, and the church lay close together surrounded by the land of the village, which although it might be individually owned was for the most part farmed in common by the inhabitants. The land was graded into three main divisions, arable, meadow and pasture, and the unit of open-field holdings in Holderness, as in the Danelaw, generally was the bovate or oxgang. The bovate in Holderness was usually an eighth of a carucate. The bovate and the carucate were both fiscal units, consisting of variable amounts of acres of arable, meadow and pasture.

The arable lay in open fields around the village settlement, in two, three or more open fields, which were subdivided by baulks or turf that provided access into smaller rectangular areas known as flatts, furlongs, shotts or falls. The flatts in their turn were subdivided into strips of land known as selions, riggs or lands. The arable fields, in the open-field system were cultivated in alternative years, the fallow field being used for pasture and thus fertilized, a system generally known as infield-outfield. It was for this reason necessary for men to have an approximately equal number of holdings in all fields, their strips being scattered among the flatts but often occurring at regular intervals in each flatt. The demesne lands of the lord of the manor lay among the strips of his men as did the glebe lands. There were, however, many villages where the lord used his authority to rearrange the strips so that they lay in blocks; from which it was but a short step to creating enclosed fields. Examples of enclosure can be found throughout England from the early Middle Ages, and in Holderness it occurred from the twelfth century onwards in the common fields.

Between 1197 and 1210 Meaux Abbey acquired land at Arnold where a grange was subsequently built, the donor giving the abbey strips lying together in two flatts, and giving his men, who had formerly held land in those flatts land acre for acre elsewhere in the territory of Arnold. This exchange was made easier because the donor already had an enclosure in the centre of the flatts. By the middle of the thirteenth century if not earlier the grange was enclosed by a wall.

Apart from arable, the two other essential elements in open fields were meadow and pasture. Meadow was always highly valued in the Middle Ages and the processes of enclosing meadow started very early in some parts of the country. In some areas, however, meadow allotments were redistributed on an annual basis. The sources of pasture land were stubble in the arable fields after crops were harvested until March, the fallow fields, headlands and pieces of land found in corners of fields, also meadow after the hay had been cut. Additionally many settlements had large areas of common grazing of rough ground. In the Holderness region it is possible to trace the extension of villages into marshes. Immediately after the Conquest the boundaries of some villages were still undefined, but as more men began to own more animals, the increasing use of marginal lands for grazing meant that from the early thirteenth century boundaries between the various marsh areas had to be established. Subsequently the number of animals allowed on common pasture for each person was limited.

In the twelfth century there still seems to have been considerable variations in the field systems and clearly in some parts of the country the more primitive 'infield-outfield' system was still developing.

Figure 41   Early medieval colonization of waste in south Lincolnshire

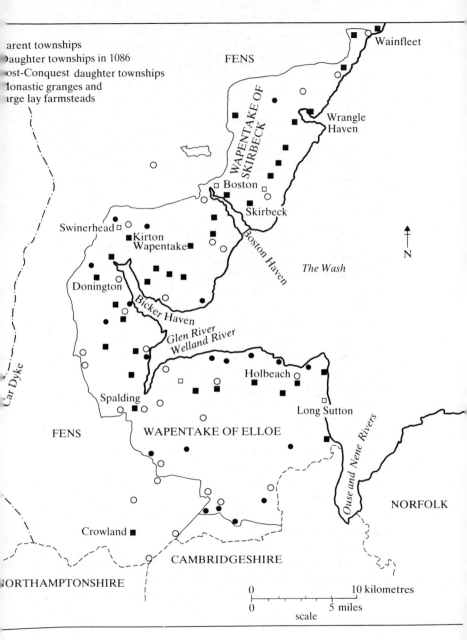

Land clearance and colonization in the twelfth century

In Chapter 4 we established that much of England was already cultivated and managed, nevertheless there remained areas of poor drainage, particularly adjacent to the east and south coasts and pockets inland as well as areas of poor soils that were not capable of cultivation. The twelfth century, however, saw the progression of such lands into cultivation, but because of the random survival of documentary evidence it appears that the grandest works were being carried out by the monastic institutions and on the large estates. While it is true that such establishments would have had the resources to undertake the civil engineering required it does not follow that groups of ordinary villagers on smaller estates and freemen as well were not involved in lesser activities. Let us again look to the area of Holderness where the Cistercian monks of Meaux were particularly active. The whole of the South Holderness coast was eventually protected by a series of walls, the first of which was recorded in 1201, enabling the land behind them to be reclaimed from marsh to pasture and subsequently to arable.

From the middle of the twelfth century there is a considerable amount of information about the making or altering of waterways in Holderness, in which the abbeys, especially Meaux, were interested. The first and most simple motive for making a dyke was to form a property boundary in a wet low-lying land such as Holderness which had no natural stone to make walls and little wood to make fences. These 'fence-ditches' occur very often in the archives, describing the boundaries of a croft, a meadow or a grange.

Industry

Much of the obvious industrial activity at the time was generated by the great monastic institutions. As early as the Domesday Book we can see traces of the incipient wool industry developing. The manors of Ely Abbey stocked over 13,000 sheep according to the record in 1086. In the Cotswolds the nuns at Minchenhampton had 17,000 sheep

256

grazing on the common early in the twelfth century. These and other suppliers were clearly providing the wool which was processed in Cirencester and other Cotswold wool towns. The Cistercians particularly led the way on the waste commons of the Yorkshire Dales and in South Wales. To some extent it was no accident that wool became associated with monasteries; wool was necessary for monks habits and cowls in the first instance, but the Cistercians were quick to realize the potential of the wool industry.

In the twelfth century the manufacture of cloth for sale, although widespread, was centred on a dozen or so towns mainly in eastern and southern England. Weavers Guilds in London, Oxford, Lincoln and Huntingdon were mentioned in the 1130 Pipe Roll and by the end of Henry II's reign in 1189 there were others at Nottingham, Winchester and York. Weavers and fullers were also recorded at Beverley, Gloucester, Marlborough and Stamford amongst other places. Towards the end of our period the water-driven fulling mills were introduced and were first recorded on land belonging to the Templars in 1185. Indeed most of the mills date from the late twelfth century and were on royal or ecclesiastical estates and this development was to prove a springboard for the subsequent industrial revolution in all trade in the thirteenth century.

One industry which clearly expanded greatly after the Conquest was that of quarrying and building. The records of the twelfth century abound in references to the right to take and transport stone, often by water, and toll exemptions on building materials were freely given to religious communities. The quarrying of building stone to meet this demand can be seen in the distribution of surviving eleventh- and twelfth-century masonry containing great oolite stone. Quarries in the inferior oolite at Barnack near Peterborough had been worked since the seventh century and in the time of Edward the Confessor, Ramsey Abbey was licensed by Peterborough for the taking of 'werkstan at Bernak'. In the twelfth and thirteenth centuries Ramsey, like Crowland and St Edmund's at Bury, obtained from its

55 The earthworks of medieval tin-working activities on Dartmoor: the oval-shaped mounds on the right, known as pillow mounds, were probably constructed as rabbit warrens

Northamptonshire benefactors grants of land including concessions and leases of strips of ground in Barnack quarries. Sawtry Abbey had a special canal made from Whittlesea Mere to bring in Barnack stone. St Edmund's at Bury had a permanent grant of a right of way from Barnack to the wharves at the Welland ferry, over a mile distant. Norwich cathedral took its Barnack stone down the Welland, round the coast and up the Yare in the early fourteenth century. The church at Levenham in Suffolk, sixty miles away, is also built of Barnack stone.

William I had Battle Abbey built on the site of his famous

victory but as suitable stone could not be found in the vicinity the king arranged for Caen stone to be fetched from Normandy at his own expense. Eventually, however, a quarry was opened at a site near the abbey which proved adequate for the building which was supervised by monks brought from Marmoutier near Tours. It is recorded that

56 The earthworks of medieval coal pits on the Clee Hills in Shropshire. The earliest reference to coal mining here dates to the twelfth century

259

between 1165 and 1171 £550 was laid out on the works of the king's houses at Windsor and large quantities of stone were brought from the Egglemont quarry at Totternhoe in Bedfordshire, presumably by water.

Along with stone, metals were in increased demand for building as well. Iron mining and smelting were located mainly in the Forest of Dean until the thirteenth century. The forges of St Briavels supplied picks, shovels, axes and anvils to Ireland on the occasion of Henry II's expedition there in 1172 and horseshoes and other iron ware went with Richard I's crusade in 1189–91.

During the second half of the twelfth century tin production became particularly important when the deposits of south-west Devon produced nearly all Europe's tin. Tin working was organized in 'stannaries', each with its own warden or supervisor and the miners had to take their products to one of the stannary towns in order that the correct duty might be levied. A castle tower was built at Lidford in 1195 as a special prison for offenders against stannary laws. In 1198 a new royal official, the warden, replaced the Lord of Lidford manor as supervisor of the stannaries.

A myriad of other industrial activities took place in the twelfth century mostly at a local level, for local consumption, but the documents only rarely hint at these. Just how much these were influenced by the institutional and tenurial changes brought about by the Conquest is impossible to say.

Postscript

Thus by 1200 England, and to a lesser extent Wales, was enjoying a degree of prosperity – a prosperity that was to remain for another century and a half. Everywhere there is evidence of great energy and industry. The imprint in this intense activity is still with us today both in town and country. Without the Normans would the towns have been expanded and redesigned, would the churches, cathedrals and monasteries have been rebuilt and would hundreds of castles have been erected? No doubt some of these developments would have occurred irrespective of who was ruling; it is impossible to say. What does seem certain is that the Normans were different enough from the Anglo-Saxons to see themselves as 'conquerors' and acted accordingly. Many of the activities of the eleventh and twelfth centuries happened because the Normans had the wealth, energy and ruthlessness to impose a new face on an old country. What would have happened to the Normans if they had failed at Hastings? No doubt they would have gone the same way as the other French kingdoms and duchies. We would certainly not have had very much by which to remember them. The Norman Conquest gave the Normans an entity which they would otherwise not have enjoyed, as well as respectability. It is no accident that in 1066 William, 'the bastard', becomes William 'the Conqueror'.

Appendix 1

Translation of the section of the Domesday Book shown in Plate 1

Land of the Bishop of Lincoln in Dorchester Hundred

Of the land of the manor of THAME, Robert holds 10 hides from the Bishop; Saewold 4 hides; William 3 hides; Alfred and his associate 6 hides. In lordship 10 ploughs.

    16 villagers with 21 smallholders and 8 slaves have 10 ploughs. Total value £20.

In (Great) MILTON Aelfric holds 6 hides from the Bishop; William 3 hides and 3 virgates of land. In lordship 2 ploughs.

    10 villagers with 4 smallholders and 4 slaves have 4 ploughs.

    A mill at 8s. Total value £6.

Of the land of the manor of BANBURY, Robert holds 4 hides from the Bishop; Jocelyn 5 hides; another Robert 2½ hides; William 5 hides; Humphrey ½ hide. Land for 12½ ploughs. In lordship 8 ploughs.

    13 villagers with 3 smallholders and 12 slaves have 4 ploughs.

    A mill of one of them, Robert son of Walkelin, at 5s 4d; meadow, 4 acres.

Total value before 1066 £11 10s; when acquired £9 10s; now £14.

Of the land of the manor of CROPREDY, Ansgered holds 10 hides of land of the manor from the Bishop; Gilbert 5 hides; Theodoric 2 hides; Richard 3 hides; Edward 6 hides; Roger 1 hide and 1 virgate; Robert and another Robert 3 hides less 1 virgate. Land for 34 ploughs. In lordship 13 ploughs.

    28 villagers with 27 smallholders, 4 Frenchmen and 10 slaves have 18 ploughs.

    3 mills at 35s 4d; meadow, 22 acres; copse, 5 acres.

Total value before 1066 £27; when acquired £29; now £30 10s.

Roger of Ivry holds YARNTON from the Bishop. It is Eynsham Church's. 9½ hides. Land for 9 ploughs. Now in lordship 2 ploughs.
20 villagers with 3 smallholders have 7 ploughs.
Meadow, 200 acres less 20; pasture, 80 acres.
One Mainou had 1 hide there; he could go where he would.
Total value before 1066 £10; value now, with the fishery and the meadow, £14.

Robert holds 2 hides of the Bishop's *inland* in WYKHAM.
Land for 3 ploughs. Now in lordship 2 ploughs; 4 slaves.
5 villagers have 1½ ploughs.
A mill at 30s.
The value was 60s; now 100s.

Saewold holds WATERSTOCK from the Bishop. It is of the Holding of St Mary's of Lincoln. 5 hides. Land for 5 ploughs. Before 1066, 5 ploughs; in lordship 3. Now in lordship 3 hides of this land; 2 ploughs there.
A mill, 9s 5d; 5 slaves; meadow, 36 acres.
The value was 20s; now 50s.
Alfwy held it freely.

In (Little) BALDON Isward holds 5 hides from the Bishop and Bricteva 2½ hides. Land for 7 ploughs.
10 villagers with 3 slaves have 6 ploughs.
Meadow, 1 acre.
Value before 1066 £4; now £7.

Land of the Bishop of Bayeux

The Bishop of Bayeux holds COMBE from the King. 1 hide.
Land for 4 ploughs. Now in lordship 2 ploughs; 2 slaves.
6 villagers with 6 smallholders have 3 ploughs.
A mill at 3s; meadow, 15 acres; woodland 1½ leagues long and as many wide.
The value was £6; now £10.
Alwin and Algar held it freely.

The Bishop also holds DEDDINGTON. 36 hides. Land for 30 ploughs. There were 11½ hides in lordship, besides the *inland*.
Now in lordship 18½ hides; 10 ploughs; 25 slaves.
64 villagers with 10 smallholders have 20 ploughs.
3 mills at 41s and 100 eels; meadow, 140 acres;
    pasture, 30 acres; from the meadows 10s.
Value before 1066 and later £40; now £60.
Five thanes . . . .

The Bishop also holds STANTON (Harcourt). 26 hides which paid tax before 1066. Land for 23 ploughs. Now in lordship 1 hide and 1 virgate of this land, besides the *inland*; 5 ploughs; 12 slaves.
  55 villagers with 28 smallholders have 17 ploughs.
  3 mills at 40s; 2 fisheries at 30s; meadow, 200 acres; pasture as much; woodland 1 league long and ½ league wide; value when stocked 25s.
Value before 1066 and later £30; now £50.
  Alnoth held it freely.

The Bishop also holds (Great) TEW. 16 hides. Land for 26 ploughs. Now in lordship 6 ploughs; 14 slaves.
  31 villagers with 8 smallholders have 16 ploughs.
  Meadow, 300 acres less 12; pasture, 101 acres.
Value before 1066 and later £20; now £40.
  Alnoth of Kent held it.

In LEWKNOR Hundred
Ilbert of Lacy holds 2½ hides in TYTHROP from the Bishop of Bayeux. Land for 3 ploughs. Now in lordship 1 plough.
  4 villagers have another (plough).
  Meadow, 10 acres.
The value was 60s; now 40s.

Wadard holds 2½ hides and 12 acres of land in the same village. Land for 3 ploughs. Now in lordship 1 plough; 2 slaves.
  2 villagers have another (plough).
  Meadow, 10 acres.
The value was 60s; now 40s.

Hervey holds (Little) HASELEY. 9 hides. Land for 9 ploughs. Now in lordship 2 ploughs, with 1 slave.
  8 villagers with 3 smallholders have 6 ploughs.
  Meadow, 30 acres.
The value was £7; now £6.

Hervey also holds 2 hides in BRIGHTWELL (Baldwin). Land for 6 ploughs. Now in lordship 2 ploughs.
  5 villagers with 5 smallholders have 2 ploughs.
  A mill at 20d; meadow, 6 acres; woodland, 20 acres.
The value was 50s; now 70s.

Roger holds 2 hides and the third part of 1 virgate in COWLEY. Land for 2 ploughs. They are there, in lordship, with
  4 smallholders and 2 slaves.

Meadow, 4 acres; pasture, 2 acres.
The value was 60s; now 40s.

Reginald Wadard holds SOMERTON from the Bishop. 9 hides.
Land for 9 ploughs. Now in lordship 2 ploughs, with 1 slave.
  17 villagers with 9 smallholders have 7 ploughs.
  A mill at 20s and 400 eels; meadow, 40 acres; pasture, 156 acres.
The value was £9; now £12.

He also holds 6 hides in FRITWELL. Land for 4 ploughs.
Now in lordship 1 plough, with 1 slave.
  4 villagers with 1 smallholder have 1½ ploughs.
  Meadow, 12 acres.
The value is and was £3.

Adam holds 2 hides in *SEXINTONE* from the Bishop. Land for 3 ploughs.
  6 villagers have them.
The value was 40s; now 60s.

Alfred holds 1½ hides in *SEXINTONE* from the Bishop. Land for 1½
ploughs. Now he has 1½ ploughs in lordship.
  3 villagers with 4 smallholders have 2 ploughs.
The value is and was 30s.

Wadard holds FRINGFORD from the Bishop. 8 hides. Land for 8 ploughs.
Now in lordship 2 ploughs; 4 slaves.
  18 villagers with 8 smallholders have 6 ploughs.
  2 mills at 10s.
The value is and was £8.

In the same village he also holds 2½ hides. Land for 1 plough.
It is in lordship, with
  4 smallholders.
The value was 20s; now 40s.

Robert holds 2 hides in FINMERE from the Bishop. Land for 2 ploughs.
His men have 1 plough.
The value was 30s; now 40s.

Roger holds FOREST HILL from the Bishop. 3 hides. Land for 3 ploughs.

Appendix 2

Domesday boroughs

Bedfordshire
Bedford

Berkshire
Reading
Windsor
Wallingford

Buckinghamshire
Buckingham
Newport Pagnell

Cambridgeshire
Cambridge

Cheshire
Chester
Rhuddlan

Cornwall
Bodmin

Derbyshire
Derby

Devonshire
Barnstaple
Exeter
Lydford
Okehampton
Totnes

Dorset
Bridport
Dorchester
Shaftesbury
Wareham
Wimborne Minster

Essex
Colchester
Maldon

Gloucestershire
Bristol
Gloucester
Tewkesbury
Winchcomb

Hampshire
Southampton
Twynham
Winchester

Herefordshire
Clifford
Ewyas Harold
Hereford
Wigmore

Hertfordshire
Ashwell
Berkhamstead
Hertford
St Albans
Stanstead Abbots

Huntingdonshire
Huntingdon

Kent
Canterbury
Dover
Fordwich
Hythe
Rochester
Romney
Sandwich
Seasalter

Lancashire
Penwortham

Leicestershire
Leicester

Lincolnshire
Grantham
Lincoln
Louth
Stamford
Torksey

Middlesex	Staffordshire	Wiltshire
London	Stafford	Bedwyn
	Tamworth	Bradford on Avon
Norfolk	Tutbury	Calne
Norwich		Cricklade
Thetford	*Suffolk*	Malmesbury
Yarmouth	Beccles	Marlborough
	Bury St Edmunds	Salisbury
Northamptonshire	Clare	Tilshead
Northampton	Dunwich	Warminster
	Eye	Wilton
Nottinghamshire	Ipswich	
Newark	Sudbury	*Worcestershire*
Nottingham		Droitwich
	Sussex	Pershore
Oxfordshire	Arundel	Worcester
Oxford	Chichester	
	Hastings	*Yorkshire*
Shropshire	Lewes	Bridlington
Shrewsbury	Pevensey	Dadsley
Quatford	Rye	Pocklington
	Steyning	Tanshelf
Somerset		York
Axbridge	*Surrey*	
Bath	Guildford	
Bruton	Southwark	
Frome		
Ilchester	*Warwickshire*	
Langport	Warwick	
Milborne Port		
Milverton		
Taunton		

Appendix 3

The Assize of the Forest, 1184
This is the first official act of legislation relating wholly to the
forest and is sometimes cited as the Assize of Woodstock,
since Henry II is known to have made legislation dealing
with the forest at a council held there in 1184. In its present
form it is composite in character, with several clauses derived from a variety of sources: some are restatements or
modifications of earlier decrees, and some additions formulated at Woodstock in 1184.

This is the assize of the Lord King, Henry, son of Maud,
concerning the forest, and concerning his deer in England;
it was made at Woodstock with the advice and assent of the
archbishops, barons, earls and magnates of England.

1 First he forbids that anyone shall transgress against him in
   regard to his hunting rights or his forests in any respect;
   and he wills that no trust shall be put in the fact that
   hitherto he has had mercy for the sake of their chattels
   upon those who have offended against him in regard to his
   hunting rights or his forests in any respect. For if anyone
   shall offend against him hereafter and be convicted thereof,
   he wills that full justice be exacted from the offender as was
   done in the time of King Henry, his grandfather.
2 Item, he forbids that anyone shall have bows or arrows or
   hounds or harriers in his forests unless he shall have as his
   guarantor the King or some other person who can legally
   act as his guarantor.
3 Item, he forbids anyone to give or sell anything to the
   wasting or destruction of his own woods which lie
   within the forest of King Henry: he graciously allows them

to take from their woods what they need, but this is to be done without wasting and at the oversight of the King's forester

4 Item, he has commanded that all who have woods within the bounds of the royal forest shall install suitable foresters in their woods; for these let those to whom the woods belong act as sureties, or let them find such suitable sureties as can give redress if the foresters shall transgress in anything which pertains to the Lord King. And those who have woods without the bounds of the forest visitation but in which the venison of the Lord King is covered by the King's peace shall have no forester, unless they have sworn to the assize of the Lord King, and to keep the peace of his hunt and to provide someone as keeper of his wood.

5 Item, the Lord King has commanded that his foresters shall have a care to the forest of the knights, and others who have woods within the bounds of the royal forest, in order that the woods be not destroyed; for, if in spite of this, the woods shall be destroyed, let those whose woods have been destroyed know full well that reparation will be exacted from their persons or their lands, and not from another.

6 Item, the Lord King has commanded that all his foresters shall swear to maintain his assize of the forest, as he made it, according to their ability, and that they will not molest knights or other worthy men on account of anything which the Lord King has granted them in respect of their woods.

7 Item, the King has commanded that in any county in which he has venison, twelve knights shall be appointed to guard his venison and his 'vert' together with the forest; and that four knights shall be appointed to pasture cattle in his woods and to receive and protect his right of pannage. Also the King forbids anyone to graze cattle in his own woods, if they lie within the bounds of the forest, before the King's woods have been pastured; and the pasturing of cattle in the woods of the Lord King begins fifteen days before Michaelmas and lasts until fifteen days after Michaelmas.

8 And the King has commanded that if his forester shall have demesne woods of the Lord King in his custody, and those woods shall be destroyed, and he cannot show any just cause why the woods were destroyed, the person of the forest himself and not something else shall be seized.

9 Item, the King forbids that any clerk shall transgress either in regard to his venison or to his forests; he has given strict orders to his foresters that if they find any such trespassing there, they shall not hesitate to lay hands upon them and to

arrest them and to secure their persons, and the King himself will give them his full warrant.

10 Item, the King has commanded that his 'assarts' (deanings), both new and old shall be inspected, and likewise both 'purprestures' (pastures) and the wastes of the forest; and that each shall be set down in writing by itself.

11 Item, the King has commanded that the archbishops, bishops, earls, barons, knights, freeholders and all men shall heed the summons of his master-forester to come and hear the pleas of the Lord King concerning his forests and to transact his other business in the county court, if they would avoid falling into the mercy of the Lord King.

12 At Woodstock the King commanded that safe pledges shall be taken from any who shall be guilty of one transgression in respect of the forest, and likewise if he shall trespass a second time; but if he shall transgress a third time, for this third offence no other pledges shall be taken from him nor anything else, except the very person of the transgressor.

13 Item, the King has commanded that every male attaining the age of twelve years and dwelling within the jurisdictions of the hunt, shall swear to keep the King's peace, and likewise the clerks who hold lands in lay fee there.

14 Item, the King has commanded that the mutilation of dogs shall be carried out wherever his wild animals have their lairs and were wont to do so.

15 Item, the King has commanded that no tanner or bleacher of hides shall dwell in his forests outside of a borough.

16 Item, the King has commanded that none shall hereafter in any wise hunt wild animals by night with a view to their capture, either within the forest or without, wheresoever the animals frequent or have their lairs or were wont to do so, under pain of imprisonment for one year and the payment of a fine or ransom at his pleasure. And no one, under the same penalty, shall place any obstruction whether alive or dead in the path of his beasts in his forests and woods or in other places disafforested by himself or his predecessors.

Further reading

Chapter 1 The coming of the Normans
Brown, R. Allen, *The Normans and the Norman Conquest*, London (1976).
Davis, R. H. C., *The Normans and their Myth*, London (1976).
Douglas, D. C., *William the Conqueror, The Norman Impact upon England*, London (1964).
Douglas, D. C., *The Norman Achievement, 1050–1100*, London (1969).
Gibson, M., *Lanfranc of Bec*, Oxford (1978).
Haskins, C. H., *The Normans in European History*, Boston & New York (1915).
Le Patourel, J., *The Norman Empire*, Oxford (1976).
Loyn, H. R., *The Norman Conquest*, London (1965).
Stenton, F. (ed.), *The Bayeux Tapestry: A Comprehensive Survey*, London (1957).

Chapter 2 The Norman dynasty in England
Chambers, J., *The Norman Kings*, London and Edinburgh (1981).
Stenton, F. M., *Anglo-Saxon England*, London (1943).

Chapter 3 Castles of the Conquest
Allen Brown, R., *English Castles*, London (1976).
Beresford, M. W. and St Joseph, J. K., *Medieval England: An Aerial Survey* (second ed.) Cambridge (1979).
Colvin, H. M. (ed.), *The History of the King's Works*, London (1963).
Renn, D., *Norman Castles in Britain*, London (1968).

Chapter 4 The English landscape at the time of the Conquest
Crossley, D. (ed.), *Medieval Industry*, London (1981).
Galbraith, V. H., *The Making of Domesday Book*, Oxford (1961).
Darby, H. C. (ed.), *A New Historical Geography of England*, Cambridge (1973).
Darby, H. C. (ed.), *Domesday England*, Cambridge (1977).
Lennard, R. V., *Rural England 1086–1135: A Study of Social and Agrarian Conditions*, Oxford (1959).

Poole, A. L. (ed.), *Medieval England*, Oxford (1958).

Sawyer, P. H. (ed.), *Medieval Settlement: Continuity and Change*, London (1976).

Chapter 5 The towns of the Conquest

Aston, M. A. and Bond., C. J., *The Landscape of Towns*, London (1976).

Beresford, M., *New Towns of the Middle Ages*, London (1966).

Platt, C., *The English Medieval Town*, London (1976).

Chapter 6 The impact of the Conquest on the church

British Archaeological Association, *Medieval Art and Architecture at Worcester Cathedral*, British Archaeological Association, Leeds (1978).

Clapham, A. W., *English Romanesque Architecture after the Conquest*, Oxford (1934).

Gibson, M., *Lanfranc of Bec*, Oxford (1978).

Knowles, D., *The Monastic Order in England* (second ed.), Cambridge (1963).

Loyn, H. R., *The Norman Conquest*, London (1965).

Zarnecki, G., 'Romanesque Sculpture in Normandy and England in the Eleventh Century', in *Proceedings of the Battle Conference 1978*, ed. R. Allen Brown, Ipswich (1979).

Chapter 7 Forest, park and woodland

Beresford, M., *History on the Ground*, London (1957).

Colvin, H. (ed.), *The History of the Kings Works*, vols 1 and 2, London, (1963).

Young, C. R., *The Royal Forests of Medieval England*, Leicester (1979).

Chapter 8 The Norman impact on Wales and the Welsh borderlands

Beresford, M., *New Towns of the Middle Ages*, London (1967).

Nelson, L. H., *The Normans in South Wales 1070–1171*, Austin (1966).

Millward, R. and Robinson, A., *The Welsh Borders*, London (1978).

Rees, W., *An Historical Atlas of Wales from Early to Modern Times* (1972)

Chapter 9 Norman heritage

Cameron, K., *English Place Names*, London (1961).

Darby, H. C., *A New Historical Geography of England before 1600*, Cambridge (1976).

English, B., *The Lords of Holderness*, Oxford (1979).

The English, Welsh and Scottish Tourist Boards have produced a booklet entitled *Discover Norman Britain* (1979), written as an introduction to a series of Norman heritage trails in Britain.

Index

Abergavenny (Monmouthshire), Benedictine priory at, 240
Abingdon (Berkshire) traders at, 110; monastery at, 156, 211
Abbotsbury (Dorset), monastery at, 156
Aethelwig, Abbot of Evesham, 169
Ailred, Abbot of Rievaulx, 172–3
Aldington (Kent), 94
Alexander, Bishop of Lincoln, 52–3
Alfred, King, 61
Alnwick (Northumberland), planned town of, 147
Amesbury (Witlshire), nunnery, 178
Anarchy, the, 51–5, 59, 64, 138, 177; *see also* King Stephen
Anglo Saxon Chronicle, 57, 62, 88, 197, 205
Anselm of Aosta, Archbishop of Canterbury, 31
Anselm of Lucca (Pope Alexander II), 31
Antioch, 42
Arden, Forest of (Warwickshire), 204
Arnulf of Pembroke, 231
Arundel (Sussex), 125, 210, figure 7
Arwystli, cantref of, 222
Ashford (Kent), town plan of, 151
Aspall (Suffolk), Domesday fair at, 110
Aston Eyre (Shropshire), 165; tympanum, plate 39

Augustinians, 170

Baldock (Hertfordshire), place name of, 247
Baldwin, Abbot, 107
Baldwin de Redvers, 52, 74
Baldwin V, Count of Flanders, 34
Bamburgh (Northumberland), castle at, 79
Banbury (Oxfordshire), burgage plots at, 151
Bangor, bishopric at, 239
Barford St Michael (Oxfordshire), plate 47
Barker, Philip, 69
Barlow, Frank, 18
Barnack (Northamptonshire), stone from, 111, 257
Barton (Oxfordshire), 90
Bath, 118
Battle (Sussex), market at, 147; abbey, 167–8, 232, 258; figure 26
Bayeux Cathedral, 14, 22, 73
Bayeux Tapestry, 13–16, 28, 68, 70, 73; plates 2, 3, 7, 8, 18; figure 5
Beaudesert castle, 151
Beaumont (Essex), place name of, 146
Bec, Normandy, abbey at, 31, 161, 169
Beckermonds (Yorkshire), place name of, 249
Beckley Park (Oxfordshire), 212
Bedford castle, 52
Bere, decline of, 134
Beresford, Maurice, 138

Berkhamsted (Hertfordshire), castle at, 67, figure 8
Berkley (Gloucestershire), castle at, 73; Domesday market at, 110
Bernard de Newmarche, 231
Bestwood Park (Nottinghamshire), 213
Bignor (Sussex), quarry at, 111
Bigod, Hugh, 52
Bishop's Cannings (Wiltshire), 128
Bladon (Oxfordshire), Domesday potters at, 111
Blenheim Palace, Woodstock, 211–12
Blythe, parish church of, 189
Bohemond of Hauteville, 42
Boothby Pagnell, (Lincolnshire), Norman house at, plate 5
Bordesley, Redditch (Worcestershire), 173
Borough Green (Cambridgeshire), park at, 208
Botcheston (Leicestershire), place-name of, 247
Bottisham (Cambridgeshire), Domesday record of, 94
Bougle (Suffolk), place-name of, 246
Bourne (Kent), Domesday pasture at, 102
Bowes castle (Durham), 79
Box (Wiltshire), Saxon stone from, 111
Brackley (Northamptonshire), town plan of, 151
Bramber castle (Sussex) figure 7
Brecon, new town of, 222, 231, 240, figure 39
Breura (Cheshire), place-name of, 246
Bridgnorth (Shropshire), 138
Bristol, castle, 50; Domesday town of, 104
Brown, Capability, 212
Brown Clee (Shropshire), Saxon hunting at, 199, 208
Bruern (Oxfordshire), place-name of, 246
Bryanston (Dorset), place-name of, 247

Brycheiniog, princedom of, 231
Buckingham (Buckinghamshire), market at, 121
Builth, new town of, 231
Burford (Oxfordshire), merchant's guild at, 122
burhs, Anglo Saxon, 61, 105, 117–21, 125
Burnham (Sussex), Domesday record of, 105
Burton-on-Trent (Staffordshire), burgage plots at, 149
Burwell castle (Cambridgeshire), plates 12, 42
Bury St Edmunds (Suffolk), origin of town plan at, 106–7; plate 26; figure 15
Byland (Yorkshire), Cistercian foundation at, 173

Caen (Normandy), town of, 32, 33, 138, 161; castle at; stone from 33, 259; plate 10
Caerleon (Monmouthshire), 117, 222
Caernarvon market at, 132; castle at, 223
Cainhoe castle (Bedfordshire), plate 11
Caister (Norfolk), Domesday salt pans at, 112
Caldew (Cumberland), place name of, 249
Camarthen, 231
Cambridge castle, 43, 64, 72, figure 7
Canterbury (Kent), St Augustine's, 14, 157, 163, 169, 179, 182, 186, 190, 191; foreign merchants at, 106; castle at, 64, 79; town of, 118, 122; figure 7
Cardiff, market at, 132
Carisbrooke castle (Isle of Wight), 51, 52, 74
Carlisle (Cumberland), 50
Castle Cary, 55
Castle Pulverbatch (Shropshire), 99
Castle Rising castle (Norfolk), 81
Caus (Shropshire), 233, plate 53
Cefnllys, decline of, 134, 234–6

Celtic Fields, 101
Ceredigion, 225–6
Cerne, monastery at, 156
Chaumont (Normandy), 49
Charles, the Simple, King of the Franks, 24
Chelmsford (Essex), allotments at, 149
Chepstow, castle at, 73, 77; town of, 233; Benedictine priory at, 240; plate 19
Cheshire, Domesday, waste in, 46
Cheshunt (Hertfordshire), traders at, 110
Chester (Cheshire), castle at, 43; trade at, 106; site of, 117; monastic foundation at, 166; figure 7
Chipping Campden (Gloucestershire), town plan of, 151; plate 37
Church, Domesday record of, 99–100
Church Brough (Westmorland), 63; plate 15
Church Pulverbatch (Shropshire), 99
Chute (Wiltshire), forest of, 204
Cirencester (Gloucestershire), Domesday market at, 110, 257
Cistercians, 70, 170–8, 240
Clanville (Hampshire), place name of, 249
Clare castle (Suffolk), 131, plate 32
Clee Hills (Shropshire), coal mining at, plate 56
Clifford castle, 221
Clifford, Walter, 89
Clipston (Nottinghamshire), park at, 213
Clothaire, 24
Clovis, 24
Clun (Shropshire), castle town of, 144–6, figure 22
Cluniacs, 166, 170
Cnut, King of England, 35, 49, 87, 197
Colchester (Essex), castle at, 49, 59, 77; monastic foundation at, 166, 169; figure 7

Combe Abbey (Warwickshire), 177
Commote, 223, 225
Conway castle, 223
Corbet, Roger, 233
Corfe (Dorset), castle at, 51, 55, 79; town of, 204, figure 7
Cornbury, Domesday forest at, 211
Crispin, Gilbert, Abbott of Westminster, 163
Cydewain, cantref of, 222

Danelaw, 62, 160, 253
Dapifer, Eudo, 64–5
Darby, H.C., 91, 100–1
Dartmoor (Devon), forest of, 199, 201; rabbits at, 215; plate 55
David, King (earl of Huntingdon), 208
Davis, R.H.C., 17–18, 26, 32, 39
Dean, Forest of (Gloucestershire), 110, 199, 206, 260
Deer farming, 207; figure 35
Deerhurst (Gloucestershire), church at, 159
Degannwy castle, 223
De Lacys, at Ludlow, 142–4
Delamere (Cheshire), forest of, 204
Derby, 86
Deserted medieval villages, 251, 252
Devizes castle town (Wiltshire), 54, 128, 214, plate 30, figures 19a, 19b, and 36
Dieulacres (Staffordshire), place name of, 246
Dinan, Brittany, castle at, 73
Disafforestation, 201–2
Dol, (Brittany), castle at, 73
Dolforway, decline of, 134
Domesday Book, 13, 46, 63–6, 69, 73, 87, 88–113, 125, 145; forests in, 201–2; parks in, 206–8, 210; commotes in, 223–5; French language in, 248; plate 1; figure 6
Doué-la-Fontaine, castle, 61
Douglas, D. C., 91

Dover (Kent), Roman lighthouse at, 78; guildhall at, 106; castle at, 77; figure 7; plate 21
Driffied castle (Derby), 79
Droitwich (Worcestershire), Domesday salt working at, 111
Dryslwyn, decline of, 134
Duns Tew (Oxfordshire), 89
Dunthrop (Oxfordshire), 90
Dunwich (Suffolk), French burgesses at, 106
Durham, castle, 48, 50; cathedral, 184, 189; plate 43; figure 7

Eadmer, 19
Ealred, Archbishop of York, 181
Eamont (Cumberland), place name of, 249
Earldoms, 87–8, 221
Earl's Barton (Northamptonshire), church at, 159
East Grinstead (Sussex), Domesday iron works at, 110
Eaton Socon (Bedfordshire), castle, 65
Edmund, King, 107
Edric, the Wild, 43
Edward, the Confessor, 15, 35–6, 62, 155, 157, 181, 218
Edwin, Earl, 43, 87
Ely, (Cambridgeshire), abbey of, 90, 157; castle at, Domesday record of, 256; figure 7
Emma, Queen, 35
Enville (Staffordshire), place name of, 249
Epping Forest, 200
Ethelred II, King of England, 35, 158, 211
Evesham, refugees, at 45
Ewyas Harold (Herefordshire), castle at, 63, 73, 221; Benedictine priory at, 240; plate 14
Exeter, castle, 43, 52, 72; figure 7
Eye (Suffolk), Domesday trade at, 106; street plan at, 131; plate 31
Eynsham (Oxfordshire), 153, 156
Eyton, R. W., 238

Faulston (Wiltshire), place name of, 247
Fécamp (Normandy), 29
Feudalism, 38
Field systems, 101
Fisheries, in Domesday, 104–5
Flamston (Wiltshire), place name of, 247
Florence of Worcester, 19
Fontevrault, 178
Forest Laws, 51, 197–204
Fountains Abbey (Yorkshire), 174, 213, figure 29, plate 42
Freeman, A. E., 16
French burgesses, Domesday record of, 106
French language, influence of, 254
Fulk Nerra, Count of Anjou, 61

Galbraith, V. H., 91
Garsington (Oxfordshire), strip agriculture at, 101
Gem, Richard, 186
Geoffrey of Coutances, 31, 48, 50
Geoffrey de Mandeville, 52, 65
Geoffrey Martel, Count of Anjou, 59
Geoffrey of Monmouth, 240
Gervaise de Pagnell, 213
Gilbert de Lacy, 142, 143
Gilbert fitz Richard, 225
Glaber, Raoul, 188
Glamorgan, 222
Glastonbury (Somerset), abbey at, 176
Gloucester, castle at, 64; abbey of, 157, 188; figure 7
Godwin, 157
Goltho (Lincolnshire), 63
Gontard, Abbot of Jumièges, 49
Goscelin, 85
Great Malvern Priory (Worcestershire), 188
Great Shelford (Cambridgeshire), 95, figure 12
Griffth ap Llewelyn, 229
Guildford (Surrey), park at, 210
Guiscard, Robert, Duke of Apulia and Calabria, 41

Gundulf, Bishop of Rochester, 77, 163, 184
Guy, Count of Ponthieu, 15
Gytha, 43

Hainault forest, (Middlesex), 206
Haltemprice (Yorkshire), place name of, 246
Halley's Comet, 15
Haresfield (Gloucestershire), Domesday potters at, 111
Harold II, King, 15, 36, 87, 155
Harptree, castle at, 55
'Harrying of the North', 36, 45, 99
Hastings, battle of, 15, 36, 87; castle at, 16, 73; figure 7; plate 18
Hatfield Chase (Essex), 200–4
Hay, new town at, 231, 232
Hayling Island, 160
Hedingham castle (Essex), 81
Heighington (Durham), figure 13
Hen Domen castle (Montgomery), 69, figure 9
Henley-in-Arden (Warwickshire), new town of, 151
Henry I, King, 51–2, 190, 211
Henry II, King (Plantagenet), 39, 55, 131, 232; at Woodstock, 199, 211
Henry III, Emperor, 83, 155, 205
Henry VIII, King, 243
Henry of Anjou, 27
Henry of Huntingdon, 19, 211
Hereford, town of, 120–1; castle at 63, 74, 125; French borough at 106; figure 7
Hereward, 48
Hermann, Bishop, 182
Holderness, 250, 256
Hook Norton (Oxfordshire), font at, plate 46
Howton (Herefordshire), place name of, 247
Hugh, son of Roger de Montgomery, 69
Hugh D'Avranches, Earl of Chester, 221
Hugh de Lacy, 143
Hugh de Muskham, 213

Huntingdon (Herefordshire), castle at, 43, 64, 72; failed town of, 233, 236; figure 7

Icknield Street, 124
Iffley (Oxford), St Mary's church, plate 38
Ipswich, markets at, 124
Isembard Teutonicus, 31
Ivry castle, 61

Jesmond (Northumberland), place name of, 249
John, King, 39
John of Fruttuaria, 31
John of Hexham, 54
Jumièges (Normandy), abbey at, 32, 169, 181

Kearsney (Kent), place name of, 246
Kenchester (Herefordshire), 117
Kendal (Westmorland), 126
Kenilworth castle (Warwickshire), 79
Kesteven (Lincolnshire), 204
Kidwelly (Carmarthenshire), 132, 231
Kilpeck (Herefordshire), 134, 192, 238, plates 34, 48
Kington (Herefordshire), borough of, 236
Kington-in-the-Fields, 236
Knights Templars, 179
Knowles, Dom, David, 156

Lanfranc of Bec, 31, 35, 48, 156, 160
Langport, market at, 121
Lastingham, (Yorkshire), 189
Launceston (Cornwall), castle at, 125; street plan at, 131
Lavendon (Buckinghamshire), park at, 213
Laxton Park (Nottinghamshire), 213
Leicester, 86, 120
Leo IX, Pope, 34
Leofwin, Earl, 87
Leominster (Herefordshire), 159, 165, plate 40

Lewes (Sussex), castle at,
    Cluniacs, 170; figure 7
Lichfield church (Staffordshire),
    190
Lidford (Devon), 260
Lincoln, Jew's House at, 99;
    castle at, 55, 63, 72; town of,
    86, 123; cathedral of, 182;
    figure 7; plate 4
Lisieux, Archdeacon of, 155
Little Tew (Oxfordshire), 89
Llanbadarn, 225, 231
Llandovery (Carmarthenshire),
    231
Longville (Shropshire), place
    name of, 249
Ludlow (Shropshire), castle at,
    55; French borough at, 137;
    charter at 138, town of,
    139–44, 233, 238; figure 21;
    plates 35, 36
Lyme (Dorset), Domesday salt
    workers at, 112
Lynn (Norfolk), second town at,
    137
Lyveden (Northamptonshire),
    late Saxon furnace at, 110–11

Macclesfield Forest (Cheshire),
    204
Macegarth (Yorkshire), place
    name of, 246
Mainstone (Hampshire), place
    name of, 247
Maitland, F. W., 26, 90
Malerbe, Robert, 176
Malet, Robert, 48
Malmesbury castle, 53
Maminot, Gilbert, Bishop of
    Lisieux, 49, 89
Mancroft (Norfolk) new borough
    of, 138
Manor, administrative unit of, 87
Mantes (Normandy), 49
Marcher revolts, 219
Margam, Cistercian foundation
    at, 240
Market Brough (Westmorland),
    plate 15
Marlston (Berkshire), place name
    of, 247
Matilda de Mules, 213

Matilda, Empress, daughter of
    Henry I, 152
Matilda, Queen (wife of William
    I), 34, 110
Meaux (Yorkshire), abbey at,
    173–6, 210, 254–6
Melbourne church, (Derbyshire),
    plate 49
Methleigh (Cornwall),
    Domesday fair at, 110
Middleham castle (Yorkshire), 81
Middleton Stoney (Oxfordshire),
    63, 74, 202
Middlewich (Cheshire),
    Domesday salt industry at, 112
Minchenhampton, Domesday
    record of, 256
Mondrem (Cheshire), forest of,
    204
Monmouth, castle at, 73;
    Benedictine priory at, 240
Montacute (Somerset), place
    name of, 245
Montgomery, 222
Mont-St-Michel, (Normandy),
    29, 31
Morcar, Earl, 43, 48, 87
More (Shropshire), 238, plate 54
Morville (Shropshire), 158, 164–5
Motte and bailey castles, 66–70;
    figure 8
Mountferaunt, castle at, 70
Muchelney (Somerset),
    monastery at, 156
Much Wenlock (Shropshire),
    Cluniac foundation at, 170
Mynton (Shropshire), waste in,
    99

Nantwich (Cheshire), Domesday
    salt industry at, 112
Neath, Cistercian foundation at,
    240
Neroche Forest (Somerset), 201
Neustria, 24
Nevern (Pembrokeshire), 231
Newark castle, 33
New Buckenham (Norfolk), 53,
    plate 33
Newcastle, 48, figure 7
New Forest, 204

Newport (Pembrokeshire), 117, 232
Newport Pagnell (Buckinghamshire), park at, 213
Nicholas, Prior of Worcester, 185
Nigel, Bishop of Ely, 53
Norham (Northumberland), castle at, 79
Norman Conquest, attitudes to the, 16–18; impact of, 36–8; landscape 86–113; impact on the church, 155–95
Northampton, market place at, 121
Northwich (Cheshire), Domesday salt industry at, 112
Norwich (Norfolk), castle at, 48, 63, 79; town of, 123, 138, 149; Domesday churches at, 160; plate 22, figure 7
Nottingham 86, 121; castle at, 43, 72; French borough at, 135, 137; park at, 210: place name of, 248; figures 7, 20

Odo Bishop, 14, 31, 50, 73
Offa's Dyke, 221, 222, 223
Old Dynevor, decline of, 134
Old Sarum (Wiltshire), (see also Salisbury), town plantation at, 126–7, 147; cathedral at, 126, 182; castle at, 126; place name of, 246; figure 23a; plate 29
Ongar (Essex) park at, 207, figure 34
Ordericus Vitalis, 19, 40, 45, 57, 72
Osmund, Bishop, 126
Oswestry (Shropshire), 222
Outremer, Kingdom of, 42
Owen, Clifford, 204
Oxford, town of, 120, 121; castle at, 64, 77, figure 7

Painswick (Gloucestershire) place name of, 247
Parish formation, 165
Parks, 208–15, figures 34, 35, 36; *see also* deer farming
Paul, Abbot of St Albans, 160–1, 162, 184

Pembroke, 231, plate 52
Penrith (Cumberland), 126
Perfeddwlad, 225
Peterborough church, 190
Pevensey (Sussex), castle at, 77, figure 7
Philip, King of France, 49
Picot de Say, 145
Pipe Rolls, venison recorded in, 205; weavers guilds recorded in, 257
Place name evidence, 25, 159, 245–9
Pleshey (Essex), 63, 131; plate 16
Pontefract (Yorkshire), markets at, 131; French borough at, 137; place name of, 245
Pontoise (Normandy), sacking of, 49
Porchester castle (Hampshire), 51, 81–2, plate 25
Port Meadow (Oxford), 102
Potterne (Wiltshire), 128
Premonstratensians, 177
Princes Risborough (Buckinghamshire), Domesday salt trading at, 112

Quarries, 111, 257
Quarr (Isle of Wight), Saxon stone from, 111
Quatford (Shropshire), 138

Rabbit warrens, 215
Rackham, Oliver, 103, 104
Ralf, Earl of Hereford, 218
Ramption (Cambridgeshire), castle at, 65
Ramsey Abbey, 257
Rannulf, Earl of Chester, 52
Ranston (Dorset), place name of, 247
Reading Abbey, 54, 165, 179, 190
Remi, Bishop of Fécamp, 182
Remigius, Bishop of Lincoln, 89
Remy abbey church (Normandy), 32
Rennes (Brittany), castle at, 73
Repton (Derbyshire), Saxon foundations of, 156
Revesby Abbey (Lincolnshire), 177

Rhuddlan (Flintshire), 106, 221, 229, plate 51

Rhys ap Griffith (the Lord Rhys), 232

Rhys ap Tedwr, 222

Richard I, 'Richard Coeur de Lion', 56, 201

Richard II, Duke of Normandy, 35, 181

Richard fitz Gilbert, 225, 226

Richard le Scrob, 237

Richard's Castle (Shropshire), 63, 134, 233–8, figure 40

Richardson (Wiltshire), place name of, 247

Richmond (Yorkshire), castle at, 81; town of, 131; French borough at, 137; place name of, 245; plate 24

Rievaulx (Yorkshire), Cistercian foundation at, 170–3, figure 28

Robert de Belleme, 225

Robert 'Curthose', Duke, 42

Robert, Duke Robert 1, Robert the Magnificent, 32

Robert of Jumièges, Archbishop, 157

Robert de Mowbray, Earl of Northumberland, 50

Rochester (Kent), castle at, 50, 77, 78; cathedral at, 184; monastery at, 169; figure 7; plate 20

Rockingham castle, figure 7

Roger de Clinton, bishop of Salisbury, 52, 128, 165

Roger de Lacy, 139, 142

Roger de Montgomery, Earl of Shrewsbury, 69, 99, 145, 167, 221, 222, 225

Roger de Mowbray, 173

Rolf or Rollo, 24

Rolleston (Wiltshire), place name of, 247

Romanesque, 181, 191–5

Roman fortifications, 74–6

Rouen, palace at, 15; town of, 22–5; castle at, 61

Round, J. H. 17, 105

Rowlstone, (Herefordshire), place name of, 247

Royal Forests, 197–206, figures 32, 33; see also Forest Laws

Rudheath (Cheshire), 204

Rufford monastery (Nottinghamshire), 177

Rural sees, transfer of, 163

Rye (Sussex), new borough at, 106

Ryedale (Yorkshire), Cistercian foundations at, 173

St Aethelwold, 161

St Albans, cathedral, 184

St Asaph, bishopric at, 239

St Briavels, 260

St Étienne, Caen (Normandy), 31, 32, 33, 34, 50, 182

St Gervais, Priory of, 49

St Oswald's church of St Mary Worcester, 185–6

Salisbury (Wiltshire), castle, 53; town of, 147; figures 7, 23a, 23b; see also Old Sarum

salt making, 112

Sawley Abbey (Yorkshire), plate, 41

Sawtry Abbey, 258

Sayles, G. O., 17

Scarborough (Yorkshire), burgage plots at, 149

Scrooby Park (Nottinghamshire), 213

Seacourt (Oxfordshire), deserted village of, 252

Selby (Yorkshire), monastic foundation at, 166

Sempringham, the order of, 177

Shawbury (Shropshire), 165

sheep farming, 173–4

Sherborne castle, 53

Sherwood Forest, 137, 204, 210

Shirelett (Shropshire), forest of, 199

Shrewsbury, town of, 43, 117; castle at, 52, 64, 73; French burgesses at, 106; abbey at, 158, 167; figure 16; plate 27

Sicily, 41, 42, 212

Siegeworks, construction of, 52

Simeon of Durham, 45

Simon, Earl, 52

Skenfrith (Monmouthshire), decline of, 134

Sleaford castle, 53

Southampton (Hampshire), French burgesses at, 106
South Muskham, park at, 213
Southwark, hospital at, 179
Stafford, castle at, 43, figure 7
Stamford (Lincolnshire), castle at, 64; late Saxon furnace at, 110–11; market at, 121; French at, 135
Stanstead Abbots, French burgesses at, 106
Stanton Lacy (Shropshire), manor of, 139
Stenton, F. M., 17
Stephen, King, 51–5, 65; see also 'The Anarchy'
Stephenson, Carl, 122
Stigand, Bishop of Canterbury, 157, 161, 181
Stokesay (Shropshire), place name of, 247
Stoke St Milborough (Shropshire), 94
Strata Florida, Cistercian foundation at, 240
Strata Marcella, Cistercian foundation at, 240
Stratford-upon-Avon (Warwickshire), burgage plots at, 149; figure 24
Stretton Sugwas (Herefordshire), tympanum, plate 45
Sulgrave (Northamptonshire), earthwork enclosure at, 63
Suppo of Fruttuaria, 31
Swansea, 231
Swyre (Dorset), Domesday meadow at, 102

Tackley (Essex), 160
Tamworth (Staffordshire), 125
Tancred, 42
Tanshelf, 131
Tavistock Abbey (Devon), 215
Taynton (Oxfordshire), Domesday quarries at, 111
Temple Bruer (Lincolnshire), place name of, 246
Tewkesbury (Gloucestershire), Domesday market at, 110; monastic foundation at, 166; abbey church at, 188

Thame (Oxfordshire), burgage tenements at, 149; market at, 151–2; figure 24
Thetford (Norfolk), Cluniac foundations at, 170
Thornbury (Gloucestershire), Domesday market at, 110
Thornton Abbey (Lincolnshire), 177
Tickford Priory, tithe of venison to, 213
Tinchebrai, battle of, 50
Totnes, castle, figure 7
Tours, 169, figure 26
Tovil (Kent), place name of, 249
Tower of London – see White Tower
Town plantations, 138
Treaty, St Clair-sur-Epte, 24
Trim castle (County Meath, Ireland), 81
Tudbury, place name of, 248
Tutbury (Staffordshire), Domesday trade at, 106; street plan at, 131

Unceby (Lincolnshire), charter for, 177
Urban II, Pope, 42

Val-ès-Dunes, battle of, 32
Vaughan, Sir Griffith, rebellion of, 234
Vineyards, in Domesday book, 105; figure 14

Walcher, Bishop of Durham, 48
Wales, conquest of, 219–25; church in, 239–41; figures 37, 38
Wallingford (Berkshire), castle at, 55, 64, 125–6; plan of, 120; market at, 121; French burgesses at, 106; figures 7, 18; plate 28
Walter, Abbot of Evesham, 161
Walter of Coutances, Archbishop of Rouen, 56
Walterstone (Herefordshire), place name of, 247
Waltheof, Earl, 48, 87, 88
Wareham castle (Dorset), 51, 125

William Longchamp, Bishop of
  Ely, 56
William of London, 157
William of Malmesbury, 19, 156,
  161, 182, 185, 186, 211
William de Mondeville, 131
Walter L'Espec, 173
William le Gros, 210
William of Montpellier, 212
William of Poitiers, 15, 19, 85
William of Volpiano, Abbot of St
  Benigne, Dijon, 29–31, 181
William de Warenne, 48, 170
Williamston (Northumberland),
  place name of, 247
Wilton (Wiltshire), 54, figure 23a
Winchester castle at, 120; treaty
  of, 55; town of, 118–20, 148;
  monastery at, 156, 157; parish
  church at, 189; figures 7, 17
Windsor, castle at, 125; forest at,
  202; council at, 163; figure 7
Wirral (Cheshire), 204
Wisbech (Cambridgeshire), 131
Woodstock (Oxfordshire), assize
  of, 199; park at, 199, 211–12
Woolmer (Hampshire), 204
Worcester, castle at, 55, 125;
  market at, 106, 121; hospital
  at, 179; cathedral of, 184–8;
  plate 44, figure 7
Wulfstan, 169, 184–6
Wychwood, demesne forest of,
  211

Yeldon (Bedfordshire), 65, plate
  17
York, castle at, 43, 63, 72; French
  burgesses at, 106; market at,
  106; town of, 120, 122, 149;
  hospital at, 179; figure 7
Yorkshire, Domesday waste in,
  46

Warwick, castle at, 43, 64, 72;
  figure 7
Waste, 46–7, 97–9, figures 6, 41
Watermills, in Domesday, 105–6
Waterston (Dorset), place name
  of, 247
Waverley Abbey (Surrey), 170,
  202

Wawne (Holderness), 250–1
Weavers' guilds, 257
Weolfstan, 163
Westminster Abbey, 16, 181, 188;
  figure 31
Westbury (Wiltshire), Domesday
  potters at, 111
West Runton (Norfolk), late
  Saxon furnance at, 111
Weybridge (Huntingdonshire),
  forest at, 204
Whatt (Nottinghamshire),
  Domesday millstone quarry
  at, 111
Wharram Percy (Yorkshire), 252
Whitecastle, decline in, 134
White Tower (of London), 52, 59,
  76–7, figures 7, 11, plate 13
White Ship disaster, 51
Wigmore castle, 73, 221, 236
William I, the Conqueror, King
  of England, in Normandy,
  33–9; in England, 46–50, 72–3,
  88–9; attitude to the church,
  160–1; Forest Laws of,
  197–201; figure 10
William fitz Alan, 52
William fitz Osbern, Earl of
  Hereford, 73, 136, 221
William de Braos, 236
William Rufus, William II, 50–1
William of Jumièges, 15, 19